HEALING MILES

GIFTS FROM THE CAMINOS NORTE AND PRIMITIVO

Healing Miles

Gifts from the Caminos Norte and Primitivo

Susan Alcorn

Shepherd Canyon Books
Oakland, California

Shepherd Canyon Books
Oakland, CA 94611, U.S.A.
backpack45.com

Publisher's Cataloging-in-Publication data

Names: Alcorn, Susan, author.
Title: Healing Miles : Gifts from the Caminos Norte and Primitivo /
Susan Alcorn.
Description: Includes bibliographical references and index | Oak-
land, CA: Shepherd Canyon Books, 2017.
Identifiers: ISBN 978-0-936034-06-5 | LCCN 2017913917
Subjects: LCSH Alcorn, Susan --Travel--Spain--Santiago de Com-
postela. | Alcorn, Ralph--Travel--Spain--Santiago de Compostela. |
Camino de Santiago de Compostela--Description and travel. | Hik-
ing--Spain, Northern. | Hiking--Spain--Santiago de Compostela.
| Christian pilgrims and pilgrimages--Travel--Spain--Santiago de
Compostela. | Adult children of aging parents. | Caregivers. | BI-
SAC TRAVEL / Europe / Spain & Portugal | TRAVEL / Special
Interest / Hikes & Walks | TRAVEL / Essays & Travelogues
Classification: LCC BX2321.S3 .A43 2017 | DDC
263/.0424611--dc23

20 19 18   2 3 4 5

Dedication

To Ralph, with love, because he has made all of this possible

Contents

Introduction . . . 1

1 How It All Began

El Camino de Santiago . . . 7

2 Setting Out along the Northern Coast

Camino del Norte, Spring 2015 . . . 15

Interlude 1 A Change of Plans, a Life Transition

Spain and California, Spring and Summer 2015 . . . 53

3 Our Second Stretch of the Norte

Camino del Norte, Fall 2015 . . . 77

Interlude 2 Between Caminos

Spain and California, Fall and Winter 2015-16 . . . 159

4 Primitivo All the Way!

Camino Primitivo, Spring 2016 . . . 165

5 The Third Time's the Charm

Camino del Norte, Spring 2016 . . . 225

Reflections from Home . . . 244

Planning Your Camino—Resources . . . 247

Comparing Norte, Primitivo and Francés Routes . . . 247

Distances; Time Requirements . . . 249

When to Go: Weather and Events . . . 250

Transportation to /from Norte & Primitivo Routes . . 253

Pilgrim Statistics . . . 254

Terrain and Level of Difficulty; Route Finding . . . 256

Passport, Credential, Compostela, and Certificate . . 259

Accommodations . . . 263

Packing Lists and Hints . . . 269

Susan's Packing List . . . 270

Before You Leave Home . . . 276

Transporting Baggage and People . . . 281

Bicycles on the Northern Routes . . . 285

It's All about the Food; Tipping . . . 286

Guidebooks and Other Sources of Info . . . 289

Emergency numbers . . . 292

Acknowledgments . . . 294

Index . . . 296

About the Author . . . 301

Introduction

For my part, I travel not to go anywhere, but to go. I travel for travel's sake. The great affair is to move.
~ Robert Louis Stevenson *Travels with a Donkey*

My husband Ralph calls what we do—hike long trails—obsessive behavior; I call it an addiction. We say these things tongue-in-cheek. When we are being serious, we note that we find our long walks, including the Camino routes, rewarding physically, mentally, and spiritually. We like seeing our physical strength increase and our bodies become more toned. We enjoy meeting and bonding with other pilgrims. We find joy in our natural surroundings—seeing the sunrises, the wildflowers, the rocky outcroppings. We savor gourmet meals that we find in cities, and hearty and freshly well-prepared foods from the farms. We find much that humans have created fascinating—grand churches, museums, and bridges, as well as simpler stone walls, old barns, and slate-roofed houses.

Ralph and I have been taking long-distance hikes ever since we were married in 1989. At the time, Ralph was working as a computer professional and I was a teacher. He had paid vacations and I had part of the summers free. My two sons from my first marriage, Tom and Scott, were adults, out of the house, and with their own careers underway. We were able to take backpacking trips that lasted a couple of weeks.

Beyond the Camino hikes we have completed, we have also section-hiked the John Muir Trail, the Pacific Crest Trail, the "O" or Circuit Route in Torres del Paine, Chile (Patagonia), and climbed Mount Kilimanjaro.

As many trips and miles as that represents, those miles are a fraction of what we have hiked near home in the San Francisco Bay Area. We regularly hike in the hills near us to stay reasonably healthy and fit, and whenever possible, we hike with friends.

When Ralph and I hiked the best-known Camino de Santiago route, the Camino Francés, in 2001—at ages sixty-five and sixty respectively—we had no inkling that this would lead to multiple other trips to Europe to hike other Camino routes. We proceeded to hike the Le Puy route (GR65) from Le Puy-en-Velay, France, in three stages (2004-2006); the Camino Portugués from Porto (2007); the Arles, France, route (which becomes the Camino Aragonés in Spain) in three stages (2008-2010); a bit of the Camino Mozárabe from Granada, Spain (2011); and Geneva, Switzerland, to Le Puy in two stages (2012-2013).

Choosing the trails less traveled

For Ralph and me, choosing to hike the Camino del Norte and Primitivo routes seemed like logical next steps. We were confident in our ability to hike long distances; we had learned a lot about preparing physically (the training walks at home); we knew how to pack; we were familiar with the options for accommodations; we knew that we could get by with our basic Spanish; we enjoyed the people and the land.

Some people may ask, "If the Camino Francés is the most popular, why would you choose the Camino del Norte or Primitivo?" The briefest of answers: the trails were new to us, less traveled, and more challenging. Read on and you'll see why Ralph and I found these two trails leading to Santiago beautiful, sometimes remote and quiet, sometimes energetic and pulsing with activity, and well worth recommending.

But would I be able to hike again?

As it turned out, it took a while before we could hike another long-distance trail because of what I eventually termed "Susan's medical mystery tour." In the spring of 2014, Ralph and I had gone to the Galapagos. Though some hiking was involved, it was not as much as we regularly did back home. When we returned we went on one of our familiar walks—a hilly six miles. The next day my legs were sore, but I chalked it up to our two-week hiatus. However, the pain did not go away. I made an appointment with my chiropractor, who had worked wonders for me previously with sporadic episodes of back problems. This time his treatments didn't help.

As time went by, the intensity and the location of the pain varied—often day to day. Sometimes my hips, sometimes both legs, sometimes my ankles and toes were involved. Some days I could walk five miles, other days I couldn't go a mile.

Still, we were optimistic that this was a temporary setback and that gradually I would return to normal. That June, we made reservations to fly to Spain and start the Norte in September. I continued searching for a diagnosis and trying various remedies. But in August, we had to cancel our reservations. I couldn't go up our steep driveway without pain. My left leg could not bear weight long enough to climb a flight of stairs normally; I had to tackle them like a toddler, putting each foot on each step.

Through that fall and winter, I kept trying new treatments: rest as recommended by my general practitioner, additional visits to my chiropractor, swimming and water aerobics, Pilates, deep-tissue massage, cortisone injections in my leg, and physical therapy. Nothing worked consistently. My diagnosis was changed from spinal stenosis to musculoskeletal disorder to weakness of the ACL (anterior cruciate ligament, one of four ligaments that help stabilize the knee).

I eventually got fed up with all the visits, treatments and differing opinions and went back to what had always worked best for me when training for a long hike: start where I was. In other words, I would accept that this was a setback, no one really knew what had caused it, and it was best to ignore the fact that I had been previously been able to walk ten or more miles without difficulty. I stopped trying to push through; I would only walk as far as I could without discomfort. I started by walking half a mile and then turning back; gradually I was able to increase the distance. We stuck mostly to trails close to home so I wouldn't feel pressured to walk longer distances because of time invested driving to the trailhead.

By January of 2015, we felt optimistic enough to purchase tickets for a flight in May. By March, I was doing hikes of seven miles or more. In April we went to Yosemite National Park and I did a mildly-strenuous ten-mile hike. I was elated. I figured if I could hike ten miles in the high country there, I could hike ten miles of whatever Spain offered.

Another complication on the home front

As if the ups and downs of my road to recovery (being able to walk an appreciable amount) were not enough, we also had my mother's well-being to consider. Mom was then 104. She was in excellent health for her age, but she did have some memory problems and a history of falls. Over the years she had fallen many times, but she considered it a badge of honor that she never got hurt.

"I know how to fall," she would proudly announce. "I relax when I lose my balance rather than hold my body rigid."

Even so, we, the doctors, and the assisted living facility where Mom lived knew that a fall could result in a broken hip. That in turn could lead to pneumonia because of the immobility imposed by being bed-bound. We certainly didn't want that to happen, and so there had been many discussions, and measures taken, to reduce the number of falls.

Mom was doing okay when we started making our plans for Spain, but a couple of months before we were due to leave, she fell and injured her shoulder. This time she didn't bounce back, and she was in pain. We learned that we could apply for hospice care. Even though hospice was generally reserved for those in serious decline and expected to live less than six months, the attending doctor was able to certify that Mom was eligible because of her age and the fall. She was accepted into the program with the understanding that her eligibility would be reviewed periodically.

Ralph and I toyed with the idea of postponing our Norte hike once again, but when hospice stepped in, I had the comfort of knowing that there were additional people looking after Mom's needs. And, as the time for our departure neared, we were encouraged by seeing some improvement in her condition.

In the weeks leading up to our departure, I downplayed our upcoming trip whenever I went to visit. Over the years I had noticed that telling Mom about my trips beforehand seemed to increase her anxiety. However, I wrote the dates of our trip on her calendar, talked with the various caregivers, made certain my sons Tom and Scott could step in if needed during my absence, and packed for Spain.

We walk the Norte and the Primitivo

As you will discover, the hikes that Ralph and I took on the Camino del Norte and the Primitivo were quite different in certain respects. Our Norte walk was rather complicated. We did it in three segments: two in 2015 and one in 2016. The final walk ended in Melide, where the Norte joins the Camino Francés.

The Primitivo walk, all of which we did in 2016, was straightforward from start to finish. We started from Villaviciosa, which is a couple of hiking days north of the typical starting point of Oviedo, and ended in Santiago de Compostela.

That I was able to complete either one of them I see as a result of several factors: training, good fortune, resolve, Ralph's carrying more of my gear than usual, support of family and friends, and modern medicine. It would have been easier to give up on hiking than to keep fighting against the physical limitations that had been plaguing me. However, I was not ready to give up; hiking is a major part of our life and we were not ready for a more sedentary lifestyle. We were glad we persevered.

I hope you will enjoy walking with us on the Caminos less traveled.

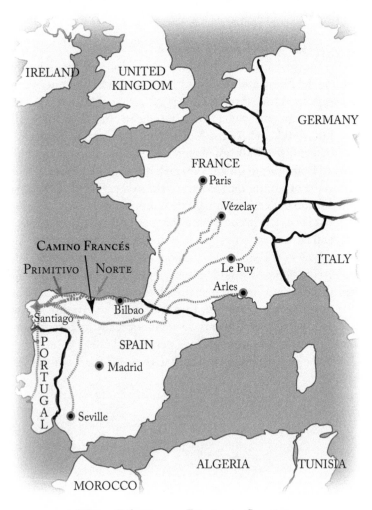

Major Pilgrimage Routes to Santiago

1 • How It All Began

El Camino de Santiago

Faith is the substance of things hoped for, the evidence of things not seen. ~The Bible: Hebrews. 11:1

Once one learns of the Camino de Santiago, it seems like a whole world opens up—literally and figuratively. Questions arise: What makes this trail special? What is its history? Who hikes the trail—and why? Usually before long, potential pilgrims find out that the history of the Camino is lengthy and the trail is not one trail, but a network of trails beginning in dozens of villages and cities throughout Europe.

All of the pilgrimage trails that are part of the Camino de Santiago eventually end, or connect to another trail that ends, in Santiago de Compostela. There, at the Santiago Cathedral, are the relics of what millions believe to be the remains of St. James.

St. James the Elder was one of the twelve apostles of Jesus. After Jesus's death, James went to Spain where he tried to convert (rather unsuccessfully we are told) the local Celts to Christianity. Later he returned to Jerusalem where he was killed in 44 CE by the Jewish king Herod Agrippa, grandson of Herod the Great.

The legend of St. James coming to be buried along the coast of Spain is also told in various versions, but probably the best-known is that he was put into a stone boat by two of his followers, the boat floated out through the Strait of Gibraltar guided by angels, and then landed on the northwest coast of Spain near present-day Padrón. The body was buried in a cave near Santiago where it lay, largely forgotten, for several centuries.

7

In 711, an invading army, mostly Moors, a Muslim people from North Africa, crossed the Strait of Gibraltar and began a campaign against the Visigothic Christians. Their inroads brought much of Spain and Portugal under Islamic rule within a decade. The Muslim forces continued their march into Western Europe and took control of parts of southern France and Sicily.

However, not all of Spain fell to the Moors—partly because of King Alfonso II (also known as The Chaste), ruler of Asturias from 791–842 CE, and partly because of geography. Alfonso was a strong leader and his forces were largely able to hold off the invaders. It also helped that the Asturias region was located along the rugged northern coast of Spain and somewhat protected along its southern boundaries by the Picos de Europa.

In 814, the legend continues, a shepherd working in a field near Padrón discovered the cave and centuries-old relics of St. James. As news of the discovery spread, the Catholic Church became increasingly interested. With the help of Alfonso II, they decreed the relics were indeed those of the apostle. A church in Santiago de Compostela was constructed—some say by Alfonso II.

Some sources also credit Alfonso II with establishing the first Camino, now called the Primitivo, or the Original Way. He ordered castles be built along the way and assigned knights to protect the travelers. That made the Primitivo a much safer route for Christians because they could avoid going through the territories to the south that Moors occupied.

The Norte route could be reached (as it still is for many contemporary pilgrims) on foot through the Spanish/French border at Irún. The Primitivo route developed as a result of its access by sea. Boats could enter the cities and fishing villages along Spain's northern coast and pilgrims could disembark and continue to Santiago on foot.

Around 1140 (almost midway through the two centuries of the Crusades), the *Codex Calixtinus* was published. This first travel guide to the Camino Francés is an illuminated manuscript (illustrated with decorative initials, borders, and miniatures, often of gold or silver) now credited to the French scholar, Aymeric Picaud. One of its sections gives practical information on walking the

Camino Francés; another provides support and encouragement to the pilgrim setting out on the arduous journey. The manuscript describes four routes. Three—from Paris, Vézelay, and Le Puy, merge before the Pyrenees, then cross from St.-Jean-Pied-de-Port and continue as the Camino Francés. The fourth—from Arles, France, crosses the Pyrenees over the Somport Pass and merges in Puente la Reina with the Camino Francés, which continues on to Santiago.

INTEREST IN THE Codex Calixtinus has never abated. In 2011, the manuscript, which had been in a vault in the Santiago Cathedral, was stolen in what turned out to be an inside job. In 2012, the manuscript was found, in good condition, in the garage of José Manuel Fernández Castiñeiras. Castiñeiras had been the cathedral's electrician for more than twenty-five years, but he had recently been let go from his job. Recovered also was a diary that Castiñeiras had kept, in which he had recorded details about stealing cash from the Cathedral's collection boxes. In 2015, he was sentenced to ten years in prison for the theft of the manuscript as well as more than 2.4-million euros and $30,000.

Things continued to evolve during the centuries of the *Reconquista* (Reconquest). These battles, from 710-1492 CE, were the attempt by Christians to retake the parts of the Iberian Peninsula lost to Moors. As the Christians reclaimed lands further south, the Camino Francés route became more established. It was easier to travel because it avoided the mountains and rivers of the northern routes, and it became the most popular.

Several factors affected the Christians' ability to make a pilgrimage, but the desire to gain *indulgence* (in the Middle Ages, the Roman Catholic Church's promise of reduction of temporal punishment for a sin) was a strong incentive. Pilgrims first had to decide which of the major destinations—Jerusalem, Rome, or Santiago de Compostela—to visit. When wars raged in one region, another destination might appear safer and draw more pilgrims. Jerusalem was heavily affected by the Crusades, which reshaped the world in the twelfth and thirteenth centuries.

In general, the route to Santiago was considerably safer, the terrain more easily traveled, and the accommodations more plentiful. The pilgrimage to Santiago de Compostela reached its peak during the eleventh and twelfth centuries when millions of people made their way across Spain.

As with the other two Christian holy cities of Jerusalem and Rome, the number of people traveling to Santiago on pilgrimage has waxed and waned through the centuries. The Moorish control lasted until 1492, when under the reign of King Ferdinand and Queen Isabella, they were forced out. In addition, the Spanish Inquisition, which began in the 1500s, the Protestant Reformation, and the wars between Spain and England and France in the sixteenth century had their effects.

In recent years, there has been a huge resurgence of interest in the Camino de Santiago and the hundreds of thousands who walk the route nowadays create a tide of travelers that affect the lands through which they travel just as their predecessors did.

Present-day pilgrims need goods and services just as earlier ones did. Though the early pilgrims often took shelter under their long, heavy, woolen cloaks at dusk, we also know that a growing number of travelers' accommodations, including pilgrim hospitals, refuges, and inns, sprang up along the more popular routes.

Today we have a range of albergues, hostals, and hotels from which to choose. Generally speaking and briefly defined: *pilgrim albergues* offer beds (often bunks) in large communal rooms. They often have kitchens, shared bathrooms, and laundry facilities. They accept donations or charge a small sum, and generally are run by religious, municipal, or civic organizations or by private owners along the Camino. *Pilgrim hostals* generally have fewer beds, more often offer some private rooms, and are privately owned. Hotels are awarded ratings and range in quality of service and ambiance from very basic to quite regal. (See Resources chapter for more.)

There are, of course, significant differences between pilgrims of old and of today. In general, we have it much easier than pilgrims of old. Early pilgrims had to walk both to and from Santiago; they rarely had groomed trails. They often traveled in groups—presumably somewhat for companionship, but perhaps more importantly for greater safety against wolves, bears, and high-waymen. They lived off the land to a greater extent, and though there were some inns and restaurants to provide shelter and refreshment along the way, they certainly didn't have the numerous places to sleep or the rich variety of foods that we now find.

Today, many still prefer to travel in small bands—in part for safety, but perhaps more for the camaraderie. Our equipment is easily obtained and lighter in weight. We have various means of transportation to get us to our starting point and then back home again, and some people use vans and buses to transport their luggage or themselves some of the distance. (*Not* using ride or luggage services is an important part of the experience for us and therefore we normally do not use these supports, but others desire this assistance. "Hike your own hike," is key.)

In both earlier times and presently, merchants have gravitated to the places where great numbers of pilgrims gathered so that they could offer their trinkets and necessities. Infrastructure grew—bridges were built to replace boatmen who charged high fees to ferry travelers over rivers. Nowadays, agencies seek to improve trails and signage to promote pilgrimage. Pamphlets, books, and websites are created to guide the traveler.

Of most significance, however, are the reasons for making the walk. We believe that most of the earliest pilgrims set out on their pilgrimage with the goal of earning their indulgence, but some had other motives. Perhaps they wanted to get away from their home or village, to make the pilgrimage in lieu of imprisonment for a crime, or as a job on behalf of a rich lord or other dignitary who didn't want to do it himself.

Nowadays, people walk or bicycle the Camino routes for a wide variety of reasons. The majority indicate when they fill out the form in the Pilgrim Office that they have made their pilgrimage for religious-cultural or religious (each about 45%), or cultural-only (11%), reasons. In casual conversation, many people say that they have done it for spiritual reasons. Often it's during a time of transition—a recent graduation, divorce, the death of a loved one, serious illness, loss of a job, or retirement—and they are seeking answers to life's questions. Others want to see the region, want to meet the people, want to try the food, need a vacation—or even to set a speed record.

Most pilgrims have carried a Pilgrim Passport with them on their journey. Obtained before they left home from an organization such as American Pilgrims on the Camino (APOC) or after they arrived in Spain or France at various pilgrim starting points, the passport has had two important functions.

First it has allowed them to stay in the pilgrim-only albergues and hostals along the Camino. Secondly, when properly filled out, it has entitled them to the *Compostela*—a beautiful document, written in Latin, which proclaims one has completed a pilgrimage. Traveling the Camino de Santiago is a unique experience and no matter their motivation for the journey, most people eagerly head for the Pilgrim Office in Santiago. There they present their Pilgrim Passport to show that they have walked at least one hundred kilometers (sixty miles), or bicycled two-hundred kilometers, into the Holy City. To receive the Compostela, pilgrims must show that they have collected two rubber stamps, *sellos,* daily for those last hundred kilometers (stamps that are easily obtained at albergues, hotels, bars, restaurants, churches, and municipal offices along the Camino routes.)

Whether their journey was for religious or secular reasons, most who reach Santiago want to visit the great Cathedral de Santiago. Before they enter, they marvel at the unique wrought-iron double staircase and the ornate stone carvings of the Portico de la Gloria (Gateway of Glory). They climb the stairs and approach a statue of Saint James atop the marble pillar, the Tree of Jesse. (Until authorities recently covered the column with protective screening, pilgrims placed their right hands in the holes worn by pilgrims over the centuries.) They climb the short flight of stairs behind the altar to hug the gilded statue of Saint James, and descend to the crypt below the altar to see the silver casket holding his relics. Traditionally, they stay to watch a pilgrim mass, also hoping to see the giant censer, the *botafumeiro*, as it swings overhead with its memorable whooshing sound, trailing clouds of smoke carrying the heady scent of incense.

It is always wise to embark on a long distance trek without

too many preconceived ideas. There's nothing wrong with having a schedule of miles to travel per day and a list of places to stay each night, but it often works out better to remain flexible. Opportunities arise and mishaps occur. Sometimes carefully-laid plans should be abandoned when a spot demands more time for exploring. Friendships are often forged on the trail; being open to hiking with new companions can be rewarding. Physical problems such as blisters or shin splints can throw a wrench into plans. Rain day after day may radically change timetables and itineraries. It's best to let the days and weeks unfold. On our first Camino trip, we did not allow for unplanned days and later regretted that we had rushed through cities and appealing locales that deserved more time.

This may not be the way you are used to traveling, but then, though you may be using vacation time to embark on your Camino journey, it will not be a typical vacation. It will be exhilarating, demanding, exciting, tiring, and rewarding—sometimes all in the same day. It's like *life*—with its ups and downs. After the journey, it may be weeks, months, or years before you are able to completely comprehend just what your experience was all about.

The Camino hikes that Ralph and I have undertaken have not had the religious elements that some people enjoy, but they have been spiritual to us in their own way. The Camino called even more strongly as we approached departure times for our 2015 and 2016 trips. Would we be able to respond to the call? Would I be able to walk across Spain one more time?

Welcome to Basque Country

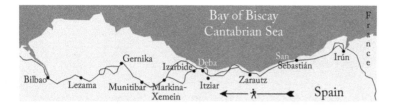

2 • Setting Out along the Northern Coast

Camino del Norte, Spring 2015

"Few people know how to take a walk. The qualifications are endurance, plain clothes, old shoes, an eye for nature, good humor, vast curiosity, good speech, good silence and nothing too much."
~ *Ralph Waldo Emerson*

On May 19, 2015, we flew to Barcelona to spend a few days before trekking our first section of the Camino del Norte along the Bay of Biscay. After our successful hike in Yosemite, we were feeling fairly confident about my fitness, though we did discuss a Plan B. If I couldn't walk, we would rent a car and tour just like millions of other tourists do. Ralph even obtained an international driver's license (which we later learned was unnecessary).

We enjoyed our time as awestruck tourists in the fascinating Catalonian capital. We did a lot of walking and exploring the many neighborhoods, Gaudi's architectural wonders, and Las Ramblas, the pedestrian-only street, with all its entertainment, shops, and restaurants.

We took a train out to Montserrat—an important pilgrim site on the Camino Catalán. This mountaintop monastery is only an hour's ride from Barcelona. We spent the day visiting the Basilica—where the revered Black Madonna of Montserrat is found—hiking to a *hermitage* (place of religious seclusion), and enjoying the spectacular views and setting. I fared well and we began to believe that the trek we had planned on the Norte would work out.

Our goal was to walk between Irún and Santander, covering

166 miles over thirteen hiking days.

Sunday, May 24, 2015
Train from Barcelona to Irún

WE WEREN'T FAMILIAR with Barcelona's Metro, so we took a taxi from our hotel to the train station. The taxi was twenty euros, the driver was great, and we avoided the stress of a transfer on the subway.

It was a six-hour train ride from Barcelona to Irún—350 miles north-west across Spain to San Sebastián, then five miles east to Irún. There are only two trips each day and we wanted to arrive before dinner, so we took the morning train, departing at 7:30 a.m.

The early part of the ride, through the countryside just out of Barcelona, was brown and barren. Then we passed by several large quarrying operations that had tremendously scarred the nearby hillsides. The train stopped a few times along the route including in the major cities of Lleido and Zaragoza.

We had purchased first-class tickets, but it seemed to us that the less expensive second-class tickets would have been fine (with maybe a bit less leg room). The train ran on electric power and the ride was fairly smooth. I was glad it wasn't a high speed train; those are faster, but you can't focus on anything out the window. It's almost impossible to take photos—by the time you see something and lift the camera, what you saw is far behind you.

Halfway across Spain I discovered I'd left my favorite Sunday Afternoons hat behind. I wondered where I'd be able to replace it, but it was pleasant watching the changes of scenery and reading a trashy novel (one from which I could tear out completed pages to lighten the load as I went). By the time we approached Pamplona and got into the hilly sections, the landscape was green and the population denser. As we climbed we went through about ten tunnels; as we neared San Sebastián and began to descend, we went through a half-dozen more. Because the tunnels were in the mountains as well as amazingly long, we figured they must have been enormously expensive to build. We would enter the dark recesses and then wait a couple of minutes to see daylight again (while I resisted thoughts of claustrophobia).

The glimpses of San Sebastián as we passed by told us little about the coastal city, but we knew that we would be back in two days' time. Irún would be our starting point; we would hike west to reach San Sebastián again. Some people start the Norte a short distance farther to the east, from Spain's border town, Hondarribia, which sits on a little promontory facing Hendaye, France. And of course many start their hikes even further away, from their homes in Germany, France, or other countries.

We reached our destination at 1:30 p.m. It was overcast, so my first impression was of a drab and tired city, but I knew Irún had a long and interesting history. The Romans founded the city (then known as Oiasso) in the first century BCE and occupied it through the third century CE. The buildings, however, didn't reflect that Roman history. Most date from the late twentieth-century, after Franco's time. Irún's population is now about 40,000.

Irún also played a role in the Spanish Civil War, as Canadian pilgrim, Randall St. Germain, blogged.

During the early days of the Spanish Civil War, Irún was important due to its location on the border with France. Weapons destined for Republican strongholds, especially in the Basque region, would enter from France, by road or carried along trails through the hills. To stop this flow of weapons, General Francisco Franco's Nationalist Army planned to take over the city in what would be later known as The Battle of Irún. On August 11, 1936, the Nationalist Army began a bombardment of the city, first from sea, and soon after, by air and ground. Although the Republican Army outnumbered the Nationalist Army, they couldn't come close to the firepower. Added to that, the French had closed the border on [August] 8, causing a shortage of weapons and ammunition. The battle lasted until September 5 when the remaining Republican Army retreated while burning any remaining buildings that they thought would aid the Nationalist Army.

WE MADE OUR way from the train station to Pensión Bowling, conveniently located near the center of town, but also right next to the underground transit; I was concerned that it would be noisy at night.

Our one-star accommodations weren't much to look at, but the middle-aged woman who greeted us was friendly. She was also quite helpful, giving us some good suggestions on where I might buy a new hat. We set out on our quest and soon found a little Chinese store, crammed to the gills. The merchandise was mostly not worth a second look, but I was happy to find a store open on a Sunday afternoon. I tried on some cotton baseball caps—too tight and poorly assembled. Next I tried a wide-brimmed, brightly colored, multi-striped had made in China with "Contents 30% paper, 70% polyester." Barcelona for the most part had been sunny, but we anticipated mostly fog and drizzle here along the coast and in the mountains. I had visions of the hat dissolving in the first rain, but it was only five euros, so we took it.

Back in our room, Ralph discovered that he had left our European outlet adapter behind in the hotel in Barcelona. We needed the device that would allow our U.S. plug to fit into Spain's round outlet holes. He went down to the lobby to ask if someone might have left one behind. On other trips, we'd seen a boxful of adapters and phone chargers stashed behind hotel counters, but in this case we had no such luck. He made a trip back to the Chinese store and was again successful.

We found that the restaurant near our pensión wouldn't open for dinner until 8:30, so we took a walk around town. It seemed that everyone else was out, too. We saw dozens of couples strolling arm in arm, families chatting and joking as they paraded by, and groups of young people playing tag and teasing one another. We expected to find a central square, as is so common in Spanish towns, but we didn't—instead of congregating in one place, those strolling chattered away as they poked their heads into the few open shops.

When dinnertime came, I was excited to see duck confit on the menu, but it appeared the duck had lived a hard life because what was served was tough and tasteless—what my kids used to call "all day meat" as they crinkled their noses with distaste. This was a far cry from the dozens of interesting and delicious meals we have previously had in Basque country.

Ralph rarely, but I always, have kept a journal on our Camino hikes. My journal entry in Irún set the stage for the journey to come.

5/24/15

I am very excited about being again in Basque country. This will be new territory for us, but we have always been intrigued by the culture and been treated warmly and graciously by the people. We are anxious to get on the trail and see what it brings us.

Tuesday, May 25, 2015
Irún to Pasajes de San Juan, 9.8 miles/16.2 km

BREAKFAST NEXT DOOR was fresh croissants and rolls with bread and jam. The orange juice, as in most of Spain, was freshly squeezed. I love to watch the automatic juicers; they look like Rube Goldberg devices, but actually they are quite efficient and functional. The server puts several oranges into a wire basket on the top of the machine; the oranges roll down a wire rack into the machine where the fruit is sliced in half, then the juice is squeezed out and fills the waiting glasses. We also asked our server to make us ham and cheese *bocadillos* (sandwiches on a roll) for our lunch.

The big walk began just before eight o'clock. Using a combination of waymarks and the help of our guidebook, a good one from Cicerone (a British publisher of hiking and trekking guides), we made it out of the center of town without any problems. We soon left sidewalks for a dirt path, which climbed up a hill to a small stone chapel. It was locked, so we couldn't go inside, but we saw that there were benches inside, which told us that the *ermita* was still in use. We turned to look back to where we had started our walk and found new views: of the Bidasoa River that separates Spain from France and runs into the Bay of Biscay, and of the city and sandy, curving beach of Hendaye on the French side.

Our climb continued, fairly steeply, until we reached a road and the Santuario (Sanctuary) de Guadalupe. We saw with some chagrin that there was a parking lot with several cars dropping off new hikers. From that point hikers had a choice of routes: a steep one up to Purgatory, or a variant that ringed the mountain. This flatter one was six hundred meters shorter.

Although the guidebooks strongly recommended that hikers take the high route because of the views of the bay as well as passing by the remains of Neolithic dolmens, towers, and castles, we decided to take the alternate. I didn't want to push too hard and injure myself on our first day out. At first, we delighted in the beautiful deciduous forest. Everything was green: grasses, ferns, and leaves. Wildflowers were fresh and abundant; birds flitted from branch to branch chirping all the while. Our path was wide, but we had to dodge puddles and rocks. After a while, we began to wish for more variety in our surroundings, but we still knew that we had made the best choice for us.

Many people passed us; about half were day hikers with small packs. When we stopped to eat our sandwiches, an elderly gray-haired fellow out walking his dog chatted with us for a few minutes about the trail ahead.

Eventually we hit a road, went awhile along the edge, then dropped very steeply on a minor trail to Pasai de San Juan, one of the tiny settlements of Pasaia (Basque; Pasajes in Spanish). We were in the province of Gipuzkoa in a quaint fishing community that is also a commercial port.

We reached the Hospital de Peregrinos Santa Ana just before 3 p.m. We were warmly welcomed by the two hospitaleros, a man and a woman, who we judged to be in their sixties. He was especially helpful; he went down a steep flight of stairs to retrieve my pack that I had set down for a rest. Since we had just climbed many steep sets of concrete steps ourselves, I was glad of the assist. Even though we had arrived an hour earlier than the posted time for the albergue to open, our hosts checked us in and offered us tea. We learned that he had been hospitalero at another town, and this was his first year at this one.

We were soon off to the showers. I was grateful for the warm water, but it did require some experimentation to get it. I finally figured out that the first push of the knob started the flow, which then ran for maybe twenty seconds, then stopped. I had to push again and again to repeat the entire process.

After we had cleaned up and changed clothes, we went down into the center of the village, which was on the water, and found a small place that served delicious *pintxos* (bite-sized, often creatively designed snacks that we usually call tapas in the U.S.

When we returned to the albergue, we found that more pilgrims had arrived—all men. One from Germany, one from Korea, and one originally from Estonia, now living in New Orleans. I dubbed him "New Orleans' Guy" in my mind. He was hiking with Musician Guy, who was also from New Orleans. Musician Guy brought in his guitar, which he was carrying on the Camino because he couldn't stand the thought of six weeks without it. He started to play, and we knew from the beginning that he was no amateur.

It was magical: the right time, the right place. I felt warmly enveloped by the ethereal music. He played several pieces, Rodrigo to Bourbon Street blues, and later confirmed that he was a professional and used his passion for music to support his other great passion: travel.

At bedtime I was greatly relieved that only six of the twelve beds were taken. Most pilgrims go all the way from Irún to San Sebastián in one day, but this village partway between the two larger cities was so charming that I was glad we stopped. It had been a fairly hard day because of the climbs, but we did well. It was fun to check my new Fitbit and see that I had 10.5 miles, 32,437 steps, and 148 flights of stairs recorded.

I had time to send and respond to several friends by email.

Tuesday, May 26, 2015
Pasajes de San Juan to San Sebastián, 6.3 miles/10.2 km

AFTER OUR BRIEF (couple of minutes) pedestrian ferry ride across the water to Pasai de San Pedro, the second of the three scenic seaside villages on the harbor, we turned and walked toward the sea along the concrete quay. Before we reached the mouth of the river, we found the trail again and turned left to begin an ascent. We climbed up multiple sets of narrow concrete steps.

Back in the mountains, then on the bay side, we followed a dirt footpath more or less on contours with the water. We passed remains of a former aqueduct, but like most other hikers presumably, we didn't walk atop the deteriorating stone arch, but followed the safe path alongside. Eventually the trail divided; again we had to decide whether to stay within view of the water or to go inland. We chose the views and the rocky paths for a while, then turned inland. It was a lot more appealing to walk through wonderfully green forests filled with birdsong rather than tree farms with their uniform rows and columns of one kind of tree such as we have seen elsewhere. Though the guidebook didn't mention accommodations in this section, we saw a couple of what looked like guesthouses.

We crossed through a county park with multiple hiking trails, but it wasn't difficult to keep to the Camino as the trail descended gradually into San Sebastián. The day was overcast, but the city's long, sandy beaches were stunning. No one was swimming, but a dozen surfers in wet suits were plying the waves. I figured if the sun came out the next day as predicted, we'd see more bathers.

Because our walk was short, we arrived early at our hostal, the Alemana. The receptionist greeted us kindly, but told us that noon was too early to check in. She offered to stow our packs behind the counter, and we went for a walk in the surrounding area and ate lunch.

We came back at 2:00 p.m. as had been suggested and went up to Room 201, electronic key card in hand. Once in the room, I noticed that the hand towels were hanging askew in the bathroom, and there was only one bath towel. I asked Ralph to go downstairs to ask for more towels. Then I noticed a toiletry kit on the bathroom counter. I was really surprised to see we'd been supplied with a full-sized tube of Colgate—usually we were lucky to get a travel-sized one. It also seemed a bit odd that a toothbrush had been supplied, but was not sealed in cellophane. However, the room's description in the guide book had said that all toiletries would be provided so I dismissed my thoughts.

I went back into the bedroom to unpack and opened the closet door. Sitting on a shelf was a neatly-folded, blue, nylon sports jacket. This was not exactly the terry-cloth robe that one might expect! I pushed open the other sliding door and saw a stack of handkerchiefs and polo shirts, all folded, sitting on the shelves, and a pair of beige, dress slacks hanging on the clothes rod.

Just then Ralph came back in shaking his head. He told me that the manager was very embarrassed and apologetic about giving us a room that was already occupied. I was just glad we hadn't found any people in the room (which we'd had happen on a previous trip back home).

The contrast between the state of the stranger's room and what our hotel rooms usually looked like when we were on a long-distance hike was striking. If someone entered our room mid-day, they would find an empty soda can on the bedside table along with whatever portion remained of my torn-up paperback. Ziploc bags filled with toiletries would litter the vanity counter. Wet clothes would be strung above the bathtub, or draped over the radiator, or hung from a window, or on a hiking pole reaching from chair to chair. I also wondered how many handkerchiefs one person really needs.

Ralph had the key to Room 204. We picked up our packs and moved. From our new room, we had a limited view of the Bay of Biscay from the tiny balcony, but we were glad to be in the city and in a comfortable room. My legs were tired and I was happy to sit.

We got a call from Mom's assisted living facility. The health coordinator informed me that Mom was not responding normally: that her speech was incoherent and that she was sleeping most of the day. Her vitals, however, were normal and she was comfortable. Because this was such a big change from her normal behavior, I called both of my sons. Tom, who I can always count on to follow up my calls with a friendly call to his grandma, promised to do so again. Scott, being an attorney with a penchant for getting to the bottom of things, said he had already talked to Blanca and grilled her for more information. Things didn't seem great, but they were under control.

Because of the nine-hour time difference, I waited until after dinner to call Mom. She was not her usually cheery self, but it was encouraging that she was being fed some soup. Even so, Ralph and I were both worried about her and so talked about our options. I thought he would be upset with me if I even mentioned the possibility of going home, but he surprised me.

"I think it would be the right thing to do if her condition worsens," he said. "We've already had a good vacation, our time in Barcelona." I felt very relieved to know that he would not be disappointed if we cut our trip short.

Nurse Wilson from hospice called to say that Mom was doing okay, "She's comfortable; we gave her medication for her shoulder and put her arm in a sling." Her call reassured me.

My doctor had sanctioned four 200-mg tablets of ibuprofen every eight hours to reduce my leg pain, so I took a full dose and went to bed. I wished I didn't need that much, but I was happy to have completed two full days of walking. I was also looking forward to taking a day off to explore San Sebastián.

Wednesday, May 27, 2015
Zero Day (no-mileage day) in San Sebastián

I HAVE WANTED to visit San Sebastián for more than forty years. In the '70s, I became friends with Carmen Sanchez, a neighbor who had been born in San Sebastián. Because she was a teacher, she was able to return to her hometown to visit her mother during the summers. I had found her photos of northern Spain mesmerizing.

When Carmen retired, she moved back to San Sebastián and

I lost contact with her, but while we were wandering through the city's streets on this trip, I fantasized about bumping into her. My luck didn't extend that far.

Ralph and I marveled that the sun was shining because we knew that rain was not unusual at any time of year. As we made our way across town, we saw there were still only a few people on the beach. I was impressed by how clean it was and saw that machines were working along the surf line to pick up detritus. A century ago San Sebastián's beaches were lined with mansions, but the 2.5 kilometer-long 'Queen of Beaches' is now bordered mostly by huge apartment houses. Even so, its beautiful sandy shoreline is internationally known for its surfing.

Still in the heart of the city, we walked along the shoreline until we reached the base of Monte Urgull. Our goal was to reach the old fortress, Mota, atop the mountain. We had many routes to choose from: a gradual, wide, asphalt path that wound around the mountain; many shortcuts on narrow dirt trails; and concrete steps. We took a combination. On each level, we dutifully admired the views of the city. We came upon a plaque in the English Cemetery and learned that the English had been involved in the Peninsular War, which (simplistically speaking) was an effort by the Spanish, aided by the English, to push Napoleon's French forces back over the border in 1813.

Inside the old fort at the top was a museum (admission free) depicting earlier times here. The wide-range of exhibits—everything from farm implements to military uniforms—reflected the rich history of the city.

After descending to the streets of old town once more, we went to the Basilica Santa Maria to admire the church and to get our *sellos* in our new pilgrim passports. Next stop was the San Telmo Museum. The entrance and lobby were squeaky clean, very modern, and used wood and glass to good advantage.

When constructed the museum retained some of the original building: a sixteenth-century Dominican convent with a core of old archways that looked out at a neatly trimmed lawn. When a modern wing was added in 2011, some people hated it, but designer Nieto Sobejano envisioned that native vegetation from Monte

Urgull would in time take hold in the holes of the exterior's thin layer of perforated aluminum panels and win over the critics.

This museum of Basque ethnography was well worth seeing. Exhibits included archaeological finds, old and new art, artifacts from centuries back to present day. Stone *stele*s (funerary art) had been collected from the Basque lands as well as neighboring ones; one of the corridors was lined with the ancient grave markers made of marble, limestone, or sandstone. There was an extensive collection of knives and other weapons that dated from the fifteenth century to the twentieth. I enjoyed the wall devoted to headdresses—most of cloth twisted into unique shapes that indicated social status and position.

After lunch we continued on foot to the top of another of the hills that surround the city to go to the national art museum. Its vast collection of religious art was overwhelming, but it was interesting to be looking at work from the fourteen hundreds and even earlier.

Many paintings were framed in ways unfamiliar to us. Some of the earliest were constructed of a single piece of wood that had been carved out to provide a flat surface for a painting. Most frames were ornate and gilded. Others were miniature altarpieces surrounding the religious art. Frames were individually made to fit a particular piece of art. Because they were so time consuming to build, and required specialized skill, they often were designed and built by furniture makers.

After our busy day came some relaxed moments. We made our way to two different bars that specialized in pintxos. Fourteen euros for two small glasses of *vino tinto* and six pintxos seemed reasonable. From our samplings, came two new favorites: slices of baguette topped with half a deviled egg topped with pickle relish, and slices of baguette topped with sardines and shrimp. Pintxos have names, just like Chinese Dim Sum items do. Since we didn't know the names, we just studied the artistic creations and pointed.

After the appetizers, it was time for dinner. We were happy to find a good, upscale restaurant that let us in even though we were wearing hiking clothes.

After dinner, it was great to connect with friends by email. Deborah, who with her husband Dennis, lives half the year in France along a Camino route and half the year in Colorado, asked how my leg was doing. I wrote back, "Major improvements since we saw you in March, but I do pay for it at night when the pain is much worse. Remains a mystery that a something diagnosed as a muscle problem would last so long, but we are doing well so far."

I wrote Amy, a terrific hiker and friend, that we were having a Zero Day in San Sebastián bragging that we did *only* forty-eight flights of stairs.

She replied, "Yesterday I took off my Fitbit midday, to take a shower, and forgot to put it back on; I hate it when that happens!!!"

Most importantly, I was able to communicate with my son about my mom.

> **From:** Susan
> **To:** Scott:
> Talked to Mom both yesterday and today;
> someone was there to pick up the phone for her.
> Anyway, she is better today than yesterday: at least
> coherent, though speech is still somewhat slurred.
> This morning she apparently got fed up about being
> stuck in bed and suddenly threw her feet out of bed,
> followed by throwing the blankets off the bed. I think
> staff was alarmed about this, but I think it is a good
> sign that she isn't going to just be a vegetable. At some
> point, they helped her up so she could sit on the sofa.
> Later, I talked to Gretchen from hospice. She said that
> Mom was still restless, but more alert.
> I suspect that she either had a mini-stroke or has
> had too much medication for her shoulder. Time will
> tell.
> Thanks, Scott, for talking to the assisted living
> folks yesterday, I was too distraught to ask the right
> questions. Your call, and the one from hospice,
> was reassuring. We were ready to abort this trip if
> necessary, but things now seem much calmer. I think

it would take us two days minimum to get home.

I think Ralph will miss seeing the topless sunbathers on this city's gorgeous beaches as we hike into the mountains again!

Love,
Mom

Thursday, May 28, 2015
San Sebastián to Zarautz, 11.47 miles/18.6 km

AFTER LEAVING SAN Sebastián, we climbed up steps to resume the Camino trail. Before long we passed through the hilly neighborhood of Igeldo, with its population of barely a thousand. The inhabitants must be a determined lot. They wanted their independence from San Sebastián, and in 2013, they started the legal process. However, they were stopped by a local court.

Once again, we generally followed the contour lines, keeping the bay on our right, making it a relatively flat walk. The humidity was high because of the fog; sweat soon soaked my clothes. Some of the way we were in lush open forest and the young trees allowed streams of light to get through. It was refreshing to see ferns and wildflowers; back home most of the wild vegetation was drying out and turning gold or brown because of California's multi-year drought. Some of our walk was on cobblestones, slippery from the recent rain.

Lunch was fish bocadillos in a café-bar on the plaza in Orio. We met a young German woman on her first hiking day. She looked even more exhausted that I felt, and was going to stop at the local pilgrim albergue.

We went on to our destination of Zarautz. We were starting to get into the rhythm of the walk and I took advantage of our early arrival by writing in my journal and sending emails.

5/28/15

All in all this day's hike wasn't as challenging as Tuesday's into San Sebastián. The climbs out of there and out of Orio weren't too bad, so even though the distance was longer, we were okay.

We saw more people on the trail today, more than twenty, and many seemed to be using the baggage carrying services.

It has occurred to me that I am speaking much more Spanish that usual. On other trips, I have been so afraid of looking foolish that I have let Ralph do all of the talking. This time around I feel comfortable. I have no idea why the change, but I like it.

We arrived at our pensión, the Hotel Ekia Pentsioa. The room is newly decorated in the "plain vanilla" style: all white except for two abstract posters on the wall, but it's very clean and I am happy to be here. When we saw it had a radiator, I was pleased because it would help our laundry dry faster. Unfortunately, we soon found out it had been turned off for the season.

From: Susan
To: Friends and family

We have passed through San Sebastián; the shops there are gorgeous. However, as usual, I am not doing any shopping because I don't want to carry anything extra. We have now reached Zarautz. We saw farmhouses along the way, but in town it's all huge apartment houses rather than single-family homes.

Pintxos here in Basque country are so much fun; we enjoy going from one bar to the other to try different kinds. We have now completed three hiking days (and have ten to go). I think the trail veers away from the coast on tomorrow's hike and will become a little less difficult. Mostly we have gone down to the cities on the Bay of Biscay and then had to climb up into the surrounding mountains each day. Today my little Fitbit toy told me that we had climbed the equivalent of three-hundred stories.

Ralph has been patient with my slow pace, and

has been carrying my extra clothes. He trained with thirty pounds at home to be ready for the additional weight, but when we tried to fit all my extra clothing, toiletries, and paperbacks into his pack, we found that he didn't have enough room. That means that I am carrying more than planned. I have about twelve pounds, which I didn't have time to train with.

We appreciated seeing the sun today though the humidity keeps me very wet. Most of our walking has been on paved lanes and roads, but we've also walked on narrow dirt trails through the countryside with many cows, goats, pigs, and chickens to capture our attention. The hard surfaces are very hard on our feet, so I was happy to put my feet up at our pension tonight.

Happy trails,
Susan

From: Amy
To: Susan

I can see that you understand my obsession with my Fitbit! Yesterday, I too explored a trail through the countryside with many cows, goats, pigs, and chickens. Actually, it was the train track from Healdsburg to Windsor, my favorite way to see the backside of this otherwise posh California wine country. It nabbed me and my Fitbit 25,000 steps! Love the reports from Spain.

From: Susan
To: Amy

38,900 steps today, but who's counting!

From: Amy
To: Susan

Well, I am most inspired by your 38,900 steps (but who's counting). I myself was pretty tired after hiking to Windsor. And I was hard pressed to make a base level 10,000 today. I was reduced to toddling around the block from time to time, unwilling to make a major hiking commitment, but still seeking that minimal 10,000. Finally, at around 9, Mickey said, "Why do you keep going outside? What's going on?" I explained my new passion. Hmmm, still only 9,510. I may have to go around the block one more time.

Sleep well and hike far!

Friday, May 29, 2015
Zarautz to Itziar, 12.4 miles/20 km

THE WEATHER FORECAST for today was for overcast skies, but no rain. I hadn't expected to hear cars driving on wet streets or to see so many people walking with open umbrellas when I looked out the window from our room in the pensión. We put on our full rain gear before we set out. That turned out to be a good choice, because though it was only misting, we have found that eventually we'd end up soaking wet.

After being so tired at day's end yesterday, I was worried about this day's mileage because it was a mile longer. However, it was wonderful to start out at sea level from Zarautz. We made our way along a promenade of aggregate stone with an attractive metal railing. Our beautifully paved route ran parallel to the beach the entire three kilometers into the next town, Getaria.

Getaria has been home to a couple of notable citizens in its history. Cristobal Balenciaga, the famous fashion designer, was born here in 1895. I would have enjoyed a visit to the Cristobal Balenciaga Museum, but it was on a hill overlooking the city and too far off our route. Balenciaga spent much of his childhood in Aldamar Palace, which is now part of the museum, because his mother was a tailor for the owners of the palace.

Getaria was also the hometown of seaman and explorer, Juan Sebastián Elcano. Elcano was an officer with Fernando Magellan's expedition to the Spice Islands in 1521. The expedition began with 241 men and five ships. When Magellan was killed by natives in the Philippines, Getaria took command of the Nao Victoria. In 1522, he and the seventeen remaining crew returned to Spain with the one ship—thereby completing the first known circumnavigation of the world.

We stopped for soda, coffee, and finished off some leftover cake from breakfast. Our route left the sea and climbed on paved roadway, then on very muddy and slippery goat paths, and along the edge of a busy highway.

We enjoyed the green fields and the grazing sheep. We'd seen white and black ones before, but here we also saw some gray-colored ones. The last third of the walk was the most difficult: up and down on a detour to make our way around a freeway. On the final climb, Ralph slipped and fell: luckily on a grassy bank and not in the mud. He had some laundry to do.

Anemone del Camino, a Facebook friend on the Camino forum, also found difficulty in this region. Coming down the hill just after Zumaia, she found a spot that was difficult for her to manage—too steep and too eroded. She solved her problem and wrote, "If you just sit on your toosh you'll make it down ok. Just don't go thinking you are a mountain goat."

Our day ended well with a glorious sunset. The Hotel Kanala was much pricier than we expected—almost a hundred dollars. I hoped we wouldn't run into such high rates again. We were surprised to end up with three single beds, but the décor and the printed draperies were cheerful.

For the last three years, my niece Karen and I have exchanged daily email messages that give a brief account of something that brought us joy, for which we felt gratitude, that we appreciated, and that gave us a sense of satisfaction.

From: Susan
To: Karen

Joy competing 12.5 mile day. *Gratitude* that our hotel is nice and it's now sunny (though it drizzled during much of our walk.) *Appreciated* out ocean views. *Satisfied* that I did not fall in the mud. Ralph did, but he's okay.

From: Karen
To: Susan
    Did you only smirk a little?

From: Susan
To: Karen
    Only had thoughts of gratitude that it was not me
    in the sheep muck! I have to be nice to Ralph because
    he is carrying a bunch of my clothes☺.

Saturday, May 30, 2015
Itziar to Izarbide, About 6 miles/10 km

TODAY STARTED WITH a, mostly downhill, walk of four kilometers into Deba. The fun part about getting into the city was taking two separate elevators that lowered us down the very steep hillside into the heart of the city. There we stopped for beverages and slices of delicious Spanish tortilla. We bought apples at a grocery and poked around a tiny farmers' market.

We visited the Church of Santa María, a heritage site. The main entrance (the *cover)* was richly decorated with polychrome, carved figures. A man, probably in his sixties, encouraged us to enter through the closed doors where we a found a gorgeous cloister.

A young African was absorbed with carefully painting the gold-colored trim of a railing in the sanctuary, but he looked up when he saw me. I was attracted by his melodious accent and his warmth so I stopped to chat. He said he had come from Senegal five or six years back, but that it hadn't been easy being in a new place where the jobs come and go.

We could understand why Deba was a popular tourist stop; it was an attractive seaside town. Those walking the Norte in August might be able to join in the festivities for San Roque, the town's patron saint. Events during the town's most important fiesta traditionally include the *encierros* (running of the bulls), bullfights, traditional dances, and outdoor parties.

After leaving Deba, we climbed steeply: first on a concrete

road, then on packed dirt trail alongside pastures with cows, sheep, chickens, geese, and donkeys. There was one short section of my preferred type: soft, nicely packed forest bed.

We stopped at the chapel, Ermita del Calvario. There as back in Deba, were some curious large, concrete blocks with metal handles attached. The stones' weights were marked on one side: one read "1600 kilos" (about 3,500 pounds). In front of the blocks was a *probadero* (a concrete pad, or runway). I later learned that this set-up was for a popular traditional contest held in these parts known as the *idi probak*. The competition is between oxen, who are challenged to pull the weighted block as fast as possible to the far end of the track. Another version is for men to lift, instead of pull, the heavy weights (but it's certain the concrete blocks the men lift do not weigh nearly as much as the ones the oxen pull).

While we walked, Ralph and I discussed why we were seeing so few people on the trail. When we started the Norte, back near San Sebastián, we saw more; we wondered where they had gone. Had we not seen them because we had generally stayed in private hostels or hotels rather than in pilgrims' albergues? Or was it because some were cherry-picking the route and busing ahead?

We arrived in Izarbide early afternoon. It had been a short day's hike for which I was grateful. I was happy to rest my feet and write in my journal.

5/30/15

We are in a new private albergue, the Izarbide Aterpetxea. It's well-organized with two rooms holding a total of thirty-two beds. There are separate men's and women's rooms and also separate showers and bathrooms. It costs twelve euros per bed and we have paid the extra fee for a communal meal.

The albergue has some very strict rules. Boots and hiking poles must be left by the entrance. This is to help keep the sleeping rooms clean.

More complicated is dealing with the backpacks; they must be unpacked in a locker room. You can take out your clothing and so forth to use, but the pack stays in the separate room. This is all about trying to keep bedbugs out. We have read about this precaution being implemented on French Camino routes, but we haven't encountered it before. I am all for the high standards; it was just a surprise.

As I sit here writing this, other pilgrims have come in. There are now several hikers from the U.S. There's a bi-continental couple—he from the UK and she from New Zealand. They look to be in their sixties and seem very nice. A man, also about sixty, has arrived along with his two sisters and a niece. They are also from the U.S. but they aren't very responsive to my attempts at conversation, so about all I have learned is that they are from Montana. Even when I mentioned that Ralph was born in the Big Sky Country, there was no attempt at sharing trail stories.

We got to talking with Andrea and Terry, the Kiwi/UK couple. This is the first Camino trip—in fact their first long-distance walk. They have been together for twenty-five years, and have spent seventeen of them sailing around the world. I can scarcely imagine being out of sight of land for days, much less weeks.

Terry said, "Sailing is the easy part of what we do; the hard part is that something is always breaking down. Every time we come to a port the first thing we have to find is a way to get needed repairs." He added, "The hardest time was when we were sailing out of India and we lost our autopilot. We had to take two-hour shifts for ten days until we reached another port."

They now feel that the boat is no longer strong enough for long trips and have decided they don't want to tackle the Pacific. Andrea, like me, is finding this hike extremely hard; neither of us likes ending the day so tired and feeling that we don't have any reserve.

Terry is a very optimistic sort. Meeting them is a bit of luck—what we call trail magic. We all hit it off instantly. Our conversations go quickly from when and where we started on the Camino del Norte to more personal topics such as parents, children, and grandchildren. They have a home and a family in each country, so they spend roughly half the year in each place. They invited us to stay with them if we come to New Zealand to hike one of their trails.

Another group of hikers comes in including a good-looking, friendly man from France. French Guy's story is that he sold his business a few months back and wants to do the Camino alone during this transition. Two young women come in looking quite exhausted and shaken; they ended up on the alternate route today after splitting off from their hiking partners. The women are inexperienced hikers and their friends are supposed to be helping them. Apparently there was a lack of communication, and what appeared to be some carelessness, because the friends should have not left the "newbies." They still don't seem to know where their friends are.

Dinner was good basic fare with generous portions. The first course was a lettuce, egg, carrot, tuna, and pasta salad. Next was a chicken-stock soup with a bit of pasta. The main course was chicken and French fries. Of course this was all accompanied by vino and bread. We felt the cost for our stay was quite reasonable—our beds, dinners, and breakfasts cost sixty euros total, but the family from Montana decided it was too expensive for them, changed their minds about staying, and hiked on.

Sunday, May 31, 2015
Izarbide to Markina-Xemein, 11.2 miles/18 km

I WAS A bit apprehensive about communal sleeping last night, but even though we had eight people in our dorm, it was surprisingly quiet with very little snoring. Rest was good!

After breakfast Ralph and I set out alone, but we weren't

that way very long; there was a walkathon going on and we must have met and dodged about two-hundred participants coming towards us on their 10K walk.

We came to an open area where we enjoyed seeing large swatches of deep red violet foxglove, yellow buttercups, and a few patches of purple larkspur.

We followed a quiet road up a steep hill and at the top came upon two little girls sitting behind a small table in their driveway. We stopped at their homemade lemonade stand and were delighted to find that they also sold cold beers. We enjoyed supporting the local entrepreneurs.

A short distance before we reached Markina-Xemein, we came to the extraordinary *San Miguel de Arrechinaga* (Archangel). This uniquely designed hexagonal-shaped church and hermitage was constructed in the eighteenth-century to replace the ruins of an earlier building.

Inside, three massive boulders stood on end, leaning toward each other. This created an open space where a small altar with a statue of San Miguel (St. Michael) and St Pollonia, a local saint, stood. Some have claimed that the three boulders were *dolmen* (a megalithic tomb), which would have required the stones be altered and moved here by people. Most authorities have agreed that the boulders are remnants of a huge rock outcropping from an eroded hillside near here, and date back hundreds of millions of years to the Tertiary period.

The rocks practically filled the interior and left only a small space around them for worshipers to gather; there were few benches and chairs on which to sit. There has long been a local legend associated with the site: that if a man wishes to marry within the year, he must pass between the stones three times. I had a hard time figuring out how anyone could squeeze through the open spaces between the stones. When I tried to take photos of the interior, I found the space was so confined that I couldn't back up far enough to get all of the rocks in the picture.

Coming into Markina-Xemein involved a very steep descent. I was already missing seeing the ocean; we'd be away from the coast for a couple of days. The hike had been hot and difficult for me on the long uphill stretches. The trails had varied from concrete to dirt track, some of it with slippery patches of mud. I was, however, pleased that I managed 34,000 steps. We were pleasantly surprised when we arrived at our accommodations to be given a private room decorated in cheerful shades of yellow. It was set up with single beds, but we were happy to have any bed.

We met up with Andrea and Terry again and had dinner together. We all loved talking about food and were in agreement that Basque cuisine was top notch. We feasted on paella, filet of beef, French fries, rice pudding, wine and bread provided by the hostal's owner.

There have been more exotic choices on the printed menus we've seen in this region—*marmitako* (fresh tuna and potato stew), *chipirones en su tinta* (baby squid in their own ink), or *kokotxas* (cheeks of large fish such as hake (*merluza*) or codfish (*bacalao*) in green sauce, but the daily specials were usually were tasty and cost about ten dollars per person.

I included updates on Mom's condition in my journal.

5/31/15
   I've read through the small print of our airline's cancellation and change policies and figure that it would cost about six-thousand dollars to make all the necessary changes for flights and other transportation in order to go home earlier than we have scheduled. And it would take a minimum of two days to get there. After that sobering news, I made my call home crossing my fingers and hoping for some improvement in Mom's health.
   This time I talked to someone else from hospice, Laura, who told me that Mom is comfortable and that the 24-hour watch has been extended until 4 p.m. (their time) today. At that point, the charge nurse will evaluate Mom's condition and decide if they will do another twenty-four hours.
   Laura said, "If we leave, she will jump out of bed

and fall." So they are doing what they can to keep her in bed. They can't use restraints (thank heavens), so about all that can be done is to stay with her and not let her get out of bed unassisted.

They report that she is not reading, which is unusual for her. When she is feeling normal, she spends most of her day sitting on the sofa with a dog-eared romance novel. Apparently Mom is alert, but when she talks it's clear that she's confused. Of course since they have been giving her morphine, I am not exactly surprised.

Apparently Mom's right shoulder still hurts. The sling on her arm is to help her avoid moving it and to let the shoulder rest. They have already figured out that she is not a complainer, so the fact that she is telling anyone something hurts means that it really does.

It 's a good sign that she is eating something: a bit of scrambled egg, some banana, and chocolate ice cream. As far as I am concerned, she can eat all of the ice cream that she wants.

Monday, June 1, 2015
Markina-Xemein to Munitibar, 6.9 miles/11.2 km

WE HAD TO be out the door by 8 a.m., but found a coffee bar nearby for *napolitana de chocolate* (chocolate-filled puff pastry much like the French *pain au chocolate*) and beverages. We walked at a leisurely pace, and stopped often to take photos. We planned to go only eight or nine kilometers, passing tiny Bolibar along the way and staying at the medieval Monasterio de Zenarruza at Ziortza-Bolibar. Although we did have one patch of muddy track, the climb wasn't very steep. Shortly before the monastery, we spotted an albergue, and bar that was open, but we continued on.

At this point we were playing leapfrog with Andrea and Terry. Sometimes we were ahead, other times they were, but we reached the monastery at the same time. The monastery has some significance, but what I admired most were the wooden supports and beams of the cloister. The covered porch was built during the Renaissance of lumber used from much larger trees than any of those that can be found in the area these days. The unique carvings in the wood were skillfully done.

While we were looking around the exterior, one of the monks approached and invited us to look inside the sanctuary. The Church of Santa Maria, a Gothic-style building, dates from 1379. The church's small east door had an image of an eagle with skull in its claws, which related to the legend of how the church came to be. It seems that while nearby villagers were celebrating Ascension Day Mass in 968 CE, an eagle picked up a skull from the cemetery and dropped it on the present-day site of the church.

The monk also suggested we visit the small store operated by the order. While the rest of us sipped tea, Andrea selected some notecards to take home for family. We asked about accommodations. The guidebook had said there were some available; but we understood the monk to say that there were none. It was only 11:30, so we had plenty of time to go ahead to find somewhere else. If we'd stayed, there'd have been many hours with nothing much to do.

As we were leaving the grounds, Terry saw the local mail carrier, a stocky, middle-aged woman, who told him that all the services that we would need could be found in the next town. She indicated that we had only one-and-a-half kilometers to go.

That brought us to the village of Gerrikaitz, but we found no facilities there either. Then we lucked out; at four-and-a-half kilometers along, we found a bar-restaurant serving lunch. We gorged on green salad and tomatoes; cauliflower and potatoes; garbanzo beans and sausage, and *bacalao*. For dessert we saw that there was Manchego cheese and a popular confection, *membrillo*, available. I had never heard of it. Andrea had, and she explained that it's a thick, sweet, jelly made by cooking the pulp of the quince fruit over low heat.

We again discussed our earlier confusion at the monastery and concluded that the monk had been trying to tell us to come back mid-afternoon, after 3:30, when they opened up the room with beds.

Andrea went online and found a listing for the Casa Rural Garro. When we arrived, our host, Jose Angel Uberuaga Etxebarria, welcomed us into a converted Basque stone farmhouse that has been owned by the Garro family for hundreds of years.

It turned out that our host, Ube (as Uberuaga Etxebarria is referred to in professional circles), was a famous sculptor. He showed us pieces of his work both inside and outside his house. Most of his studio work is stark, contemporary, and political. I generally prefer gracefully flowing pieces in the style of Rodin, but I admired the way that Ube had combined stone, metal, and wood.

Everywhere there were artistic and graceful touches: the well-tended gardens with roses and irises in bloom. Exposed beam ceilings, ten-foot high wardrobe closets. The bathroom modernized with both tub and shower. A romantic bedroom with crocheted white coverlet, starched lace curtains at the window, and a hand-carved bed wonderfully made up with fine linens embroidered twelve inches deep. I could hardly believe our luck in landing there; I had to pinch myself to see if it were true.

It was a comfort to write in my journal that night.

6/1/15

Once we were settled I called Mom. She made no sense; she pushed the phone away. That has never happened before. I wasn't at all sure that she knew it was me. Hospice tried twice to give the phone back to her, but she continued to push it away. It was reassuring that hospice was still there on the 24-hour watch so she wouldn't try to get up and then fall and injure herself again. After that distressing phone call, I just sat on the bed and tried to focus on the beauty and comfort of our room.

I went out to find the others and found Andrea. We talked a lot: about women being torn between mates', children's, parents', and our own needs.

She was a very good listener and has had her own challenges within her family. I told her my tales of woe, not only about Mom worries, but also my leg problem. She commiserated with me about the sadness that comes up when one has to consider giving up something important to them—as with me with hiking. How wonderful that we have met Terry and Andrea and such a strange twist of fate that we are all facing big new challenges now.

We had known beforehand that we would not be served dinner at this home, which was why we'd had the huge lunch. We made do with our energy bars. The walk today was rather good. My Fitbit recorded 22,705 steps and 115 flights of stairs.

Tuesday, June 2, 2015
Munitibar to Guernica/Gernika, 8.5 miles/13.7 km

THE TRAIL STARTED alongside a creek, which was quite pleasant to follow. It seemed like whenever we passed homes with gardens, we saw gorgeous robust roses. Although there were still some wildflowers in bloom, the trees here are crops: pines planted in rows plantation-style. We also saw a few huge scars caused by clearcutting. We continued played leapfrog with Terry and Andrea.

There were many *PUDS* (pointless ups and downs). We took a welcome detour that avoided one steep climb and walked along a road that had a bar where we could stop for lunch. The official route would have missed this pleasant stop.

This Camino trip has been different from most of our other Caminos: on most others we have purchased meat, cheese, and bread ahead of time for picnic lunches during the day. On this trail we have almost always found an establishment where we could stop to eat.

The weather report had indicated rain was possible, but we were determined to walk to Guernica—a scene of horrible bombing of the Basque instigated by Francisco Franco and carried out by the Germans and Italians.

We arrived in Guernica-Lumo (Basque name *Gernika*) and found lodging at the Pensión Bolina. It seemed clean enough at first glance, but I noticed that the chair pad was very soiled, which made me wonder about the level of housekeeping.

We explored the center of the city and soon found the Assembly (the Basque meeting house) and the Oak Tree Memorial. The Assembly, which has operated from the Middle Ages into the present day, is where the representatives of the villages along the Bay of Biscay meet and govern. In the earliest times the meetings took place under a large tree; that symbol has survived. The Republican resistance in Northern Spain during the Spanish Civil War of 1936–1939 put them at odds with Franco's right-wing leanings. Guernica, being the Basque center of government, became a prime target for Franco. A devastating bombing took place on April 26, 1937, and people fled from their homes. The younger men were already at the front, but more than a thousand women, children, and elderly men were killed. Sources give varying percentages, but some claim that eighty-five percent of the buildings were totally destroyed.

The General Assembly building and the symbolic oak tree survived. It was the third-generation oak planted on the premises; the Father Tree was planted in the fourteenth century and lasted 450 years.

After visiting the meeting house, we set out to wander again without a map. We came to Pedro de Elejalde Street and a full-sized, ceramic tile reproduction of Pablo Picasso's famous painting, *Guernica*. The original was made in 1937, expressing his outrage at the bombing and devastation. Beneath the ceramic tile work here was an inscription expressing a desire of the local people—that the original canvas be displayed in the town whose suffering had inspired Picasso's original creation.

There was more to see in Guernica than we were able to see in only a few hours. We'd have been interested in the *Museo de la Paz* (Peace Museum) with its exhibits that portray the Basque history, including the dramatically told story of the Guernica bombing and its aftermath. There was a tourism office that offered guided visits that give insight into how life was the day of the bombing and included a visit to one of the air-raid shelters. If we'd been there on a Monday, we would have spent time at the lively farmer's market.

Guernica, with only 16,225 residents, is much smaller than either San Sebastián (186,125) or Bilbao (350,000), which may explain why we observed so many people stopping to talk with friends on the street. Here as in much of the country, we enjoyed people-watching and I was enthralled with the differences between how the Basque and the Americans interact with their children.

First of all, the kids here seemed to have a lot more freedom to run around in the parks and plazas; the parents were not hovering. Here, while the adults were sitting on park benches, chatting at bistro tables, or sampling vino and pintxos at a bar, the youngsters were tearing around with their friends playing tag, riding bikes, or playing soccer. They practice and play soccer from about the same time they start walking. If the children get hurt, there's no coddling. That's not to say that parents ignore serious injury, but minor scrapes and falls hardly merit adult interference.

At the same time, when Basque parents were with their children eating together, or walking somewhere, they (like many of their contemporaries in the U.S.), were very warm and affectionate. A noticeable difference however, between customs here and back home, was that here when a man runs into friends and acquaintances on the street, he doesn't appear to be afraid to admire the kids. He's not worried about being thought of as less of a man, nor afraid of being labeled a deviant, just because he's warm and friendly to the children.

Dinner, usually a highlight of the day, was disappointing. When we have burned a large number of calories while walking many miles, food takes on a greater than usual importance. It also may be that we have been spoiled by all of the tasty Basque foods that we've had. Whatever the cause, the salad mixta of iceberg lettuce, carrots, matchstick cut beets, hard-boiled egg, stalk of white asparagus, and tuna was tasteless. I gave it a C-. Afterwards, we went to a nearby *super* (strangely, "supers" are usually not very large here) market and bought a box of six chocolate-covered ice cream Popsicles and ate all of them.

After finishing my treats, I turned to my journal.

6/2/15

I talked this evening to both the nurse and the case manager at Mom's place, but both conversations were difficult. I had to pry information out of the nurse, and the case manager's accent was so thick that I found it difficult to understand her. From the two, however, I learned that Mom was agitated and was given two doses of codeine earlier today; this concerned me because normally she takes no medication and I wondered if it would have a stronger effect on her than on most people. I felt better when they added that her pain level had decreased and they were going to switch to Tylenol.

Hospice is going to stay, around the clock, one more day, because Mom is still not considered stable. They removed the sling from her arm, but she still can't feed herself. She was sleeping so I wasn't able to talk to her.

Though some of their reports were good, they also delivered some bad news: I have twenty-four hours in which to decide if Mom should be moved to the memory care section (in the same facility where she lives now, but on a different floor) or whether she should stay where she is in the assisted living section.

The 24-hour watches by nurses from hospice has been a comfort for the last few days, but that will likely end tomorrow. Once they decide she is stable, that level of care will end.

The benefit of moving her to memory care is that the staff-to-patient ratio is much better: about five to one versus twenty to one, but I have never seen the section they would move her to. Clearly, there's no way that I can check out the facility myself within the time given. If the majority of the other residents in the new wing have advanced dementia, that could be a very upsetting situation for Mom. Except for her poor short-term memory, she is lucid and can have meaningful conversations—at least she could until this whole episode started. I have no idea what activities and programs would be provided in the new setting, or whether or not she would be able to see her old friends at meal time.

The only other option offered by hospice was to hire a sitter; this would be someone who sits with Mom for fall prevention, but does nothing else. That doesn't solve the remaining new problems: providing complete care in feeding, dressing, toileting, bathing, and grooming as she is too weak to do most of these things for herself.

Whichever route we go, this will be an even more expensive situation. Ralph is already concerned that we are dipping into funds that we may need for our own care not too many years down the road. I feel completely stressed.

I sent a message to Scott explaining the dilemma and asking if he could check out the facility. I felt a flood of relief a couple of hours later when I checked my emails again and found one from Scott. He has agreed to go check out the memory care unit tomorrow.

Maybe the fact that I hit over 30,000 steps and walked ten miles today, combined with this good news from Scott, means that I will be able to sleep well tonight.

Wednesday, June 3, 2015
Guernica to Lezama, 13.6 miles/22 km

AFTER LEAVING OUR hotel, we stopped at a bar for croissants and beverages; Andrea and Terry came in. Though they hadn't stayed where we had, there were few choices on our route for breakfast. Andrea, always efficiently researching accommodations, had come up with an Agro Tourism (aka Casa Rural) place. Ralph and I hadn't stayed in accommodations of this sort before, so we weren't sure what to expect. Would there be mechanical bull riding contests like in the 1980s film *Urban Cowboy* and chores such as milking cows? Trusting her instincts, we asked Andrea to reserve a room for us too. We started out on the route with them, but soon separated because we hiked at different speeds.

Just outside of Guernica, we had a big ascent, three-hundred meters in five kilometers. We entered a logging area, but all was quiet. We reached the fork in the trail called the *Meakaur Turn-off*. Those who wanted to reach Albergue Meakaur would turn right and take the BI-2121 two kilometers to reach it, but since we were continuing on, we went to the left. We soon had to duck and crawl under a couple of downed trees lying across the wide dirt trail. I supposed some people would find this kind of hiking annoying, but I liked the challenge of getting over and around obstacles (in moderation). I was reminded of the many places where we had to crawl over and under dozens of trees along the Pacific Crest Trail. We found a few puddles to dodge along the way, but it had been several days since it rained so things had dried out a lot.

Trail markings were spotty. We missed a turn and climbed higher up a hill than we needed to, but we were saved from climbing even farther out of our way by a local hiker who came along at just the right time. He pointed out the correct path. We thanked him profusely.

When we passed a flock of sheep in a field, I realized we had not been seeing the large numbers of them as we had at the start. Along this stretch, most of the farms and fields were smaller land-holdings. I liked seeing the small, tidy vegetable gardens and the well-cared for flowers along the way. We passed through rural Goikolexea and Larrabetzu and could have stopped at a bar for lunch, but the restaurant where we had eaten breakfast had prepared a bocadillo for us so we ate picnic style alongside the road.

We reached the outskirts of Lezama. Bilbao may be the

home of the professional *football* (what we call soccer in the U.S.) team Athletic Bilbao, but Lezama is home to their training headquarters. They often go by the nickname, *Los Leones* (The Lions), because their stadium was built near a church called *San Mamés* (Saint Mammes). Mammes was a semi-legendary, early Christian thrown to the lions by the Romans. Mammes pacified the lions and was later made a saint. The Athletics have a Basque-only policy and they support promising players as they come up through the ranks. They are one of Spain's top teams and immensely popular. We have seen flags bearing their name everywhere along the way.

6/3/15

The Casa Rural is two kilometers off the Camino—a fact that seemed less important this morning than it did at the end of the day when we were tired. We came upon Andrea and Terry at the bottom of the last hill up to the casa and managed to drag ourselves up the last bit.

The property is a combination of working farm and guesthouse—a lovely, fairly new house. It's my favorite place so far. Of course my feelings might be influenced by the fact that we are again with Terry and Andrea and we are the only guests.

Both dinner and breakfast are included in our room rate. That's a good thing because, other than a nearby gourmet restaurant where dinner goes for two-hundred euros per person, there's no place else to eat in the area.

Our hostess is very friendly and helpful. Because it is just the four of us, I was surprised that she offered several options for dinner. Everything we ate was from her family's place or nearby. The flavorful salad of greens and tomatoes was dressed lightly. The chicken was from their farm, and was accompanied by *patatas fritas* (French fries). Ralph and I had the decadent profiteroles for dessert. Even the rosé we enjoyed had a local connection—it was produced by our hostesses' family in Galicia.

After dinner, Ralph made reservations through Booking.com for the next two nights in Bilbao. We had decided on private accommodations because we are going to take a Zero Day and want to be in the center of old town instead of at one of the albergues on the outskirts. We are going to pay 177 euros, including breakfasts, for both nights, which seems reasonable for a city of that size. It appears to cost an additional ten euros to book through Booking.com, but it's easier for Ralph than calling the hotel and having to use his limited Spanish.

I managed to reach someone at Mom's assisted living place. Hospice has gone home. I only hope that Mom stays put, doesn't try to get out of bed, and doesn't fall. I am sitting on pins and needles waiting to hear what Scott thinks of the memory-care unit. The nine-hour time difference makes communication very difficult.

This, our ninth walking day on the Norte, was the longest distance yet. Though I felt tired some of the time, overall I felt better and stronger than I had on the previous few days. I am looking forward to reaching Bilbao tomorrow for our two days in the city.

Thursday, June 4, 2015
Lezama to Bilbao, 9.1 miles/14.7 km

BREAKFAST AT THE Agro Tourismo was just right. The simple meal of toast, packaged jams, juice, and sliced cheese and ham provided energy and didn't leave us feeling stuffed. But then, because our schedules were diverging, we said goodbye to Terry and Andrea. Though we hoped we would run into them in Bilbao, we knew that it was such a huge city that unless one planned a meeting, it would be difficult to find someone.

We felt very sad and their hugs told us they felt the same way.

I felt that we were all wondering if this chance acquaintanceship would become a permanent friendship after we all returned home.

Their company helped provide comfort, fun, and distraction from what is going on at home with my mom. Meeting up with this wonderful and supportive couple had been just what I needed to make it through the worst days of worry and indecision—of not knowing how deep Mom's decline would go, wondering whether to continue this trip or not.

We have also found a lot of things to laugh about during shared dinners and beer stops. Their company has also made it easier to climb some of the steeper hills. We've all hiked at about the same pace, fairly slowly, so though we didn't often hike with them, we would run into them occasionally through the day.

MUCH OF THE day's walk was on pavement, but climbing up and over Monte Avril kept us away from a string of industrial towns. At the highest point of the trail, we had a wide, expansive view of the city including the Gothic-style Basilica de Begona. We were away from the noise of the freeway and after we topped the mountain, we came down through a couple of large, tranquil, green parks with lots of benches. At that point, we were about two to three kilometers from Bilbao's *Casco Viejo* (old quarter). We had to go through the suburbs before getting into the heart of Bilbao, but we didn't mind. It was not as nice as hiking through open country, but it was an interesting contrast.

By the time we reached the outskirts of Bilbao, I was exhausted and covered with a sheath of sweat. I noticed a sign displaying the temperature as 39 C (102.2 degrees Fahrenheit). I didn't believe it was that hot, but it was far from comfortable for hiking. We stopped at a bar for beers and pintxos. I thought one type was worth duplicating at home—a spoonful of tuna salad on French bread with a bit of pimento to give it a nice zesty taste.

We reached the center of the city and headed for the Petit Palace. The hotel was in a perfect location for someone on foot because there were lots of shops and good pintxos bars nearby and it was only a twenty-minute walk to the Guggenheim Museum designed by Frank Gehry. We asked around and found out that it had hit 100 degrees during the day—no wonder I was suffering toward the end of the walk. Even with the heat, however, this had been the easiest day for us so far.

We went out to survey our surroundings and found the Plaza Nueva, a huge open square surrounded by restaurants, bars, shops, and hotels. It looked like all the boys in town were playing soccer. Sometimes in Basque country girls join in the ball games, but here they all appeared to be spinning tops or coming up with dance routines.

We were gazing at the various buildings surrounding the plaza when all of a sudden Terry popped up; he and Andrea had checked into a nearby hotel and their room overlooked the plaza. Andrea was still in their hotel room changing clothes, but eventually she came down and joined us. We talked for a while and then all went our own way to have food.

I ate too much. I had hoped that all of this walking would help me shed a few pounds, but apparently there's a limit to how freely the vino tinto and such can flow without consequences. The food and wine were too good.

As Ralph and I walked down a pedestrian-only street toward our hotel, a man and his young daughter caught my eye. One moment they were walking hand-in-hand coming towards us. Then, only fifteen feet in front of us, they both suddenly stopped. The man, quick as a wink, pulled down the youngster's shorts, pushed up her shirt a bit, scooped her up in his arms with a practiced move, and held her over a grate in the street so that she could pee into the openings.

Back in our room after our full day, I checked my emails to see if there was any news about Mom. Without fully realizing it, Ralph and I had walked the final miles of our first stretch of the Camino del Norte. I turned to my journal.

6/4/15

Scott emailed that he had visited the memory care unit and gave a favorable review. "I don't see anything negative about it," was how he put it. So, Ralph and I made the decision to have Mom moved so that she can be looked after more.

We asked assisted living to go ahead. The next step will be getting her stuff moved ASAP. I know that the new room will be smaller; I'm trying to find out how much. I want to make her new room as much like the old one as we can—her pictures on the walls and a few pieces of her furniture in place.

I think that the hardest thing for her to give up will be her bed—and because of her sentimental attachment, it will be the most difficult thing for me to get rid of. She and my dad shared the four-poster bed for their entire 51 years of married life. Because of my dad's service in WWII, his job changes, our growing family (my two brothers and me), and eventually their retirement, my parents moved a lot. The mahogany bedroom set went with them from house to house through more than twenty moves. After my dad died, the sturdy set moved along with mom another four times. Now she has to give it up in order to change to a hospital bed.

This has been a weird trip in several ways: not only because of the Mom situation, but also wondering for almost a year if I'd be physically able to do it. My emotions have been up and down, but it has been wonderful to see this much of the Basque Country on my own two feet. It has also been rewarding to have the camaraderie of other pilgrims (including Ralph!).

RALPH AND I discussed where we would go next. Because we hadn't hiked as many miles as we had originally planned, we were no longer on schedule. We had to decide how to spend our remaining days before returning to Madrid for our flight home on June tenth. We decided to bus from here to Santander, stay two nights there, and then fly home.

Interlude 1

A Change of Plans, A Life Transition

Spain and California, Spring and Summer 2015

Friday, June 5, 2015
Zero Day in Bilbao.

I think Ralph and I were both feeling a bit off-kilter today because of our change of plans. We enjoyed our day, but didn't feel very ambitious. Instead of going to the Guggenheim to see the exhibitions, we spent our time looking at its exterior and the surrounding sculptures. We were satisfied with that; when we were in Bilbao a few years back, we found the exterior of the museum even more interesting than the interior. The soaring, curving building was clad with glass, titanium, and limestone. It was amazing viewed from any angle and I could spend hours walking around it.

Right next to the museum was a sculpture by American artist, Jeff Koons. His *Puppy* was modeled after a West Highland Terrier, and was covered with flowering bedding plants. Some sources have said that it was based on topiary sculptures of eighteenth-century formal gardens, but I have never seen a forty-three-foot high topiary.

I was surprised to learn that benevolent *Puppy* was almost caught up in a political plot. Days before the Guggenheim was to open in 1997, the ETA (Euskadi Ta Askatasuna) attempted to plant twelve grenades. On October 13th, three Basque separatists appeared wearing gardeners' outfits and carrying pots of flowers of the sort that were being placed on the sculpture. They tried to place the plants at the feet of *Puppy*. In the pots were the grenades—set to go off using remote-controlled devices. Some sources say their goal was to bomb the museum; others say that the objective was to sacrifice *Puppy* in an attempt to kill King Juan Carlos I and Queen Sofia of Spain on the evening of the October 18th opening ceremony.

Police foiled the plot. Officers on duty at the museum became suspicious of a van parked nearby, checked and found out that the license was fake. When the separatists spotted the police, a gun battle began; one policeman, Jose María Aguirre, was killed. The suspects took off running. One was arrested on the spot, the other two were apprehended shortly thereafter—and a cache of firearms and ammunition was also found. The opening ceremony went forward when planned and tributes to the slain officer were made.

The Basque regional government has been highly involved in the construction of the museum. Among other things, they paid the $100-million construction cost, donated $50-million for new acquisitions, and cover the museum's $12-million annual budget.

We also spent time studying another sculpture near the Guggenheim—*Maman*, by Louise Bourgeois (which has not been involved in any political controversy as far as we know). The almost thirty-foot-high bronze, marble, and stainless steel spider was impressive. Doubtless, those with arachnophobia should keep their distance, but I found the delicately-formed arachnid, complete with egg sack, graceful and beautiful.

On the way back to our room, I had another "first" sighting: a woman breastfeeding her baby while walking down the street with her family. I didn't think it was a bad thing, but it was unexpected. In general, we in the U.S. are much more uptight about breastfeeding in public.

6/5/15

I am back in our room and trying to get some information on our flight home from Madrid. We have heard on the news that the air controllers at

Madrid's airport, the Madrid–Barajas, are threatening a series of walkouts. One of the strikes is scheduled for June 10th at 10:00 a.m. That's our departure date and we're scheduled to fly out at 10:45.

The Spanish government is insisting that 70% of the flights go as scheduled. Ralph pointed out that we have encountered this situation before and it was no big deal. I'm glad that I am the only worrier in our family.

Now that I able to hike more, I am hoping that we can do another hiking trip this fall. It's too early to make that decision, though, because much depends on Mom's condition. And I'm afraid this increased level of care is going to be a huge financial hit for us.

From: Susan
To: Tom

I'm glad you could communicate with your grandma; I haven't been able to do so for about four days. The last time I got her on the line she was unintelligible and pushed the phone away. It has been extremely stressful trying to get a clear picture and having to make important decisions from a distance. Let me know how the visit goes, please.

Saturday, June 6, 2015
Bus ride to Santander

As we waited for our bus, I managed a few emails. The bus station in Bilbao was rather filthy and in a run-down part of town so it was nice to have the distraction. I wrote to Deborah because I thought she and Dennis might have explored Santander and have some trip advice. I wrote to Andrea and Terry because we already missed them.

From: Susan
To: Andrea and Terry

I don't think I could possibly have expressed well enough how invaluable your support and camaraderie were to us. I think if we had not run into you when we did at the albergue, I would have been a basket case the last few days. As it was, you lifted our spirits and granted us a good time!

I'm sitting here in the Bilbao bus station. It took only 3,959 steps to reach, so I guess we will get to wander around Santander a bit this afternoon. Thunderstorms are predicted, so that should be interesting.

I am dreading the return home with the need to immediately do the move for Mom, but as Terry would say, "the nearer you get, the clearer things are."

Love to both of you as you carry the pilgrim staffs ahead. We'd love to keep in touch and we also have a spare bedroom with a modest futon available for as long as you'd care to stay in the SF Bay Area. We also have the Napa Valley wineries, many microbreweries, fabulous food, and great hiking trails all only a short drive away.

Love, Susan and Ralph

From: Andrea
To: Susan

Hello, you two good pilgrims! Thank you for your lovely company—friendship and support work both ways you know.

We are still in Bilbao, having spent an expensive morning in a clinic trying to sort out my annoying cough that prevented us sleeping till 4:00 a.m. last night. The noise did not help either. After x-rays and a VERY thorough examination it seems that it may be my BP [blood pressure] meds that are causing it. The choices of old age!!!

We will walk on tomorrow constantly with thoughts of you in our hearts. Take care and good trip!

P.S. We are sure we will see you somewhere
sometime xxx

BECAUSE SANTANDER WAS on the Norte, we had planned to reach
it by backroads on foot not on freeway and bus. Nevertheless,
we enjoyed the different perspective. Leaving Bilbao we passed
through several industrial areas. We knew that some pilgrims
took public transit to avoid them.

When we drove into Loredo to let several passengers off, I
noticed there were many single-family homes, which was a change
from the huge apartments and condos we had seen in the larger
cities. After that stop, the landscape became open and green. We
traveled through a marshy area, and then we were in Santander.

The weather also changed as we traveled—from gray and
overcast at the beginning, to rain midway, back to slightly overcast, ending with clear skies and a pleasant temperature here in
Santander.

We had reached our destination in an hour and a half. We
liked it at first sight—another beautiful city sitting on the Bay
of Biscay. We started the walk to our lodgings from the bus station (which I was happy to note was relatively clean). We made a
slight detour to take a look at the pilgrim albergue. It's immediate
neighborhood was a mixed lot: several rundown buildings—one
with trash stuffed into its broken windows. However, only a block
away from the sketchy area were fairly good shops and adequate
restaurants, and the more upscale part of town was still within
walking distance and had many places to eat.

Our reservations were farther away; the route took us along
the waterfront. Though our future on the Camino del Norte
was still unclear, when we watched a ferry from Brittany arrive,
I started dreaming about sailing from England before resuming
our trek. That would be fun. I did a little research and learned
Brittany Ferries sails from Plymouth and Portsmouth, England,
to both Bilbao and Santander. Though primarily for cars and vans,
there are occasionally openings for passengers on foot. ORCA's
Wildlife Officers are on board several months each year conduct-
ing surveys and educating the public about marine animals. It

would be exciting to see some of the whales and dolphins that live in these waters.

Many sailboats were out on Santander Bay. The signal flags were green along the sandy beaches, indicating that swimming and other water activities would be safe.

It took more than an hour on foot to reach our lodgings because of the distance and our stops—once for a tart at a *pasteria,* and then for a beer at a restaurant. We were on a flat, broad walkway within view of the water the entire time. The houses along the street opposite the sea were huge and impressive; there's clearly a lot of money in the city. If we had been here as pilgrims, we probably wouldn't have wanted to walk as far from the station, but since we were off the Camino and here for two nights, we weren't concerned about the distance.

We reached our accommodations at the Hosteria Santander. Our room was delightful—sparkling clean and with a nautical look using white walls, marine-blue drapes, and a photo mural of a dock behind the headboard. We had partial views of the bay. I was happy to sit to read and write for a while.

At dinner time we set out again. Our hosteria was above a restaurant—one of several along the street with tables, chairs, and umbrellas set up outside. I wondered if there would be noisy crowds in the evening.

We discovered that we were staying only one block from the Belle Époque casino. The large, spiffy-looking, white building was buzzing with activity. Cars were arriving to deliver scores of guests. Maybe they weren't quite up to the James Bond dress code, but we knew we would not be welcome in our casual attire.

We spotted a Thai restaurant and decided we'd like a change from Spanish cuisine. The place was almost deserted. Nevertheless, we were starving and went on in. After enjoying the delicious food and good service, we decided the lack of customers was more likely due to the time we were eating—eight o'clock is early for dining in Spain.

When we returned to the hosteria, we found that most of the restaurants on the street had already closed and that the area was well lit. It was relaxing to sit and check my emails.

From: Susan
To: Terry and Andrea:

Now that we have jumped ahead of you by taking the bus, I want to let you know that we think Santander is quite lovely. We haven't seen any monuments yet, but think tomorrow we may go to the maritime museum. Watched the ferry from Brittany come in and lots of sailboats. Beautiful walk along the bay, but that is not on the Camino route.

Happy trails,
Susan

From: Deborah
To: Susan

We have never been to Santander so I can't be of much help. The Michelin Green Guide for Spain lists the cathedral and gives a star to the Regional Museum of Prehistory and Archeology. There is also a fine arts museum with a Goya portrait of Ferdinand VII.

6/6/15

Ralph and I had time to talk again about what we had been through and what we may face when we get home. We think we have made the best of a highly stressful situation—our sadness that Mom is declining combined with deciding whether or not she should be moved. Everything we'd read said that moving is usually harder for the elderly, but we hoped that the new unit would provide more care.

Of course we had zero information on the new place. I desperately needed someone to look at the setting and decide if it was suitable. I didn't want Mom in a place where everyone was incoherent and just sitting all day long watching TV. At the same time, I didn't know if she had declined to that point herself.

It was great that we had Scott back home where

he could check out the new room and let me know that things looked okay. It wasn't so great when I began receiving multiple emails a day from hospice giving me a countdown to when they thought they would be leaving. "Only two hours . . . . . . "

When we finally settled that we would go ahead with the move, I had to arrange how to deal with all of Mom's furniture and other belongings. Even though Mom had been in a studio apartment, the new room into which she had moved wouldn't hold all of her things.

I've tried to get information from assisted living about the process. Did they have anyone on staff who could assist with the physical move? Could they recommend a mover? What window of time did we have to make the transfer before we would have to pay double rent? I didn't get much help, but I learned we had to move her stuff from the old apartment this coming Thursday if we want to avoid paying extra.

We won't be getting home until late Wednesday night. I'm sort of dreading it all, but I know I'll be happier when the logistics are taken care of. I'm relieved that, thanks to Google and email, Ralph found a mover.

IN GENERAL, BOTH Ralph and I prided ourselves on being relatively self-sufficient; we didn't often call on friends or family for help. However, at that point in our lives, we knew we could use some aid. I knew before I even heard back from those I asked, that they would be there for us.

From: Susan
To: Patricia and Tom
The big news is we've ended our walk in Bilbao and bussed to Santander. We're not too happy about it, but the next stages were twenty-three to twenty-four kilometers long, the accommodations spotty, and we

had no leeway on time.

Mom has now been moved. Assisted living wants us to vacate the old room by the 11th . . . That's the day after we get home, but I am going to try to make that happen so that we aren't paying double rent as well as the huge increase in cost of the additional care.

Speaking of work, is there any chance that you could help us get Mom's belongings from her old room to her new one? We could look for pizza and beer afterwards.

AFTER PATRICIA EMAILED back that they would help us, I again wrote her.

From: Susan
To: Patricia

Thank you so much, you can imagine how difficult it has been to try and handle this while hiking and with the time difference. Indeed the time and date for the move are tentative, so I'll provide info as things progress.

I'd prefer to stay in Spain, or anywhere, another six months rather than come home to the work and worry ahead, but that isn't an option.

Sunday, June 7, 2015
Zero Day in Santander

As SOON AS we got going, we walked over to the Peninsula of Magdalena, a public park near by our hotel. We really knew little about it, but it was a large green space on our city map. Several food trucks were parked alongside one of the roadways and people were in the process of setting up long tables and folding chairs. A temporary stage had been erected. It was clear that preparations were underway for a big event. We spotted a cardboard sign on a lamppost—*Dia Infantil de Cantavaria* (Children's Day of Cantabria) it proclaimed.

Small groups of adults and children came by headed for the grassy area in front of the stage. The participants were dressed in colorful, traditional costumes—the women and young girls in brightly-colored full skirts, white blouses, floral-printed scarfs, and white socks. They carried tambourines decorated with ribbons; many of the women had burden baskets made of straw and covered with fabric. Most of the men wore long, dark-colored pants, white shirts, vests, and wide black cummerbunds, while the young boys were dressed in white shirts and pants, red cummerbunds, and carrying wooden castanets decorated with long strands of ribbon.

Ralph and I walked to the far side of the field to see the craft booths. Most things for sale were handmade and of excellent quality. I was attracted to a display of wooden whirly gigs—complex carvings of scenes such as a couple dancing, a farmer milking a cow, and a man with a shotgun aiming at a bear. CDs with Celtic tunes were offered. Food booths with huge mounds of homemade breads and buns lured us.

Groups of participants continued to arrive and assemble with their clans to get ready for performances. I snapped photos as mothers made final adjustments to their daughters' costumes—scarves at the correct angle, skirts straightened. A stocky woman took charge of lining the girls up properly, shortest child first, tallest the last, for the entrance onto the stage.

Not far away, a ring of people, mostly men, gathered to watch a contest of strength. Contestants would pick up a heavy weight in each hand and circle the track as many times as possible. By the time they finished their laps, sweat was pouring.

We stayed for quite a while—watching the folk dancers and singers. We felt very lucky to have stumbled into this celebration.

Continuing our tour through the large and well-maintained park, we followed a path along the bay past a small zoo, two beaches, a place to feed seals, and replicas of three Spanish galleons by navigator Vital Alsar Ramírez. I took photos of tree stumps that had been creatively shaped into seats we could actually sit on; I hoped to inspire our own city parks to follow suit.

We climbed a short rise to the Palace of La Magdalena, which sits on the highest point of the park. The huge palace, which is open for tours, was built as a summer residence for King Alfonso XIII and Queen Victoria Eugenia and used by the monarchs and their children between 1913 and 1930.

From: Susan
To: Karen

Joy happening on a Cantabrian folk festival today. This was a treat with kids and adults in colorful, beautiful traditional costumes doing dances and singing or playing music. *Appreciated* the Celtic music. One of those thrilling things that you run into by chance. It was better than our Renaissance Pleasure Faire and *free* unlike the big festival at home.

I knew nothing about this city previously except that it had a university, but it also has wonderful shops, classy mansions, and an incredible beach. *Satisfied* doing 20,000 steps today while looking around. *Gratitude* for the beautiful weather.

From: Susan
To: Andrea and Terry

The parks and beaches here are immense and very popular. I imagine all the apartment dwellers need someplace to play. I loved seeing all the activity and as you noted, Terry, no vandalism beyond graffiti.

By the way, we tried to order tap water at a restaurant last night and at first were politely refused. As you know, they much prefer to sell bottled water. After a while, the waiter seemed to take pity on us and brought over a couple of glasses.

Tomorrow we'll be taking the RENFE train to Madrid. I hope we can visit the Prado Museum, but I have to check to see if they are open on Tuesdays. On our previous visit there, I was so jet-lagged that I couldn't really enjoy it.

Love, Susan

Monday, June 8, 2015
Train to Madrid

WHILE WE SAT waiting for the RENFE to take us south to Madrid, we tried to focus on the day's journey rather than the days ahead. The four-and-a-half hours on the train were pretty much a blur. We read, talked, ate, and enjoyed views out the windows. The landscape became flatter, drier and browner the further south we traveled. From the train station we took the Metro to the Puerta del Sol station and then walked from that public square to the Hotel Petit Palace Arenal. Being in the center of the city, we were also able to easily walk to the Plaza Major for its restaurants and other activities.

Tuesday, June 9, 2015
Zero Day in Madrid

IT WAS A day of playing tourist and winding down. We made it to the Museo de Prado where we'd hoped to see Picasso's Guernica, but I'd made a mistake—Guernica was at the Museo Reina Sofia. By the time we discovered this, it was too late in the day to go over there.

Picasso generally avoided political statements, but he was asked by the Republican Government to paint something that would bring the realities of the Spanish Civil War to the attention of the rest of the world. His painting of the tragedies caused by war achieved that goal and became Picasso's best known piece.

Back at the hotel, I called the airlines to confirm our flights for the next day and to find out about the strike situation. The latest update was that one strike was scheduled for 10 a.m. to noon and another for a couple of hours in the afternoon. Ralph said that in previous strikes, international flights had gone on as scheduled; it was only domestic ones that were affected. I wouldn't even let myself think about the complications of a delayed return home.

Wednesday, June 10, 2015
Flights from Madrid to San Francisco

Since we hadn't received word about the strike from our airline, we headed for Madrid's Barajas airport as planned. We breathed a sigh of relief when we learned we weren't going to be affected by the threatened air controller strike and were allowed to board. The flight departed as scheduled.

We changed planes in Dallas. The closer we got to home, the more I worried about Mom's condition. I mentally replayed the plans for the next day—I was to grab a stack of old newspapers and collect some bubble wrap and boxes before the "packing team" arrived. The movers were to meet us at assisted living between 9-9:30 in the morning, and our friends Tom and Patricia and our daughter-in-law Lynn were to show up a bit later to help with the packing. With all that had happened so far and all that awaited, this would go down as the most stressful trip we'd ever had.

As expected, it was a long, long day. We arrived home after nine p.m. and managed to fall into bed almost immediately.

Thursday, June 11, 2015
Home

I think both Ralph and I woke a couple of times during the night due to the time changes, but we tried to rest in bed as long as we could before getting up to eat and make the twenty-minute drive to Mom's. This being our first time in the memory care section of her building, we had to become familiar with the procedure for getting into the section. We buzzed from the corridor and one of the staff members let us in through the locked double doors.

Mom was still sleeping when we arrived, but she woke when we came in to see her. She smiled and recognized us, but talked very little. She drifted back to sleep.

We talked with staff about helping Mom into her robe and wheelchair so that she could be moved from her room to the common room while we were bringing some of her clothes and pictures downstairs from her former, upstairs room.

We got a call that the movers had arrived. Ralph went out front to coordinate moving most of Mom's furniture out of the building and into a self-storage facility not far away. We planned to store most of her things off premises until we knew whether this move was a permanent or a temporary one.

When Tom, Patricia, Lynn arrived we began packing everything the movers hadn't taken—dishes, pillows and other bedding, books, lamps, clothes, and photos. As the old room was emptied out, the new one was set up. I was so jet-lagged that I felt completely useless, but Ralph said I got plenty of credit for arranging and organizing the move.

Mom didn't seem too distressed by all of the moving activity, but then she was not acting like herself. There was one moment of levity when Lynn asked Mom what she thought of the arrangement of pictures and other wall décor that Lynn and Patricia had spent considerable time hanging. Mom pointed to one of her favorite paintings, a quiet seascape, and said, "It's not straight."

Though we had promised everyone we'd treat them to pizza and beer, we were all too tired to make the effort. They took a raincheck and Ralph and I headed home.

I was thrilled to get an email from Andrea. Because they had continued on after Ralph and I left the trail, they'd reached Santander only a few days after we left there. They had a different take on the city then we did, and they walked longer days than we had.

From: Andrea
To: Susan:

Just a quick email to assure you that we will
not be repeating the thirty-kilometer trip any time
soon! It was a needs/must day and yesterday was
only nineteen kilometers, which was much more
enjoyable. Terry was pretty chuffed to know we could
cover the distance though if we needed to. I was less
impressed!!!

No snow here, but raining today so we are

hunkering down in our flea pit, which was all we could get in the centre of town, opposite the municipal market. The water is lukewarm, wifi drops in and out, and yesterday when I went to the toilet (about half a mile away) the toilet pan broke away and flooded the entire bathroom!!! I'm glad to say the bed wasn't too bad, if a little lumpy. Ho hum…

We will be thinking of you in the next week getting changes made. Like you I don't sleep in planes and always feel wrecked after a long trip. No need to reply as I know you will be very busy. We still miss you!

From: Susan:
To: Andrea and Terry

Mom does not look like or act like her former self, so that is hard to see. Definitely much more confused and I don't know what all to credit it to. We moved some of her things to her new room, put some in storage, and I brought home several boxes of memorabilia to sort through—including every greeting card she ever received.

I find it very difficult to get rid of anything that she has, but in reality I don't think she cares about making things as they were as much as I want to make it "right" for her. I guess in time I will better know what actually registers and what doesn't. Bottom line, I feel like I am stealing or being "bad" if I remove or discard anything; I know I have to get past this, but I haven't been in this situation before. You don't need to respond to this; I know that I have to come to terms with it and I am just getting my feelings out here.

On a more positive note, we did make it home in one piece, the house is still intact, no bill collectors were waiting at the door, and our yard looks great in spite of California's continuing drought. Our water bill came and we have reduced our consumption of water about forty-five percent, so we are happy we are doing our part.

That's it for now. Hope you have moved on to a cleaner place with a functioning toilet!

Love, Susan

THE NEXT WEEK at home passed quickly, as they always do when we return home. There were the chores: unpacking our backpacks, doing the laundry, returning phone calls and emails. There were the fun things: going to friends' houses for dinners and conversations, listening to music, working in the garden, taking short walks. And there were Mom-related things: visits to see her, discussions with nurses, hospice, and care center staff, and bills to pay.

We heard back from Andrea at the end of the week when they reached Ribadesella. Things were evolving in our relationship—she and Terry were still in Spain hiking all day long. Ralph and I were home—dealing with reentry and the "real world."

Every time one of their emails popped up on my computer, I felt warm and happy all over.

From: Andrea
To: Susan

Thank you for the lovely email with your news. Sorry we haven't replied earlier. Somehow we haven't had much liberty to keep in touch lately. We have had two milestones lately, one was moving into Asturias, and the other passing the halfway mark.

The walking during the past few days has not been too hard, though the weather in Spain overall has been dreadful. The middle of Spain has been flooded with hailstorms and we have had cold weather also. Now sunny and meant to stay so for a few days.

I am pleased that the move went smoothly for your Mum and feel quite in tune with you about the disposal of her personal items. It seems so sad, at the latter end of someone's life, to be disposing of things

which were so important to them—at the time. I had
a thought that if you wanted to check out whether the
cards are important to her now, you might slip them
into loose leaf folders and give them to her to browse.
I am sure you will soon see whether they are still really
important to her.

Oh Susan, it appears that she is slowly and surely
slipping away I feel, and that is just so hard for you
to bear. Keep remembering what good things you
have done for her in the past (I am sure). I was also
thinking about something you said on the trail—
that your mom had mentioned a name unknown
to you. I remember with my mother experiencing
similar moments. There were times when she was
"communing" with a person or people unknown to
me, but other times when I clearly knew what she was
referring to.

I suppose when you think about it, when we age,
our clearest memories are not necessarily the most
recent ones, and there must have been many people in
her life about whom you know very little, if anything
at all. Anyway, as Mr T would say, "Many g'donyas"
for doing what you have done for her, and may she be
comfortable and as happy as is possible in the final
stages of her life.

We are plugging along, some days really good,
and others not so good, not sure why but that doesn't
really matter much. We are constantly overtaken by
others and of course the Camino splits within the next
few days, so probably even fewer on our route after
that. We have decided to continue with the Camino
del Norte since that is what we started out to do, and
also think that the Camino Primitivo, being shorter, is
a possibility to do another year.

We are now only 35 km from the mountains and
the cold at nights makes us realize that it has been
lovely walking with the Picos de Europas on our port

side and the ocean on our starboard side. Also it has
not been hard walking, but that is about to change
I note. We quite like some of the seaside places. We
have been fairly lucky and only walked a couple of
hours in the rain.

Now I must close down and get some sleep in
preparation for tomorrow. It is only 20.5 km so hope
we manage ok but now that we are moving further
west food is harder to find. I imagine the last week or
two might be quite testing in that regard.

Love from us both—we still miss you but are glad
you are where you need to be.

I WROTE BACK that she never needed to apologize for delays or
breaks in responding—none of us needed more obligations than
we already had. Their support and empathy were so touching
that I cried—but I smiled when I remembered our shared time
on the trail.

From: Susan:
To: Andrea and Terry
We welcome hearing from you whenever you
feel inclined, inspired, and have the time and energy!
We love hearing from you and experiencing the trail
through your reports. Do we get to be proud of you?
Congratulations on reaching the halfway point; I only
wish we were there to celebrate with you.

Spain's weather seems to be pretty crazy this year.
I was happy that the places we stayed generally had
A/C of some sort. Not that I like air conditioning,
but the alternative would have been sweating not only
during the day, but also all night.

Here at home it's been foggy—sometimes all
day—because of our proximity to the coast, but where
my sons live, over a ridge of hills, it has been twenty
degrees warmer (80-90F). When we go that direction
to hike (which I think we will do today), we get an

early start.

Saga with Mom continues—she is eating less and less—but I guess we are all making adjustments and trying to figure out this next stage.

Andrea, I appreciate your suggestion on putting the cards into binders so we can look at them more easily. I've found that looking at old photo albums with her is usually the best way to connect—at least it was. I do have to reduce the number because we have very little storage space. Not all Californians live in MacMansions!

Just hearing of Picos de Europa sets my heart racing—how I wish that we were there enjoying the views and making the miles. I look forward to learning more about the rest of the Norte route as you progress. As you know, Ralph and I were always being passed. That's all because of me—I've tried giving Ralph a handicap by "allowing" him to carry some of my stuff, but it just doesn't slow him down!

I hope that you are feeling okay and getting the rest you need. Are there places along the way that you can do layover days when inclined?

I think I should start sending photos of places we hike around here, and of Yosemite, so that we can entice you to visit California.

Love to both of you!

Susan and Ralph

AT HOME, RALPH and I tried to maintain some sort of normalcy in our lives. We stayed close to home, but frequently took short walks in our neighborhood. In late June we took a longer one in Point Reyes National Seashore—on the Pierce Point trail—one of my favorite hikes in the whole world. The trail runs about five miles along a narrow peninsula to the very end and from it you can see both the Pacific Ocean and Tomales Bay at the same time. Our trip that day was no exception. And if feeling like I was at the end of the world wasn't enough of a thrill, we also saw dozens of the tule elk that make their home there.

Frequent trips to Mom's place continued. There were some very sweet moments. She still enjoyed our family's visits. One Saturday, Ralph and I arranged a special one. We would be there when son Tom and daughter-in-law Lynn made their hour's drive over to see her. With them, they brought Daisy, their fluffy, little white dog. Daisy, of course, was a big hit and got all of the attention. Mom couldn't really converse with the us, but she clearly was pleased when she got to hold and pet Daisy. When we all moved into the common room, Daisy made the rounds making friends wherever she stopped to be petted. Seeing the look of delight on the patients' faces, I wondered if there were local organizations that arranged similar visits.

By early July, visits to Mom had become increasingly difficult because we didn't know what we would find. We wondered if it was the move that had thrown her off. Or had the medications affected her? I wasn't exactly the most objective observer; I hoped against hope that the changes were only temporary—that the mom I remembered would return. We met with management and staff of assisted living and hospice to discuss Mom's changes. All were kind and supportive, but the message we took home was that her body was shutting down.

Soon Mom wasn't able to eat or drink on her own anymore. Sometimes when I arrived I would find a caregiver feeding her; other times I was told that she pushed away the spoon. Mom had always been a fussy eater, so I thought maybe she didn't like the food being offered. I brought in small cups of chocolate pudding—which had always been one of her favorite treats. The first time I fed her she ate like a bird, took half an hour, and finished only half the container, but I was elated that she would eat. I took staff the remaining pudding and also encouraged them to feed her ice cream (another of her favorites) whenever she wanted it. Considering that Mom's weight had dropped nearly to a hundred pounds, offering a diet that was balanced, but would not be eaten, was not sensible.

A couple of days later when I tried the same approach again, she couldn't eat the pudding without choking. I brought in cans of Ensure, hoping that the fortified drink would be both palatable and easier to use. On the first attempt, I held the cup and she was able to sip it. The next day, however, she could not. I tried offering a straw, but Mom did not have the strength to sip....

Early the next morning, on July 12, 2015, I got a call, that my mom, Vivien W. Bean, had passed away in her sleep—at the age of 104.

THE NEXT TWO months became a whirlwind of activity. Honoring Mom's wishes, there was no funeral service. Even towards the end, Mom had said, "I've been lucky—I've been very healthy, I've had a good family." I wondered at her sentiments—knowing that she had outlived her husband, both of her sons, and all of her friends from childhood and early adult years. I recalled the decades when she and my dad were in their forties, fifties, and sixties and Christmas decorations included dozens of holiday cards strung from the divider next to the living room. It seemed so sad, but it was typical of Mom to make the best of whatever circumstances she found herself in.

Ralph and I arranged a family gathering with my sons and their families, and we all had a chance to share some good memories. Then we launched into handling the logistics. I notified our extended family and Mom's distant acquaintances of her passing. We closed various accounts and filed required legal notifications. Tom, Scott, and I each selected a couple of decorative items that had special meaning to us. Old family photos went to several relatives; most clothing, household furnishings, and books went to Goodwill or the local library; and several pictures went to the assisted living facility.

There was very little that I could bear to throw in the trash. Even though the boxes of old greeting cards hadn't been looked at in decades, Ralph, understanding the importance to me of treating all of Mom's things with care, helped me lug every box home. I proceeded to look at every card: those with only a signature were boxed up and sent for reuse by charity, those with a longer message were packed away until I decided on a plan for dispersal.

We took possession of Mom's ashes and started planning a road trip to Walla Walla, Washington, to place them in the plot where my dad, brothers, and grandparents had been buried. I was surprised and dismayed when I found that she had saved not only her own college yearbooks but also my dad's. I didn't care to keep them, but strongly felt that they should be given back to the schools' library or alumni. I emailed his university and soon connected with the University Historian and Archivist, Jennifer O'Neal.

> **From:** Susan Alcorn
> **To:** University of Oregon
>
> Hi,
>   I have my father's yearbooks, the Oregana, from 1929-1932, which I would like to donate to your library, or another organization, if they would be of benefit. Please let me know your thoughts, we are driving through Oregon in about two weeks.

> **From:** Jennifer O'Neal
> **To:** Susan Alcorn
> **Subject:** RE: Oreganas 1929-1932
>   Dear Susan,
>   Yes, we would be delighted to receive an extra copy of an Oregana into our collection. Simply drop it off to our department, which is located on the 2nd floor of the Knight Library....

AFTER OUR SHORT time in Walla Walla, we headed back home, stopping overnight in Medford, Oregon, to visit a long-time friend, Jeannine. Making it a road trip was perfect; flying would have been faster, but would not have worked for us this time around. We wanted to make the stops to donate some of Mom and Dad's things, and we also needed to get away—to drive through quiet, beautiful country as we went north.

8/20/15

It's been an emotional time. Ralph and I sitting all by ourselves at the edge of the gravesite was tough. So many thoughts of earlier days when I was growing up and living at home, thoughts of the hardships Mom had gone through during her long life, missing my dad again.

But, it has not all been dreary. On the way north, we stopped in Bend, Oregon, and enjoyed a balmy evening while sitting on the deck of a restaurant alongside the Rogue River. Just a bit further on, we visited the High Desert Museum. We even did a bit of wine tasting at our hotel in Walla Walla.

It was very satisfying to deliver my parents yearbooks to their colleges and to donate Mom's and Grandma's wedding dresses to the museum in Pendleton where they both had gotten married. I'm glad that I have made the effort to give Mom's things to people who will value them. I hope that these tangible items will help her live on in people's memories.

It feels great to be here with Jeannine tonight. In the past, she has driven Ralph and me to numerous trailheads of the Pacific Crest Trail (PCT), and here she is again giving us help and support.

BACK HOME AGAIN, Ralph and I decided we wanted a longer break from all of the physical and emotional demands of sorting things out. I felt much better after our roadtrip to Washington. We decided to return to Spain to resume our hike on the Camino del Norte.

While getting ready for another trip, it seemed strange not to have to anticipate Mom's needs during our absence. I didn't have to take her to the doctor, dentist, or optometrist before we left. No need to pick up an extra supply of toilet tissue, toothpaste, or cough drops. No necessity to notify management at assisted living of our schedule and contact info. No bills or other mail to deal with. After ten years of those kinds of responsibilities, there was some relief mixed in with the sadness.

On El Brusco heading towards Noja

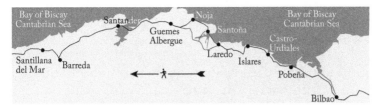

3 • Our Second Stretch of the Norte

Camino del Norte, Fall 2015

Where'er you walk, cool gales, shall fan the glade. Trees, where you sit, shall crowd into a shade.
~ Alexander Pope, *Pastorals: Summer*

For our second segment of the Camino del Norte, we planned to set out from Bilbao, where we'd left off in the spring. The trip would continue along the Bay of Biscay initially, and then turn south into the interior. Our schedule was flexible, but we thought that reaching Baamonde, which would be 342 miles/551 km over thirty-one days, would be reasonable.

Wednesday, September 9, 2015
Flights to Bilbao

Generally speaking, our flights to Heathrow and Bilbao went well, but when Ralph and I went to collect our baggage at the end of our long journey, something was missing—our duffel bag. Not good! We would definitely need the contents: hiking poles, Swiss Army knives, nail clippers and a couple of over-the-counter-medications. We had properly collected and rechecked the bag in Heathrow, but it hadn't arrived in Bilbao with us. We hoped that it would arrive on the next flight, but meanwhile we filed a missing baggage report and were instructed to check the British Airways' website for updates. We discussed what we would do if the bag didn't show up the next day.

There wasn't much else that we could do about it, so we made our way to the Hotel Petit Palace where we had stayed in the spring.

Thursday, September 10, 2015
Zero Day in Bilbao

GETTING UP THIS morning was difficult for me because I'd had so little sleep, but we found a generous breakfast buffet waiting downstairs in the hotel—an assortment of cheeses and hams, yogurt, cereals, scrambled and hard boiled eggs, fresh fruit, pastries and bread. I ate too much; it's hard to resist all the good food.

Ralph went online and found a sporting goods store, Decathlon Capital, (part of a huge chain). Amazingly, the store was just across a nearby bridge and less than a half mile away. We went out on an exploratory trip to look for hiking poles and Swiss Army knives. The store was huge: three-stories high. They had a lot of gear, but much of it was not the lightweight gear we usually buy. However, they had exactly the type of hiking poles that I had purchased back home just before we left. This was very good news because I didn't think I would be able to do this hike without poles. We planned to come back later in the day if the airline didn't find our missing bag when the next flight arrived.

Since we had been to Bilbao previously, we had already seen the Guggenheim and some of the other top sights; we wanted to see some new places. The *Turismo* (tourist office) was just around the corner from our hotel, so we got a map from them and spent some time in the newer part of town. I noticed that most of the upscale clothing shops featured displays of fashionable dresses, but ninety percent of the women on the street were wearing pants. Perhaps the window dressers knew what they are doing and that at night the number of women who want to wear skirts or dresses goes up and the stores are ready to cater to them.

For lunch, we had one of Ralph's favorite combinations: melon and prosciutto. This starter was followed by skewered fish and shrimp for me, gazpacho for him. And, of course, a full bottle of wine was included in our Menu of the Day.

As we continued our stroll to the end of Gran Via Avenue, we again saw a number of homeless—most were older white men. None of them said a word; they just sat quietly against the walls of buildings with small signs asking for donations and with small boxes for collecting any offerings. I didn't see any passersby giving money. The homeless were not setting up tents in the streets like they do in the Bay Area.

We also saw several young Nigerian men lugging suitcases full of merchandise from shop to restaurant, or trying to sell umbrellas or the like on the street. If a shopkeeper told them to get out, they did. We never saw any rudeness, and seldom saw any sales. It had to be a very hard way to make a living.

We went back to the hotel for a short nap, which helped me feel better. At 6:00 p.m., we again crossed the bridge and paid a visit to the *Museo Vasco (Euskal Museoa Bilbao* or the Basque Museum of Bilbao) at Plaza Miguel de Unamuno.

We entered at the ground floor and were pleased to learn that because it was late afternoon, admission was free. We walked through the first building and into the courtyard, which led to a baroque cloister. On the grass in the center of the courtyard was *El Mikeldi*, or "Animalus," which is a pre-Christian piece thought to be four-thousand-years old (during the Iron Age). The sandstone sculpture represents a four-legged animal—perhaps a boar or bull.

Upstairs were rooms covering the prehistory of the people, the sea and fishing way of life, the shepherding culture, and more. There was a life-sized model of an iron-making operation with an intricate setup combining the fire ring, bellows, fire wall, and water course.

On the top floor was a huge, wooden, scale model of Bizkaia (a Basque province), which filled a large room. Looking at the exhibit, I was struck by how many mountains there were in this area. It was a rather sobering to one who planned to walk the convoluted route through the valleys, beaches, and canyons. It was not going to be a straight shot like the Irún to Bilbao portion that we had already completed. We were impressed with the exhibits, the building, and the variety and extensive number of objects.

After checking again the airline's website--and seeing that our luggage was still lost, we returned to Decathlon Capital and purchased the poles for me and the knife for Ralph. For dinner, we tried pintxos and wine at two different places. We concluded that the wine served with pintxos was much better than the typical bottle of wine that was included with a meal.

Afterwards, I had time to send an email to one of my oldest and closest friends.

From: Susan
To: Melanie

Ralph and I are back in Bilbao and you know how much we enjoy this city! I know you and Bob love rock and roll, so I wanted to tell you about an annual event here just in case you are so inclined to visit. In early July, there's a rock and pop music festival. It's called BBK Live, and was first held in 2006. It's a three-day event on two stages atop Kobetamendi Hill. In past years, they've had Guns & Roses, Red Hot Chili Peppers, REM, The Police, Metallica and others. You won't be alone, however, the capacity of the arena is 40,000. Take care!

Love, Susan and Ralph

Friday, September 11, 2015
Bilbao to Pobeña , 13.6 miles/22 km

WE STARTED OUT slowly on our first hiking day; I still wasn't sleeping well because of jet lag and my leg problem. On this trip we were not married to the idea that we had to walk every step of the trail. Even with the poles, I didn't think I could walk the distance required between accommodations on some stretches, but we planned to be faithful to the trail when possible.

That said, we took a suggestion in the guidebook—to take a shortcut, saving us about ten kilometers, on the quiet, efficient, smooth suburban train to Portugalete. Strictly speaking we had walked every step of the Norte to that point so far because we had walked the bypassed stretch on our very first trip to Bilbao in 2010. On that trip we walked to the shores of the Bay of Biscay to see the expensive Basque homes that sit alongside the beach, and to Portugalete to see the world's first transporter bridge, the Vizcaya.

This time when we reached Portugalete we started hiking where the Camino bent to the west. We soon found the way-marks—the brass shells embedded in the concrete sidewalk, and yellow arrows on walls. Sometimes signage has not been great in cities, so we were pleased here they were good. The route turned onto a very new, long, elevated walkway that became a bridge and then a paved bike-and-pedestrian passage with appropriate lanes. There were quite a few other people on the trail—not only pilgrims, but also locals walking or jogging on the ten-kilometer course. The downside was that it was paved, and my feet were not used to walking on hard surfaces yet.

The elevation rose gradually as did the temperature. We passed many large apartment complexes, saw two or three city picnic areas with tables and benches, but as was to be the case throughout most of our Norte walk, saw few public bathrooms.

Another mile or so along, we came to Ortuella, a town that was part of the region's mining district during their peak in the late 1800s. The town experienced a tragic event at Ortuella's el-ementary school, the Marcelino Ugald, in 1980. On October 23rd, a plumber making repairs in the basement struck a match, which ignited propane gas that had accumulated due to leaks in the supply lines. The blast was heard more than six kilometers away. Two classrooms collapsed leaving 120 students under the rubble. Fifty-three people died—fifty children and three adults . . .

It was a long stretch with no restrooms. I had to duck behind shrubbery a couple of times to pee. Each time I hoped that I would not be spotted by some passersby (no mean feat consider-ing the number of people on the trail).

As we continued, I felt so hot, footsore, and exhausted that I had to sit down on the side of the trail and cry. Just getting that release helped. We resumed our walk and only a quarter-mile further came to Playa de la Arena, a popular beach entirely of black volcanic sand. Rounding a curve and seeing the open-air restaurants, the tables shaded by large umbrellas bearing beer logos, with shorts-clad tourists enjoying their cold beers, got me back on track.

We stopped for ham and cheese sandwiches and beers. In Spain, the delicious local cheeses and hams make an ordinary-sounding sandwich something to savor. After I took a few photos of the beach and those enjoying it, we walked the final mile to our lodging. Ralph had booked a private room in an apartment. We wanted a good night's sleep, which doesn't always happen in a pilgrim albergue.

The apartment was clean, but utilitarian—walls, ceiling, and kitchen table white, the blond wardrobe, bedside table, and small storage chest were uncluttered Ikea-style. The kitchen had all the standard appliances as well as a washer and drier, but there was no soap so that wasn't much help. I did my laundry in my usual manner: thrown in the bottom of the shower to be stomped on and soaped as I enjoyed the shower. We had a view from the balcony, but we used the elevated space to set up a folding drying rack and hang our laundry.

I liked having space to spread out our things. I sorted through the contents of my backpack trying to find some way to reduce my pack weight, but about all I could find to eliminate were the plastic containers that my pills were in. I wrote out the prescription information on slips of paper and transferred the medications to zip-lock bags. When I finished reading my two paperbacks, I'd be able to cut more weight.

The combination of new pack, lack of training with weight in the pack, the heat, and the high percentage of hard surfaces made this day exhausting, but based on previous hiking trips, I could expect to get stronger as time went by. I wished I could hurry the process.

We had made the mistake of leaving the sliding glass doors to the balcony open. Because we were very close to a tidal stream, we were also near an abundance of hungry mosquitoes. I spent a fair amount of time climbing onto chairs and our bed chasing them.

It was strange to be on the Camino on another 9/11. In 2001, we had been on the Camino Francés. I kept a journal at that time too.

Day 14, Tuesday, September 11, 2001. Santo Domingo de la Calzada.

We were at lunch today when shocking news came on TV; CNN was broadcasting explosions of the Pentagon in Washington, D.C., and at New York City's World Trade Center. But because we didn't understand what was being said in Spanish, and there were no captions in English, we initially thought they were showing forest fires in the State of Washington. Fires in the west, in the fall, were common.

But, as we watched the second of the Trade Center Buildings explode, and replay after replay of all the events, it became clearer what had occurred. We didn't know who had flown the planes into the buildings.

We were in a crowded restaurant where most of the people were part of a large, noisy group celebrating a birthday. As the broadcast continued, there were several minutes of quiet as the news was absorbed. But, gradually the celebrants started talking and laughing again. I watched them, wondering how they felt about the turn of events, and whether they supported whoever had done the bombing. But, by the end of our meal—which I finished while watching the TV broadcast with tears in my eyes and a lump in my throat, a fellow pilgrim had come over to us to express his sorrow.

We found the local library and went on the Internet. We were able to read a few headlines on the network. Then we sent messages to people at home to find out what was going on, and to see if everyone we knew on the West Coast was okay. It was there that we read that it had been an American Airlines jet flying to Los Angeles that had been hijacked and flown through the World Trade Center towers; I sat there in disbelief. It was incredible. So much was still unknown. People trapped and killed. All airports closed. We have four weeks until our scheduled flights home, but wonder what repercussions will result.

We thought we had nothing to think about regarding home—and suddenly we hear news that's worse than any disaster movie.

Saturday, September 12, 2015
Pobeña to Castro-Urdiales, 9.07 miles/15 km

BEFORE I DRIFTED off to sleep last night, I considered alternative ways that we could spend the next four weeks in Spain if I continued to be in as much pain as I had been feeling. Should we rent a car or take a train somewhere else?

I focused on what Sylvia Boorstein emphasizes in her *It's Easier Than You Think: The Buddhist Way to Happiness*—that nothing lasts. I decided I needed a week to give this hike a fair trial. So unless things get really bad, I would go on as planned. After making that decision, I slept well all night—what a difference a good night's sleep makes!

We found an open bar serving breakfast at 7:30. Many pilgrims from the nearby albergue were doing the same. By 8:15, we were walking. First we encountered a very long flight of stairs—maybe 150-200 steps. A bit later, we found ourselves on a beach.

We then climbed a hillside to reach the highway, a secondary route (N-634) roughly parallel to the superhighway that seems to have taken most of the traffic away from this stretch. In general there was adequate room to walk along the side of the road; we were relieved there was little traffic. The route continued downhill; we met up with some other pilgrims and descended on a somewhat rocky track toward the bay until we could turn left and continue south.

Just before Mioro, we stopped for beers. There we encountered another trail split; we took the shorter route, which we had read would save us about two kilometers over the alternate uphill route. Our coastal route started out along a promenade, but led to a chain link fence that blocked the trail and displayed signs advising people to stay out.

However, since this route offered a substantial shortcut, we wanted to take it. We could see that ahead were rocky outcroppings and then train tracks running through a dark tunnel. As we were pondering our next move and the likelihood of being fined or arrested for trespassing, a couple who seemed familiar with the area came along. We asked, as best we could in our limited Spanish, if the trail was open.

They explained that the tunnel on the right was probably not open and wouldn't be safe even if it was; the tunnel on the left was open, but the route was somewhat difficult. They gave us the once over—probably considering whether or not Ralph and I were good candidates for this venture through the rubble afoot. I guess we passed because they indicated they would lead us part of the way. They were in their thirties, definitely more agile than we, but they kindly waited for us at tricky passages, and when they determined we were not apt to fall to our death, went on their way and we proceeded through the tunnel on our own.

After the tunnel came an ascent, and then our path rejoined the other route on a paved walkway. We followed another promenade into the seaport of Castro Urdiales (population 32,000), where we checked into the Pensión la Mar. The room was basic, with no A/C, but was clean and fairly priced at fifty euros.

It had been a much better day for me due to the good night's sleep, the greater distance on unpaved surfaces, and the fun and challenge of finding our way through the area with the tunnels.

In November 2016, fourteen months after our adventurous day making our way into Castro-Urdiales, I was startled to read the news headline, "A man dies after falling off the cliffs of Saltacaballo," which is the hillside we had climbed just after the tunnel. The German pilgrim, thirty-seven-year-old Thomas Bellman, fell from the steep cliffs about four kilometers before Castro-Urdiales. Rescue teams tried to revive him, but were unsuccessful; his body was airlifted by helicopter to a rescue boat.

Sunday, September 13, 2015
Castro-Urdiales to Liendo, 11.54 miles/19.1 km

LAST NIGHT THERE was street noise until 1:00 a.m., followed by singing at 3 a.m., so little sleep. Being a seaside resort town, Castro-Urdiales has many restaurants and we easily found one open for pastries and hot beverages before we set out after breakfast.

The Cicerone guide described two routes. The recommended one headed for the hills for views of the bay, then took a short stretch of the N-634, went back inland for views of lofty hilltops and green valleys, and finally before descended into Liendo. That choice sounded lovely, but it was more difficult and almost five kilometers longer.

We took the highway variant because it was the shorter of the two routes. We were not, however, always on the road, nor were we always alone. At one point we were walking along a dirt track, reveling at our views of the bay on our right side and the gray, rocky hills on our left, when we came upon a herd of goats blocking our path. Most of them quickly scattered aside, but one of the males stood his ground. Ralph went on ahead; I followed right behind him holding my hiking poles crossed in front of me until the billy goat moved off the trail. We heard later than a hiker had been butted when going through the field.

We stopped for pizza in Islares, but ordered far too much. Another pilgrim came in. Since we had too much to eat, we invited him to join us and share our food. Yurdin, who I guessed to be in his thirties, was from Germany.

As we talked we learned that like many people on the Camino, Yurdin was going through a transition period. He seemed lonely, but clearly welcomed the opportunity to converse with someone about the changes occurring in his life. Originally he had been in banking, but he quit to become an insurance salesman in his hometown. He stayed with that for several years because he enjoyed working in the small, four-person office, and helping the townspeople get insurance coverage that was affordable and well-suited to their needs.

Then a new corporation took over, Yurdin explained, "They

wanted things to become more profitable. The pressure was on to sell, sell, sell and to take far less time talking to my neighbors to find out what would really work best for them." He decided that he'd had enough of the pressure and two years back, he quit. Now he was here trying to sort out his options for the future.

Yurdin stayed to finish his meal; we went on our way. Our mid-day meal had been alongside the road, but just below was a sandy beach the color of café *au lait*. It extended a half-mile back from the water. Dozens of people in wetsuits were surfing or boarding. As we rounded the next curve, we looked down and saw hundreds of trailers and mobile homes on the grounds of Camping Plaza Arenillas. Here travelers could rent tents or mobile homes or bring their own. Ralph said that pilgrims and others could rent a bed for ten euros a night.

We were well past the place where we'd had lunch when I realized that I had lost my new hat (the replacement for the one I had lost in Barcelona in the spring). Just as I was lamenting that fact, another pilgrim came up and said that our new friend Yurdin had it. The owner of the pizza restaurant had seen that I had left the hat behind and asked Yurdin to carry it until he saw us again. There was no guarantee that I would get it back; Yurdin had talked of taking the official route back into the hills.

Meanwhile we continued our trek—most of which was along the shoulder of Highway 634. It sprinkled just enough so we had to pull out our rain gear, but it wasn't cold.

9/13/15

With so little sleep last night, I am amazed that I could function today. My leg didn't bother me until the last two kilometers of the walk. It hurts more when we stop than when we are walking; I just took four ibuprofen, so we shall see. I'm sure that the hard surfaces aggravate the situation.

Ralph and I kicked around the idea that walking on the white line that divides the traffic lane from the shoulder is a bit softer (especially when the line seems to be a bit cushioned), and is therefore a bit easier on the feet.

Some may think this is crazy, but we've heard that many participants in the 135-mile Badwater footrace (Death Valley to Whitney Portal, California) run on the center white line because it is cooler. Of course this is not such a good idea on rainy days because the white line could be more slippery.

We're staying at a very new albergue in Liendo. The new, two-story Albergue de Peregrinos has sixteen beds, a kitchen, and washer/dryer.

Monday, September 14, 2015
Liendo to Noja, 12.5/20.2 km

FROM FOGGY, INLAND Lliedo, we walked the six kilometers to Laredo. I had missed seeing the bay on the days we didn't walk alongside it. Laredo's lengthy walk along the beach was beautiful. After its boardwalk ended, we made our way through city streets until we reached the western point of the town's peninsula.

Our information read that to reach Santoña from Laredo was thirty-two minutes by bus, hours if walking, but a ferry ride across the narrow Santoña Bay took only a few minutes. We weren't quite sure where the ferry would come in, but eventually we spotted a sign that read 'Puntal Santona." We continued on across the spit of land, and as we approached the water, we saw a dock and headed for it.

A tugboat approached. I've been fond of tugboats ever since I first read *Little Toot* in the 1940s. Little Toot, in the children's picture book, was a little tugboat in New York's East harbor that learned he could overcome his fears and went on to rescue an ocean liner on the open sea during a storm. In Laredo, our cute, white tugboat had tires tied to the sides to serve as bumpers. A couple dozen bright-orange life preservers were fastened to the deck's railings, and a whole host of colorful red, orange, white, green, and blue flags hung from a cable strung over the top of the cabin.

As the boat came close and closer to shore, we saw that it was not headed for the dock that we were headed for. Was it going to come up on the beach? we wondered.

It didn't quite do that, but it did pull aground only a few feet offshore. This was not the tourist ferry that I had envisioned. There was no dock from which to approach, just a narrow, metal ramp that the crew lowered. Grasping the thin, metal handrail, we made our way on board. I sat down quickly so I wouldn't lose my balance. The ramp was pulled back into place quickly and the boat immediately turned back toward Santoña. The views from the water were beautiful, but short-lived.

Santoña, at least to the extent that we saw it while walking through, was a lovely town of about 11,000 with an attractive marina. Its main industry was canning tuna and anchovies in olive oil. We made our way through a couple of busloads of tourists gathered at the waterfront. We tried not to get into snapshots others were taking, but it took some doing because so many people were taking turns posing in front of a large monument to Juan de la Cosa. He, both explorer and cartographer, created the first European world map that incorporated the territories of the Americas that were discovered in the fifteenth century. He was also the captain of the Santa Maria, which was built in Santoña and was one of Christopher Columbus's three ships.

The monument to Cosa was of stone, perhaps twenty feet high, and was built in 1949 by architect Hernández Morales. Going from bottom to top, there were two Doric columns (symbolizing Hercules' columns according to one source, but to me looking very much like a pair of binoculars). The two columns were "tied" together with a horizontal stone "ribbon" that read, "Juan de la Cosa." Above that was a metal compass rose, next up another horizontal piece, this one reading "Santoña" (believed to be de la Cosa's birthplace), and finally, a stone likeness of the Santa Maria.

Our route then took us past an enormous, old prison that was used for holding political prisoners during Franco's time. In contrast to that sobering edifice was the next beach, Berria, a popular swimming spot.

Lulled into easy walking along the beachfronts in the morning, we were not quite prepared for the route that we came to out of Santoña. The guidebook had mentioned there was a climb over *El Brusco*, as in "at the end of the beach, climb the hill." It had not mentioned that it might require pulling oneself up by grasping low-growing vegetation alongside the reddish-dirt path on the uphill, nor was there mention of the fact that a fall from the steep and narrow trail would have been injurious if not fatal.

9/14/15

On the climb up El Brusco, my poles were useless. Some of my steps were with a leap of faith and I prayed that my sore leg would not give out. At times like these, I wonder what would happen to someone who found himself/herself stuck where it would be too difficult to continue uphill, too dangerous to go back down. Once over the top of the hill, the going was good because downhill was nowhere as near as steep, and the beach was lovely.

Since that time, I have read others people's points of view about this section. Some have dismissed comments about the danger or difficulty, but a forum contributor who goes by the trail name, Anemone del Camino, shared my opinion. "Climbing up El Brusco, going from Santoña to Noja should be forbidden, or at least rated a 'double black diamond.' It's a steep hill mostly made up of sand, on the very edge of a cliff with no ropes or barrier, what have you. With 8 kg on your back you are also more likely to be thrown backwards if you lose your footing. It is so steep that at 5'4", I had to climb bits of it on my knees as I could not make the step up. If my poles had snapped or bent, I would most likely have tumbled down to my death. And yet that is the route the tourism info booth suggested rather than taking the road around it. There is a road, take a left and follow it."

And, on August 1, 2017, a forty-five-year-old French pilgrim had to be rescued by helicopter after he slipped in mud on the trail and broke his ankle.

We came through it all feeling triumphant (at least I did because of the challenge) and continued on our way another 8.8 km to Noja, with its two gorgeous, sandy, family-friendly beaches, Trengandin and Ris. We found the Hotel Las Olas. The bright-yellow building with turquoise-blue galvanized metal roof and equally colorfully-painted bar looked like the sort of place that Hemingway would have enjoyed hanging out. Our room was less picturesque—walls of varnished wooden panels, but the ocean view and ambiance provided a relaxing fifty-euro stay.

Tuesday, September 15, 2015
Noja to Güemes, 9.69 miles/15.4 km

I slept well in our queen-sized bed in Noja, a great relief. We had no air conditioning, but nice ventilation—how these things become important!

We started the day with our raingear on, soon took it off, put it back on for another short while. After the basic breakfast on the way through Noja, we were again on a combination of pavement and quiet secondary roads. During the day we went through several small villages; reaching a new town always makes me feel that we are making good progress.

Yet, we found no place to eat when we were hungry for lunch until after Bareyo where we saw a sign, "Camping los Molinos." We didn't see tents or RVs for tourists who wanted a short term stay; it was single-family bungalows with vinyl siding and tile roofs. We wandered into a large, brick building that held a bar and grocery. Though there was a dining area with many long tables, the place was practically deserted.

We shared a bocadillo and a beer—glad to be inside and warm on the drizzly day. Later in the afternoon we saw a couple more places to stop, but we decided to wait until Güemes to eat again.

Following the minor road CA-443, we spotted the handmade sign for the pilgrim albergue in Güemes. *La Cabaña del Abuelo*

Peuto (the hut of the grandfather Peuto) is widely-known for its hospitality and philosophy. The host of the house, Father Ernesto Bustio Crespo, is legendary.

We walked up a grassy lane to the gate and were greeted by two volunteers. They showed us where to leave our hiking poles; the young woman handed each of us a glass of water, and invited us to join those seated having lunch. Since we had already eaten, we declined, but we sat on a bench near the long tables and drank our water, relaxed, and listened to conversations in multiple languages taking place around us.

After a short time, the young man who had greeted us returned to show us to our room. We followed him up a short flight of stairs to the sleeping rooms on the second level of the split-level building. Walking along the covered corridor required stepping carefully to avoid stepping on Bieul, a huge, very friendly, blond-haired dog that welcomed pilgrims and townspeople. (Bieul passed away in October 2016, and was buried in the courtyard in front of the dorms.)

The guidebook had said there were fifty-six beds and that people could also sleep on the floor; our room had eleven—that included a single bed, two sets of bunk beds, and two sets of three-high bunk beds. I was relieved that two bottom bunks were still open for grabs and we quickly claimed them. I was even more pleased when I saw that our room had its own bathroom with toilet.

Our tour continued past the coin-operated washer and dryer, clotheslines, and separate men's and women's bathrooms with showers and toilets. Our guide then left us to our own devices, but told us the schedule for the evening: a "Meet and Greet" for introductions at 7:30, followed by dinner, followed by an informational talk about the place itself in the ermita. As usual, it felt like it would be a long wait for dinner, but having been in Europe several times before, we knew that we Americans were always the first ones waiting at the door for evening meals that typically weren't offered until 8 p.m. or later.

After we unpacked and took our showers, I did a little exploring of the property on my own. Out beyond our building were several small buildings, which looked like one-room cabanas. Were they rented out, or used by the many volunteers? I wondered. After taking some photos, I spent some time in the library, which had an amazing photo collection of Ernesto's worldwide travels. In the middle of the room, a long table was covered with scrapbooks full of photos of volunteers who have helped here, and of various youth and other local civic groups with which Ernesto and the Güemes albergue has been involved.

Later, as the wind whipped the trees outside, we were grateful we were inside seated on cushioned, built-in benches on the perimeter of the warm and comfortably large room called the 'Sala de Los Caminos.' Ernesto gave some introductory remarks, in Spanish, pausing after each phrase to let a graceful, young woman translate his comments into English. Initially I thought this back-and-forth process would be boring, but something about the timing and the good humor of the two kept it interesting and fun.

We went around the circle telling what country we were from; at least fourteen countries were represented. Ernesto announced that he was, no doubt, the oldest person in the room. He paused and glanced around. I couldn't let that go unchallenged; I raised my hand and pointed to Ralph. This provoked a lot of interest and laughter, then applause, because while Ernesto was seventy-eight, Ralph was seventy-nine. Even Ralph seemed to enjoy the attention. It was nice to see age respected rather than disparaged. Ernesto's beard was fuller and whiter than Ralph's, and he was pretty good looking, too.

Ernesto proceeded to tell his story. He was the youngest of his mother's children; he was born in Güemes to a family of modest means. His grandparents had fifteen children; his mother was the youngest. "They didn't have TV or condoms," he said with a smile. In 1946, his family moved to a town near Barcelona, but they kept their property in Güemes.

In 1963, Ernesto completed his studies as a priest and was soon assigned to a parish in the Picos de Europa. Some of the photographs I had seen in the library showed where he started out—in tiny communities on steep and rugged slopes in the mountains.

In 1979, he and four friends took a twenty-seven month sabbatical that they later termed *"el viaje de universidad de vida"*—the journey of the university of life. They traveled by Land Rover in Spain, France, Africa, Central and South America. Wherever he traveled, Ernesto was passionate about promoting workers' rights and social justice.

When Ernesto and his fellow travelers returned from their around-the-world tour and education, he became the priest for Güemes. He remodeled his family's original house and added other buildings for use as a retreat center. As the Camino Norte revived its popularity, La Cabaña del Abuelo Peuto became a pilgrims' albergue as well.

After the introductions, Ernesto began his daily presentation. He spoke of the 'Way', the Camino, as a master class in life. While he acknowledged that the trek could be difficult because we might encounter blisters, mountains to climb, hard pavement, rain, and chances of getting lost, he thought that a focus on the physical difficulties missed the more important lesson of the Camino, which is to find our way spiritually.

Ernesto said, "Some even carry distractions—phones and music—that block out the natural sounds: the cuckoo's call, the sparrows chirping."

The Albergue de Güemes operates entirely on donations and volunteers. He currently had about fifty: some from the local community, others pilgrims who had decided to stay longer than one night so that they could contribute their time and energy to the cause.

When the albergue opened to pilgrims in 1999, they had two-hundred visitors. This year they had already received 7,999 and were eagerly awaiting number 8,000. (In 2016, Ernesto's place reached 10,000 by October.)

Dinner was vegetarian. It started with a filling and tasty soup followed by a stew, a piece of bread, a small glass of wine, and a pear. During dinner we were welcomed; donations were requested. They explained that the albergue relied on *donativos*, rather than charged a set amount. (Some people think that *donativo* means free, but it doesn't—albergues need money to operate.).

They added that they didn't seek funds from governmental or other organizations because they didn't want to be beholden to outside agencies.

After dinner, we made our way to the ermita, which was a free-standing building designed to provide a quiet place for reflection and meditation. Hung on the walls were colorful, mural-sized paintings donated by Latin American artist Cerezo Barredo, a Claretian priest. Barredo, also called the "Painter of the Liberation," had been inspired by Ernesto to create the six pieces. They followed a common theme: people working or eating communally as they followed the Camino (life's route). Once again a talk was given in both Spanish and English, but this time by another duo. They also were interesting and entertaining.

Bedtime was a bit awkward. I wanted to change into the slip that I sleep in, but our roommates constantly came and went. Going to sleep was also difficult because I was next to the door. I couldn't remember ever before staying in an albergue that didn't seem to have a designated time for lights-out.

I didn't like having to make the decision about turning off the lights, but by 10:15 I was fed up. I asked those in the room if they minded if I turned them off. One man answered, "Some people are not in the room." I replied, "I don't think they are in any hurry to come in; they're out smoking and visiting." I knew it would be hard for some to climb into the highest bunks without the room light, but I resented the late-comers for not considering our needs.

Wednesday, September 16
Güemes to Santander, 10.5 miles/16.9 km

EVEN AFTER I turned off the lights the previous night, I was pretty wakeful. The room became increasingly warm, but I didn't feel free to open the window near me because I worried others might not like it.

At 6:55 a.m., someone's alarm went off. An alarm in an albergue? How inconsiderate is that? I thought. Because we were all awake, most of us started getting ready for the day. I noticed that one of the night owls didn't get out of bed when the rest of us did; she was going to sleep in because she wasn't going to hike.

Breakfast, a piece of French bread, peach jam, tea and coffee, was served from 7 - 8 a.m. We sat across from a Kim, a pilgrim from Korea. He looked as if he was avoiding filling up on bread, but waiting for the main course. I didn't want to be the one to break the news that this was it.

After some ups and down on roadways, we again reached the coast where we followed dirt trails along cliffs overlooking the water. We encountered small clusters of trailers, campers, and vans parked in a couple of areas where there was easy access to the bay.

The hiking was gentle; the sea was mesmerizing. We gazed into turquoise water beyond the line of breakers pounding on a shelf just offshore. Ralph pointed out that we already had tons of photographs of breakers and surf, but I didn't care; I could have watched them for hours. We stopped to read the engraving on a stone marker: *en Memoria A Los Pescadores, 25-7-97 MC* (in memory of the fisherman). It was a stark reminder that many who had made their living at sea had also died at her hands.

Eventually we descended to the beach and walked along the hard-packed sand for another kilometer. There were dozens of people surfing, or at least trying to. Many posters announced, and shops proclaimed, that they were surfing schools.

Before Somo we made a turn (as the guidebook suggested) to leave the beach at a bar/restaurant. It was crowded with day-trippers, but we managed to snag an outdoor table where we had a beer and snack. Somo was as described, "a comfortable port town," but we were dying to go on to Santander because we had enjoyed it so much in the spring. We marched through town, going slightly downhill to the port where we found the ferry that would take us directly into Santander.

Catching the ferry was not difficult—it ran every half hour. The crossing on the *Regina Pacos Sexto* was longer—a whole ten minutes—than I expected based on the few ferry rides we had taken earlier, but it, like the others, ended all too quickly for my taste. Nevertheless, it was exciting to pull into the waterfront near the center of the city.

This time around we wanted accommodations closer to the train station, which meant that we had a completely different section of town to explore. I knew that some pilgrims hate big cities, and Santander, with its population of 180,000, was one of the largest along the route, but I liked sightseeing, window shopping, strolling, and people watching.

The cathedral has withstood more than the passage of time, it also saw damage during an explosion in the harbor in 1893 and a fire in 1941. Nevertheless, the city's cathedral contains many ancient sections including a glass floor covering Roman ruins; the main portal, constructed around 1230; and the Gothic cloister.

9/17/15
This was a magnificent walk most of the way. When we arrived, I was at first disgruntled that Ralph hadn't booked us into a fancy hotel, but the *hospedaje* (hostel) Magallanes where we ended up was actually perfectly fine and close to restaurants. It was only a five-minute walk to the train station, which we discovered when we made our way over so we'll know how to do things tomorrow morning. We discovered there are two train stations—basically side by side, but in two different buildings. We're glad we figured out that we want the local line, the FEVE.

Dinner was a bit different, but good. The diminutive, but flavorful anchovies were served in a tin. The fried breadcrumb rolls known as croquettes were so tasty and well-made that their fish filling melted in my mouth.

Thursday, September 17, 2015
Santander to Santillana del Mar, 6 miles/9.6 km

MANY PILGRIMS TAKE a train out of Santander to get across the Ría de Mogro. When we were at Ernesto's, we were told various strategies for making the river crossing—some were not very appealing. One route required hikers to walk quite some distance, eleven kilometers, to and from the nearest footbridge across the water. Not only did that route add kilometers, it reportedly also went through an unattractive industrial area. Another possibility was to walk across on the railway bridge. Though the bridge was extremely short, going across the active railway on foot was illegal and flirting with danger.

The most common method was to walk from Santander to the small town of Boo on the edge of the water, then take the train across the hundred-yard wide channel and get off at Mogro, the first town on the other side. We heard that many people took the train across without a ticket because there usually wasn't an agent at the station. If they were caught without a ticket, apparently they could buy one on the train for 1.50 euros.

Because we felt the kilometers to the next accommodations were too many for me, and we were a day behind our original schedule, we decided to take the train an additional distance, to Requejada, meaning we rode for almost twenty-three kilometers, making what would have been a twenty-mile walk into a six-mile one.

The skies looked threatening when we started walking from Requejada so we put raingear on, but it didn't rain at all. Even though we were walking along fields and through rural settlements on a minor highway the entire time, the views were pleasant: a horse, some bulls, lots of corn fields, buildings with red-tiled roofs, rolling hills, higher mountains inland that were somewhat shrouded with fog and mist.

9/17/15

The outskirts of Santillana seemed like those of many other towns, but when we came to the town center, dating from medieval times, it became far more interesting. We came downhill toward the church— and a field of tourists.

Our hotel, the Casa del Organista, is charming and the manager is super friendly. Our room is the nicest we've had yet. The walls are a muted shade of yellow with a tinge of gold. The ceiling is white, setting off the dark-stained wooden beams. The wardrobe closet, the doors, and the baseboards are stained dark. The bathroom is moderately-sized, but has all the right touches: porcelain switch plates; a gleaming, white-tiled floor; white tub with French style shower faucets and a versatile wand.

Dinner was the most fun so far. We just happened to choose the restaurant where some of our new hiker friends were already eating. We were seated at the table next to them, but we soon were invited to join their conversation. There was a couple from San Francisco (she originally from Venezuela); Medford Guy, a hefty surgical nurse who had lived in the Bay Area, but recently moved to Medford, Oregon where he hoped to find himself; and a new tubby guy from Italy.

Somehow talk soon turned to how we make animal sounds and what the written words are in various languages. The SF guy came out with the American version, "cock-a-doodle-do," which put the Italian guy in stitches. It soon became just like a get-together of Pacific Crest Trail hikers—such things as age, job, and where you are from don't matter—you instantly connect because you are sharing an experience. Just silliness. No intellectual or higher level conversation needed.

AFTER WE RETURNED home, I looked online and found that our discussion was not a rare one to have—after all, chickens live in many places throughout the world. I found a blogpost by Pete Berg, who wrote about one of his entertaining evenings with friends:

'Kukeleku, of course,' said Sietse, my Dutch friend.
'Cocorico,' said Diane my French friend.
'Kickeriki,' said my Italian friend Hans who comes from the part of Italy where they speak German.

'Quiquiriquí,' said Iñake, my friend from the Basque region of Spain.

'Wo-wo-wo!' said my Swedish-Chinese friend Tee, who speaks seven languages, and was referring to the Mandarin word there. She added: 'In Swedish, we say Kuckeliku.'

Friday, September 18, 2015
Zero Day in Santillana del Mar

WE DECIDED TO stay an extra day in Santillana del Mar in order to visit the famous Altamira Cave. After a super breakfast at the hotel, we walked from the village to the cave and museum on a gentle, uphill route of about two kilometers. The original cave was declared a UNESCO protected cultural heritage site because it had nearly a hundred animals and signs engraved, scraped, or painted on its ceiling that dated from 36,000 to 13,000 years back (the Paleolithic period). The cave was discovered in 1868 by a local hunter, Modesto Peres. It was, however, Marcelino Sanz de Sautuola, an amateur archaeologist who studied the site in 1879, who first understood the significance of the discovery.

The original cave is almost nine-hundred-feet long and its twisting and turning passages and chambers are from six- to eighteen-feet high. The people who lived within it were hunter gatherers; their art work includes images of bison, goats, and horses—animals that lived nearby and were important sources of food, hides, tools and other necessities. The paints used were primarily reds and browns from the mineral pigment ochre, and the blacks and grays from the charcoal left from the cooking fires inside the caves. Over time, the millions of visitors to the original site have caused damage to the figures because we exhale carbon dioxide. This necessitated the protection of the original site.

Some visitors, primarily researchers and other scientists, still have access to the cave and its paintings, but we, like most tourists nowadays, toured what is known as the *Neocave*, a three-dimensional replica of the original. With a small group, we walked through the replica cave, and then on our own studied the other displays that showed how these cave dwellers lived. I was interested in the skillful way the early artists had integrated the uneven surfaces of the ceiling into their representations of the animals. A curving natural line in the ceiling might be used to help define the shape of a bison, for example. I wanted to like the replica and the museum, but I couldn't get past my disappointment at not seeing the real deal.

Returning to town, we had a wonderful meal with paella, white asparagus, bread, glasses of vino, and *flan*—the baked egg custard with caramel topping that remains my favorite Spanish dessert. All this was at a bargain rate of 12.50 euros each.

Paella is not as readily found in northern Spain as it is in other parts of the country. Rice doesn't grow along the northern coast, but it was brought to other parts of the country more than 1,200 years ago by the Moors. Valencia, being a port city on the Mediterranean Sea, became the home of paella. Over time, many people have come to think of it as the country's national dish, but the Spanish consider it a regional dish. Nevertheless, to my delight, we occasionally found it on menus along the Norte.

We visited the *Claustro Romanico de La Colegiata* (Collegiate Romanesque), which was declared a National Monument in 1889. It was originally a monastery, but became a collegiate in the 11th century. It housed the relics of Santa Juliana, which were brought here, according to legend, after she was martyred by Roman Emperor Diocletian in 303 CE. She had become a Christian and would not renounce her faith.

9/18/15

We did a search on the web and learned that a *collegiate* is a Catholic temple, not a cathedral, the distinction being what services can be held there. Not being Catholic, such distinctions aren't significant to us, but even though we have seen hundreds of chapels, churches, cathedrals, and even basilicas while on Camino treks, I still enjoy visiting them because of their history, beauty, music, and ceremony.

Sometimes our visits are brief; we like to see in what way they might be unique. I also enjoy visiting cloisters. This was no exception; the cloister of *Claustro Romanico de La Colegiata* was built on the northern side of the collegiate and has three wings. I liked the graceful arches, the stately columns, the carved or molded figures of the capitals.

Something not so peaceful is the fact that Ralph has numerous bed bug bites and the itching is driving him crazy. I've not had a problem and we are hoping that we are not transporting the little beasties. As a precaution, we are keeping our belongings sealed up in plastic bags and hung by a hook off the beds, furniture, and floors.

Saturday, September 19, 2015
Santillana to Comillas, 14.2 miles/22.9 km

WE STARTED OUT at 7:30 without breakfast and had to wait until the next town to eat. Maybe the tourists didn't want to get up and get going as early as pilgrims? We walked through the small towns of San Martin de Cigüenza (admiring the Church of San Martin with its fine Baroque façade), Cobreces, the youth hostel at La Iglesia, the monastery of Pando, and the village of Concha, but when we were hungry for lunch, we didn't find anyplace until two o'clock. We didn't want to go several hundred meters out of our way to eat.

One of the best things about the day was that we were on dirt trails or well-worn paths much of the way. The weather was good; I changed to shorts and tee shirt after the morning coolness had disappeared. We saw about twenty people on the trail; it seemed like a lot compared to the number we had seen on previous days. We kept leapfrogging over two women—one was from Denmark, but we didn't have a chance to talk to the other. We also ran into a trio from Australia that we had seen at Ernesto's place.

The city of Comillas was on the sea and had beautiful beaches, however, we stayed at the Esmeralda in the center of town. It seemed rather trendy and touristy, but not overly crowded.

We learned that this city was where Antonio Gaudí got his start. He was only in his early thirties when he designed *El Capricho*, a mansion for Maximo Diaz de Quijano and constructed by Christopher Cascante from 1883-1885. Quijano was an attorney of Antonio López y López, first Marquis of Comillas, and was a wealthy bachelor.

Because our accommodations were only a short distance from *El Capricho*, we were able to walk to see Gaudi's early work. It was the bargain of the day; it turned out that for five euros, we could take a self-guided tour inside and out. Lots of other visitors had the same idea, but we were able to see all of it without tripping over anyone.

The outside of the mansion was showy and whimsical—like everything much of Gaudi's work in Barcelona and elsewhere. The entrance to the villa was below a sixty-foot-high Persian minaret. From a platform in the minaret, we had great views of the surrounding city and the Cantabrian Sea.

Attorney Quijano had been interested in both music and botany. Gaudi's work reflected both interests. A wrought iron railing in the shape of clefs and other music notations surrounded the platform we stood on. The exterior of the minaret was predominately covered with ceramic tiles decorated with sunflowers.

The interior was quite beautiful; its rooms both tastefully designed and comfortable. I particularly liked the coffered ceilings and the other Mudejar influences in the ceilings, windows and tile work. Gaudí used a lot of wrought iron—undoubtedly influenced by the work of his father, who had been a blacksmith.

Gaudi had designed El Capricho's floorplan so that sunlight would come through the windows of the master bedroom early in the morning and then enter the rest of the rooms in a natural progression to match the day's activities.

I found it fascinating that though the exterior of El Capricho featured some of the zany characteristics that later showed up in many of Gaudi's works, the interior was designed to fit the personality and needs of his client.

9/19/15

Seeing Gaudi's El Capricho was an incredible experience; I'm in awe of his creativity and brilliance.

This was our longest walk of this trip, and it was tougher than recent ones because of the continual up and down. I was excited to see that I set a new personal record on my Fitbit: 40,148 steps. I haven't walked as many miles since the last of the Pacific Crest Trail in Washington State in 2010.

Ralph keeps saying I should be proud of myself. I keep focusing on the fact that we probably cannot finish this route in the time we have. Time will tell.

We had a good dinner at the hostal once we got it all sorted out. We thought our waiter offered scallops, but it turned out that we had ordered *Escalope*—veal scaloppini.

Sunday, September 20, 2015
Comillas to Serdio, 11.8 miles/19 km

From: Susan
To: Friends and family

Now sitting at a table, beer in hand, watching a playoff of some sort of bowling/nine pins game in the tiny town of Serdio. Looks like the entire population is on hand to see who the victor will be and who will take home the silver trophy.

Yesterday and today were pretty hard days, fourteen and twelve miles respectively, of up one hill and down the next.

Today's lunch was midway in San Vicente de la Barquera, a good-sized town with all accommodations. It also has an eighth-century castle, a handsome medieval bridge with twenty-eight or thirty-two arches (depending on who you ask), and a thirteenth-century Gothic church, the Santa Maria de Los Angeles, to visit and admire. We're staying in a very sweet house, the Posada la Torre. I felt very much at home when we were invited to hang out in the living room. The fifty euros we paid includes our breakfasts.

Our trail continues to take us down to the sea and gorgeous cities and then a bit inland to smaller towns. The good weather has continued and the cows, sheep, corn, and so forth seem to be very happy in their lush green fields. Since we have water rationing at home, it was a real treat to find a generously-sized tub! I emptied all of our room's tiny shampoo bottles into the water to create a luxurious bubble bath

We continue to see twenty or so other pilgrims each day—the max has been fifty—and it is especially fun when we run into the same people time after time.

Love, Susan and Ralph

Monday, September 21, 2015
Serdio to Pendueles, 1.8 miles/19 km

WE LEFT SERDIO, hiked through Pesués (which had a couple of bars for snacks), crossed the Rio de Tina Menor, took a steep, rocky, wide road downhill to pass under the A-8, and entered Unquera. We crossed the picturesque Rio Deva and then entered the region of Asturias and came to the central plaza of the mountain village of Colombres—with many fine examples of Indianos architecture.

One of the remaining buildings of that type is a gorgeous mansion known as La Quinta Guadalupe. This over-the-top building is painted several shades of blue, is three stories high, and has a couple of sailors' walkways and a cupola. The original building was constructed in 1906 for Iñigo Noriega Laso, who had left his home in Colombres for Mexico when he was four-teen. Once there, he became a highly successful businessman; he owned several mines, textile factories, and a shipping line. When he returned home, the mansion was built and then named for his wife, Dona Guadalupe Castro.

During the late 1800s and early 1900s, many men from the Asturian, Cantabrian, and Galician territories emigrated to Latin America (and some to Florida) to escape poverty and make a better life for themselves and their families back home. Some became wealthy and returned to their ancestral homes. They were called *Indianos* (or Indians) because the Spaniards called the Americas the *Indias*. In not only Columbres, but also other places in the region, many other impressive "casas indianas," or mansions, remain. La Quita Guadalupe now houses the *Museo de la Emigración*, and several of the museum's rooms are furnished typical of the Indianos' way of life here as well as in Latin America.

We stopped for sandwiches. In spite of the city's rich history, we saw many "Se Vende" signs; we'd increasingly seen them along the way. That so many places were for sale was one of several indications of the challenging economic situation in this part of Spain. Sometimes the old homes and farmhouses had simply been abandoned. It could be that there was no one in the family to take over after a death, that no one in the current generation had interest in the old places, or that family members were forced to leave the small towns and move to the larger cities to find jobs.

Another factor that has affected many of the rural towns has been the freeways. Just as back home, where highways are placed can have a tremendous impact on the well-being of municipalities. Once-thriving commercial districts may be bypassed entirely by new freeways; communities can be divided by tons of soaring metal and concrete structures.

From Columbres we stayed mostly on highway N-634 for the couple of kilometers to tiny La Franca. There we picked up a footpath, descended to a river, climbed up the other side, followed a dirt road, and got back on the N-634. We arrived in Pendueles, found the La Llobera Apartments, and were shown our room by the manager.

9/21/15

It was sunny this morning, and became overcast when we got closer to the coast. We'll see the water again tomorrow. The "steep, rocky descent" that the guidebook had mentioned didn't exist, but maybe there has been a reroute. We saw only a couple of pilgrims today; maybe that's because we are stopping between the stages suggested by the guidebook.

Another thing that we have been seeing less of for the last few days is toilet paper littering the ground. I wonder: are there cultural differences between where we are now and where we started? Has there been a concerted effort to clean up the area? Is it the fewer number of people on the trails? The smaller population here? Something else? Whatever the reason, I am happy to see the change.

Our apartment in the La Llobera is roomy. We have a kitchen, comfy chairs, and lighting that will be adequate for reading in bed. I like having someplace to sit other than the bed. We reached here at 2:30, which means that I have plenty of time for a wonderful, long shower.

Even though this was another nineteen-kilometer day, most of it on pavement, it seemed a bit less strenuous…or maybe I am getting stronger? I've been able to cut my ibuprofen use considerably. I have gone from twelve a day at the start, to six per day this week, and to only four today.

Tuesday, September 22, 2015
Pendueles to Llanes, 6 miles/10 km

AFTER BREAKFAST AT the local bar, we set out along a paved road under dreary skies. We somehow made a wrong turn, which cost us about a half mile. Once back on track, we followed the guidebook's recommended routes—the longer, but more scenic and off-tarmac track.

It soon cleared somewhat and we could see that the rugged Picos de Europa mountain range was now very close. Our up and down trail came to a fork; we continued to follow the narrow, dirt trail further through a windswept grassy field toward the ocean. A huge opening on the top of the rocky cliffs—cracks in the limestone, had created the *Bufones de Arenillas* (blowholes). We stood well back from the edge.

We met up with another couple who were also hoping to see the powerful geyser in action—maybe shoot seawater sixty feet into the air. The young woman told us that she had been there previously when there was quite a show, but she thought we were too early to see and hear the phenomena this time around. She explained it was usually best at high tide and when the sea was very rough. We waited with the two of them for about twenty minutes, but then decided we needed to move along.

We may have missed the bigger show, but it was not a total loss. Though I wished we'd arrived when the blowhole's conditions were optimal—when a tremendous spout of seawater exploded upwards as it was forced through an underground sea cave and a narrow rift—the small sprays of mist we saw, the thundering sounds we heard, and the shaking of the ground beneath us were enough for us to appreciate the power of the untamed ocean. In addition, the rugged area surrounding the blowholes was simply gorgeous—rough, gray limestone and soft, dark-green grasses.

We could have continued on the recommended trail variant, but we decided to road walk through Cue and on into the larger city of Llanes, which was touted as a mecca for tourists and hippies. It wasn't quite like seeing the Haight-Ashbury, but I was happy to be on the coast again. Even so, the heavily overcast skies undoubtedly kept most people out of the water.

9/22/15

The Posada del Rey where we are staying is warm, clean, and welcoming. The room is large, the walls a combination of knotty pine and stone. We asked about breakfast. "It's already in your room," the young woman in reception told us. Indeed when we looked behind our coffee maker, we saw that we had been supplied with packaged pastries—the typical sponge cakes, croissants, and cookies—as well as coffee, tea, and juice.

At dinner, Ralph was happy to see *Cocido de Garbanzo* on the menu and when the steaming dish arrived, it did indeed resemble the *Cocido Maragato* meal we'd had in Astorga on our first Camino. There are differences, but both are very filling dishes made of chickpeas and huge chunks of various kinds of meat. Ralph tried his best to eat what was served, but as with many meals we've had here, it was nearly impossible to finish the huge serving.

Wednesday, September 23, 2015
Llanes to Nueva, 10.5 miles/17 km

From Llanes, nestled between the mountains and the coast, we started our day with a couple of short stretches along beaches. Though tourist season was over, the coastline still held its attractions. Watching the tremendous waves hitting the offshore rocks was exciting. I held my breath while we watched a surfer head into the sea beyond the opening in the jagged rocks. I hoped he was experienced, because a novice would have been dashed to pieces when attempting to ride the waves back in. We noticed that he was the only one in the water.

We hit Playa de Poo, Celorio (with bars and more), and then crossed a promenade to walk across a second beach. Then into Barro, which provided another bar offering drinking and eating opportunities. Next we passed the former Monasterio de San Antolin and a beach of the same name. "Cross under the expressway, pass through Naves (with another bar) and through Villahormes, which has an albergue," said the Cicerone guide. We then went straight for three-and-a-half kilometers, descended to the AS-263, and crossed to the right of still another bar into Nueva. We checked into the Cuevas del Mar Plaza de La Verde Ruiz, which Andrea and Terry had recommended.

9/23/15

It was overcast this morning, followed by couple of short periods of light rain. We put on and took off our raingear two or three times.

We ran into Medford Guy and learned his name is Sean. We haven't seen him for days—it turned out he had left the trail for a week because his dad was having surgery back in Oregon.

The hike was relatively easy and time seemed to zip by. We got to the hotel at 3 pm., which is a little later than usual. We had stopped often to take photos of our dramatic surroundings—sandy beaches, rough ocean, rocky mountains, colorful towns.

Our room is great except for the fact that I am freezing; there's no heat. The days are getting shorter and chillier and we are beginning to wonder when the heaters will be turned on for the winter.

Thursday, September 24, 2015
Nueva to Ribadesella, 8 miles/12.9 km

IN GENERAL, WE have requested breakfasts at 7:30, so we could be on the trail by eight o'clock, but when we had a short day planned like this day's, we didn't mind eating later than usual.

It was a beautiful, clear morning as we walked through the small towns of Piñeres de Pría and by the Iglesia de Pría. As usual, the church was closed. It has been rare to find a church open on a weekday—far different from our experiences in France where we frequently had enjoyed popping in for a brief visit. We had read that it is sometimes possible to hunt down someone in the small towns to get a key, but this has always seemed too much of a hassle.

Although we loved the huge cathedrals, especially the ones in Burgos and Leon on the Camino Francés, we enjoyed even more the small chapels that were decorated reflecting the unique personalities of the villages and towns where they were built. The warmth of these small sanctuaries was sometimes missing in the more ornately decorated larger churches. Occasionally there were fresh flowers from a recent wedding, other times there was a handmade cart or religious figures sitting in a dark corner awaiting the next festival. I liked seeing chapel walls that were hand-painted with scenes typical of the area, or cherubs and clouds, or even the Stations of the Cross.

STATIONS OF THE Cross refers to a series of images depicting Jesus Christ on the day of his crucifixion (though there are variations). There are typically fourteen in the series; they will often be seen in churches in the form of paintings, carvings in relief, or sculptures. When Christians view them, they may say a specific prayer at each station and this can be done by the individual or with a congregation. This tradition is seen not only in Catholic churches, but also those of some other denominations such as Methodist and Episcopalian.

I optimistically had thought we would arrive in Ribadesella by noon, but it was 1:30 by the time we got there. We checked into the Marina on the Gran Via, which was only a block from the waterfront as well as the central part of town—an ideal location for exploring the city. We ate at a cafeteria; not much else was open after 2 p.m. because of the siesta.

We found the church of Santa Maria Magdalena and were pleased to see it was open. The exterior was a combination of gray stone and plaster, and above the front façade was a large statue of Christ with a taller tower on each side. This parish church was originally built in the early 1900s atop ruins from medieval times. It was almost destroyed during bombing in 1936, but rebuilt after the civil war.

The interior was quite splendid. The statues and other art range from traditional religious figures placed in frames to the glorious frescoes by *los hermanos* (the brothers) Uría Aza, who were born in the town.

9/24/15
This evening we were in the center of town and ran into Yurdins, our German Guy friend. He had a

forlorn look on his face. He'd had some difficulty at
the ATM and was short of cash. "I'm starving," he
said. We knew he didn't mean it literally, but we knew
how one's appetite grows when hiking hard.

"Would you like to go to the cafeteria—our treat?
We went there at lunchtime and they had good basic
food." We made our way over to the restaurant; we all
ordered the ten-euro menu.

"It's my birthday," Yurdin said. "I'm forty-four."
With that news, I was even happier that we had
treated him to dinner.

Friday, September 25, 2015
Zero Day in Ribadesella

OUR HOTEL, THE Marina, is well over a century old. Perhaps
it's not as glamorous as it was "back in the day," but it was still
charming and with friendly and helpful service. Our room had
a small balcony where we were able to check out the street scene
and hang out our laundry where it could not be seen. Luckily,
the street was not a noisy one.

It felt luxurious to be offered a full menu of breakfast choices
while seated at a table with white tablecloths. We were anxious
to explore Ribadesella—a picturesque fishing village with tidy,
small boats bobbing in the sparkling water, a golden sandy beach
enjoyed by sunbathers, and kayakers paddling along the Sella
River that cut the beach in half.

Our first walk was along the long quay to visit the ermita
perched on a hillside, and to have other views of the city. The
chapel was closed, but had been worth a look even with the 135
steps back down the hill. Even more exciting was watching the
experienced surfers paddling out to sea and then riding in on
the crashing waves.

We had been told we were too late as far as making reservations for the nearby Cueva de Tito Bustillo, but Ralph managed
to make them online, and visiting the cave became our afternoon's plan. It was an easy, flat walk of less than a half-mile and

the weather was perfect.

Finding which building was which was confusing, but we managed to figure it out in time to take a tour. From the main highway, one reaches the building that leads to the caves first, but the place where one checks in and gets tickets is farther down the dead-end road.

The cave and a sink hole named *Pozu'l Ramu* were discovered in 1968 by the mountaineering group, Torreblanca, and two young men from the town. One of the mountaineers, Celestino Fernández Bustillo, died in a mountaineering accident a few days after the group's discovery and so the cave was named after him. It was declared UNESCO World Heritage site because it was one of Europe's most important discoveries of prehistoric art.

Our guide spoke Spanish, so no doubt we missed a great deal, but seeing the cave's interior was amazing enough. It was staggering to be in the deep and enormous cave. The ceiling was lined with prehistoric symbols—primarily of horses, bison, and reindeer. For me, that this cave and its paintings were the real deal made it a moving experience.

I wished that the tour had moved more slowly; it felt like we were being run through with little time to really look around. The guide stopped from time to time and pointed various things out with his dim flashlight, but there was much more one could have seen if the lighting had been better. The dim lighting was necessary to protect the art, but it did create some risky situations. In several places we had to feel, with out feet, the way along the uneven cave floor, even down a few steps, because there was little light to see where we were going. I had to wonder how often people slipped; I could easily imagine someone falling and bumping into one of the stalagmites.

As usual, we had spent much of our Zero Day walking around a city. By day's end, my Fitbit read seven miles.

Saturday, September 26, 2015
Ribadesella to Colunga, 13 miles/20.5 km

BACK TO WORK after the day off. The forecast was for continued good weather. The trail dropped three times to beautiful, sandy beaches with numerous surfers during our walk; I continued to be amazed at the number of beaches and degree of public access. We wondered if most of Spain's beaches were public or private.

Based on the guidebook, we expected Asturias to be wilder and less settled than what we had seen so far. And overall, we did more climbing this day than we had for the last couple. We stayed on the coastal route—going through more forested areas than before—but we were still never far from the highway.

Again we saw about twenty hikers during the day, but we didn't know any of them and none seemed interested in stopping to talk. Probably because this was Saturday, we noticed more people in the towns gathered with friends in yards or in restaurants.

I felt sad and lonely because, while others were enjoying their parties, we were far from friends and family. I wondered how other travelers manage to get themselves invited in to local celebrations.

Then, as we passed behind a row of houses along the trail, I heard voices on the other side of a stone wall. They came closer and then a couple of teenagers came over to the wall and looked over at us. They were soon joined by a friendly, portly fellow, presumably someone's dad. He called out to us and extended a glass toward us. "¿Quieres la sidra?, he asked. "Yes, *si*," I replied.

We finally got to taste some of the hard cider, *sidra*, for which this region is known. For days we have been walking past trees loaded with small red or green apples. We've tasted a few—they've been sour compared to what we are used to at home. The cider was good, a bit tart, and complex—very different from the sweetened, homogenized beverage we are used to.

When we stopped in Colunga, we stayed at the comfortable, two-star Hotel Las Vegas. We felt very much at home in our room with knotty pine walls and burnt-red tile paver floors—just like we have in our house.

9/26/15

I am very excited about the kids' parks we've seen. There have been many and they've been very clean. The the play structures actually look like fun. We watch children as young as four riding zip-lines that are strung above the sand. Compared to what we've seen here, the play apparatuses at home look unimaginative. I think we need more playgrounds at home that are both appealing and safe.

Though this was a physically challenging day, with 34,336 steps, the friendly people who had allowed us to take a sip of sidra from their party certainly made my day.

Sunday, September, 27, 2015
Colunga to Villaviciosa, 10.5 miles/17 km (8:30-3:00)

THE DAY STARTED out clear and the weather forecast was for continued sun. I decided to try my new hiking skirt for the first time. I found it to be very comfortable when the temperatures were in the ten- to twenty-degree centigrade range—and also more convenient for pee breaks.

There was only one place listed in the guidebook to stop for food along our day's route, but we were prepared. Ralph had purchased lunch materials the night before. We've seen hardly any picnic benches and tables along this trail, but today we found a place to sit and eat in front of a pilgrim albergue in Sebrayo that hadn't even officially opened. A bit later, we spotted a restaurant that was so new that it hadn't yet been listed. With the increasing number of pilgrims on this route, we expected new places would continue to pop up.

We had more off-road hiking than usual. At times I wondered if the route along the highway wouldn't have been shorter, but it was pleasant to go through stands of deciduous trees and hear sounds of birds other than crows or pigeons.

We were slowed by the climbs, and I felt that everyone passed us, but as Ralph pointed out, we didn't know which people hadn't.

He figured we were going about three kilometers an hour, which somehow sounded better than 1.86 miles per hour.

Of course we would have gone faster if we hadn't stopped so often to take photographs. With the dramatic views of the Picos on the one side and the ocean on the other, we couldn't hurry on by. As we approached Villaviciosa, we saw the city was not on the water, but was alongside a huge floodplain that led to the ocean.

Although there are also places to drink hard cider in Basque Country, Villaviciosa is known as the *sidra* capital of Asturias and places to drink the hard apple cider abound. We quickly learned the terminology. The cider bar is *sidrerias* in Asturias, *el chigre* in Basque Country. The glass is *un culín;* the pouring of the cider is *escanciada.*

The *escanciada* is a big production. The bartender or server (usually a man) holds the bottle of cider extended high overhead with one arm, holds the glass at an angle with his other hand, looks up at the ceiling, and pours. Most lands in the glass, but much also splashes out of the glass in a fine spray, which is why there is often sawdust on the floor. The purpose of pouring from the height is to aerate the cider and allow the bubbles to remain in the liquid. Drinking sidra is often a very social event; bottles are shared and everyone drinks from the same glass. In other places, customers can draw their own beverage from a pressurized container.

How the dregs are handled varies from place to place. In Basque *chigres*, the person who takes the last drink pours the residue out onto the sawdust. In Asturias, it is usually the server who handles it. When he clears the table, if there is any cider still in the glass, he throws the remainder towards a wooden bucket near the bar or towards the front of the bar where it can then run down into a trough. Oftentimes the bar is heavily stained by its many years of service.

9/27/15

Even though some dark cumulus clouds appeared unexpectedly for a while today, the temperatures remained comfortable.

Our hotel, the Carlos I, has a two-star rating and is quite nice. I sometimes forget that ratings vary by country and don't necessarily tell you how cute, comfortable, or roomy a place is, nor how hospitable the owner and staff may be. Sometimes, they consider other things, such as whether or not a staff member is on the premises twenty-four hours a day.

Sometimes hotels or hostals serve *desayuno* (breakfast), but more often we are left to our own devices to find food in the mornings. Our considerate host here packed breakfast materials for us because we needed to leave before their 9 a.m. opening time.

We've lost the print version of our guidebook, so now each evening one of us has to write out the directions for the next day from the e-book. If we didn't do this, Ralph would have to get out the iPad at every turn.

Tomorrow we are going to come to an important trail junction—continuing straight ahead keeps hikers on the Camino del Norte, turning south takes them toward Oviedo to begin the Camino Primitivo. Ralph and I planned this trip around staying on the Norte. He's had no interest in changing the plan, but I wanted to discuss it again. After going over the choices again, I agreed we should continue as planned. We have loved the Norte so far, think we will continue to enjoy it, and figure that we can come back and walk the Primitivo another time.

Monday, September 28, 2015
Villaviciosa to Cabueñes, hike 20.8 km/12.9 miles
Cabueñes to Gijón, taxi 7.8 km/4.8 miles

AFTER A MODERATE start out of Villaviciosa, we began to climb. I joked with Ralph that whoever designed the walking route decided that the roadways weren't steep enough so they guided us onto dirt trails that could be made steeper.

A kilometer past the hamlet Casquita, we came to the junction—marked by a concrete post with Camino tiles. The marker for the Norte pointed toward Gijón; the one for the Primitivo pointed to Oviedo. The Norte route stays along the coast a while longer, but will start heading inland and southwest in about a week; the Primitivo follows a more rugged course through the mountains, but is shorter. We circled around the post taking photos of this important point.

We had met people who were going to make a detour to see Oviedo and then come back to the Norte at Avilés, but we suspected that most people who turned toward Oviedo would not return to our route.

A few kilometers later, and after the village of Nievares, we made a lengthy ascent and reached the high point of the Norte, the Alto de la Cruz. Compared to the Cruz de Ferro along the Camino Francés, this was anticlimactic—in fact we didn't see a sign at all.

We left the highway to descend onto track where a very faint arrow showed the way. The guidebook had indicated that trail markings were poor in this area, so we stayed alert. Eucalyptus leaves, acorns, or gravel would have made this stretch treacherous if the trail had been wet, but for us, on a clear day, it was easily passable.

The trail flattened, then ascended another hill. Finally in Cabueñes, on the outskirts of Gijón, we found a bar-restaurant for a beer. I was grateful Ralph knew without my saying anything that I was exhausted and in pain. He called a taxi. We took it all the way into Gijón's Best Western, the *Aguera,* saving half a day's walk and almost eight kilometers.

This had been a tough day, so I lounged a bit and sent an email.

From: Susan
To: Melanie

After sixteen hiking days, I am over the hump as far as accepting the fact that this is really happening, but because of my inability to train for this hike, I am still not at the point of feeling that my pack and I are "one"—that point when you don't put it down every chance you get.

Today was another tough one. We did almost thirteen miles and that involved going over a high point and then dropping into a valley and climbing back out. I am very grateful that the weather has been good; I don't think I could do it in the rain.

At least there is no drought here and everything is green. This region, Asturias, is the apple capital and the trees are loaded with them.

We go by a lot of small farms and I am impressed by the attempts to keep nice gardens. Not the wonderful obsession with gardening as you see in England perhaps, but the townspeople and villagers here take a lot of pride in setting out rows of flower-filled pots. Right now there are a lot of roses, hydrangeas, and geraniums in full color.

Gijón, where we're staying tonight, is a very large city and seemingly filled with huge multi-unit, multi-level apartments. I would have liked to head west to the beaches and the historic center, but I was too tired.

While I continued emailing friends, Ralph went out to find the bus stop for #24 buses for the next day's short ride. The guidebook had said that we could avoid Gijón's heavy industrial area by taking the #24 from the center of town to Camin Rebesosu on the outskirts of the city.

Dinner was at a hole in the wall, but the food was excellent—a *pastel cabracho* (fish pâté), pasta with clams, and *pescado del dia* (fried fish bits). Unfortunately, the atmosphere was more stressful than relaxing. The only other occupied table was filled with a group of loud women. To top it off, the waitress alternated between joining in with the boisterous group and standing by the kitchen door coughing. She made no effort to cover her mouth; I feared for my health.

Tuesday, September 29, 2015
Gijón to Avilés, 12.8 miles/20.6 km

WE LEFT FOR the bus stop Ralph had located the night before. We waited by the bus stop… and waited… and waited, but only #10 buses came by. So much for getting out the door early to get a good start.

We walked several more blocks and found a bus stop just as a #24 pulled in. The driver briefly opened the doors, and then quickly tried to close them—right in our faces. Why, we had no idea, but Ralph moved quickly and stuck his hiking pole between the doors. The driver had little choice but to let us on. We were just glad to get on the bus.

Ralph told the driver where we were headed. One of the other passengers overheard, and asked us if we were pilgrims. When we said yes, the matronly woman decided she needed to take care of us. We watched carefully for the signs at each bus stop. Ralph had counted the number of stops to Aoago Alto, where we thought we should get off. He had figured it would be the twentieth, but when we were one stop short of that, both the driver and the woman were quite insistent that we had to get off—at *Paugo Alto*.

We reasoned they had helped countless other pilgrims and probably knew the area better than we did so we hurriedly got off. The bus ride had saved us about four kilometers of walking.

We turned and made a short ascent toward Monte Arco Park. A sturdy wooden stand, with several shelves and roof, had been set up alongside the sidewalk. A wooden bench sat alongside. A sign's message, "Only for the pilgrims" was written in multiple languages. A cubbyhole contained two ripe lemons. The shelves held two large turquoise water containers, individual-size plastic bottles of water, and a wooden box.

A smaller sign, "Viglancia con Camaras" had been posted above the box. I was curious why a security camera was needed—were people vandalizing the stand? Was the box for *donativo*, or did it have the rubber sello stamp for our passport? Later I wished I'd satisfied my curiosity by opening the box.

Scallop shells pointed the direction, and a hand-lettered sign read, "16 km Avilés" and "320 km Santiago." We made our way through a eucalyptus grove and into the park's entrance. The guidebook mentioned a detour off the park's main track that would take us past the *dolmen de San Pablo*. This burial chamber in the necropolis is one of the largest burial mounds in Spain, and more than thirty *barrows* (elongated mounds that cover the burials) have been excavated.

We tried to find our way around, but we found the sign boards confusing (probably because they were in Spanish). When we left the main track and veered onto a dirt road, we saw signs pointing to several mounds. Smaller pathways took us closer to them. We weren't confident that we had found the Dolmen de San Pablo, but we assumed that the one mound with its stones intact was the most important site.

We backtracked to get back on the main track again, then descended the mountain on secondary roads past pasturelands into the small town of El Valle. Four kilometers later we reached Tamon and found one of its two bars. Generally the tapas in this region were not the artistic creations they were in Basque country, but they were still tasty. We liked the custom of throwing a couple of tapas in free of charge with your beverage.

The slender, young woman behind the counter didn't look particularly strong, or tough, but she held her own with the half-dozen male workers who were in for their afternoon break. Joking and teasing clearly are a way of life here in this rugged countryside and it's carried out with loud voices.

We next hit the slightly-larger town of Trasona, and then reached our day's stopping point, Avilés. My feet were so sore from the hard surfaces that I was practically limping as we walked along the sidewalk. The outskirts of the city were heavily industrial; the houses and small businesses were rundown and neglected. It was not an auspicious entrance to the city.

A car coming towards us pulled over to the curb. A middle-aged man got out and came up to us. Since it was the middle of the day and we were in a well-traveled area, we didn't feel threatened by his approach, but we were puzzled. He addressed us in Spanish, but even with our limited Spanish we understood that he when he asked if we were pilgrims.

When we answered, "Si," he continued in Spanish. Gradually we understood his message: the highway that we were walking alongside wasn't the best way for those on foot to enter the city; this was best only for *coches* (cars). He wanted us to take a more scenic route into town.

We considered his suggestion. The problem was that his alternative way could only be accessed at certain places and the nearest entry point was a few blocks back. Retracing our steps late afternoon after an eleven-mile day was something neither of us wanted to do. We hesitated.

He gestured to his car; he would drive us back. He reached to clear off the back seat and invited us to get in, but Ralph wouldn't get in. (I probably would have gone along.) Sensing our uncertainty, our guide grabbed a lightweight jacket from his car and motioned for us to follow him. At that point, we couldn't say no.

As we walked along, he stopped and exchanged a few words with a passing friends. I assumed he was explaining why he was playing ambassador to their city—he wanted us to have a 'proper' introduction to his city. He led us back a quarter-mile to a bridge that crossed over train tracks to reach a bike and pedestrian path.

After we thanked our newest trail angel for showing us his route, we followed the trail along the river right to the center of Avilés. Without our guide's help, we would have entirely missed the interesting collection of sculptures and other public art along the way. We easily found our hotel, the Don Pedro. When we saw that lounge and dining room were closed, we felt a bit sad that the hotel's former elegance had somewhat faded, but the hotel was comfortable and staff was attentive.

Wednesday, September 30, 2015
Zero Day in Avilés

WE WERE DETERMINED to take it easy; we kept our sightseeing to the old, historic part of town in which we were staying. The farthest we went beyond city center was to see the pilgrim albergue. The regular one was temporarily closed, but a modern municipal building had been put to use. The manager told us that there were only twelve people registered. "Not many people come through this time of year," he added.

For dinner, we decided to go for Mexican food. The small eatery was brightly decorated, which was quite a contrast to the more traditional and subdued décor of most other restaurants in the neighborhood. The walls were hot pink and turquoise. Colorful *papel picado* (paper cutout banners) were strung from wall to wall above the tables. We were happy to order a meal that would not leave us stuffed; we shared a quesadilla, had a couple of small tacos, and enjoyed margaritas.

My Fitbit recorded only five miles—respectable for a day off. For the remainder of the evening we rested and read, and I sent a group email.

> **From:** Susan
> **To:** Friends and family
> We are currently in the city of Avilés, which is a seaport and industrial city on the coast. The beaches are some distance from where we are staying in the old part of town, so we won't be visiting them. We are, however, enjoying a day off that I sorely need in order to get some rest. We are using our time to wander around the city center and enjoying the varied and interesting architecture.
>
> Our hotel has a collection of authentic old suits of armor on display. Since Avilés is on the coast, it's understandable why they'd want protection from foreign invaders.
>
> We think that most pilgrims have taken the

turnoff to go onto the Primitivo route; we are hardly
seeing any hikers anymore.

We did, however, play leapfrog with one for a
while. The second time we saw him, he was in the
process of overtaking us, but stopped to say hello. It's
nice to meet up with someone who speaks English;
they are few and far between.

He asked where we were from. When we said near San
Francisco, and he said, "Where?"

"Oakland," I answered

"I live in Eugene, Oregon," he said, "but I was born in
San Pablo" (which is maybe fifteen miles from us).

"In Brookside Hospital?" I asked. "That's where my two
sons were born." Small world, we agreed.

"I'm David," he said.

"I'm Susan, my husband is Ralph." I responded.

"My sister's name is Susan," he replied.

"My brother's name was David!" I responded.

Small world!

We are increasingly seeing *hórreos*, small buildings
usually elevated on thick wooden or concrete pillars,
for storing ears of corn and keeping them from
rodents. One we saw yesterday was unique (it was even
pictured in our guidebook). The tile-roofed hórreo was
surrounded by a wooden walkway and a bright red,
green, and yellow railing. Over one side of the railing,
several braids of corn had been strung to dry before
being stored.

We've now passed the two-hundred-mile point of
this hike. Wish us luck and please write: English most
welcome!

Cheers, Susan

From: Susan
To: Karen

Many tears, just depends on the day. I wish I had
started at one-hundred-percent, but I'm doing my best.

I had something like 205,000 steps last week, which is probably the biggest number I will ever see. I find it amusing that Ralph's numbers are fewer; it's because he has a longer stride.

From: Andrea
To: Susan

We were intrigued to hear of your decision about which route to take, and like you, quickly noticed the smaller number of walkers. We found that to our liking, though finding English speakers was less common. Terry's Spanish was taxed to its limits, and although he brushed up and became more fluent at communicating, he felt frustrated that his grammar didn't improve. Back to classes, I suspect, in order to improve there. I limped along with a few words and phrases, but felt I understood a good deal more by the end.

We remember Avilés and wish we had met someone to guide us as you did. It was near there that we met the "Parador pilgrims," who arrived at the trail each morning in a taxi, then were collected later on by the same, to take them to the parador hotel or upmarket equivalent. They were great fun (Spanish) and helped our pronunciation and understanding of local areas quite a lot.

Two hundred miles is a great achievement and we say a loud and long CONGRATULATIONS (or congraDulations, as it seems to be pronounced these days). You can see that I am becoming a pedantic old fossil. We liked your anecdotes also, and believe that those stories are the best bits to relate to others who rarely have much understanding of what life is like on a daily basis for people endeavoring to achieve long and difficult adventures. We used, also, to find that on the boat, when we returned it was us who had to fit in with "normal" life again, when we had realized that for us the "adventures" were our new normal or best way of living.

Love, Andrea

WE'D SEEN ON the newscasts that we'd been having the best weather in all of Spain. It was, therefore, quite a surprise when at bedtime there came a couple of loud thunder claps, and it began to pour. The thought of walking in pouring rain and lightning filled me with dread, but it stopped about as fast as it started. The clouds scuttled by and the sky became clear enough to see the moon. A good ending to a delightful day.

Thursday, October 1, 2015
Avilés to Soto del Barco, 12.2 miles/19.6 km

WE DID FINE walking the three kilometers to tiny San Cristobal, but then encountered some confusing directions in the guidebook as well as a lack of signage when we came to the larger Salinas. We successfully turned onto Calle Doctor Fleming, which was a fine, shaded street lined with well-cared for buildings and homes, but that took us away from the all of the restaurants or bars in town. We weren't sure if we had missed a turn or not, but we ended up having to make our way back to a busy street where I spotted a place we could stop for beverages and reorientation.

We walked right through Salinas (pop. 5,000) without real-izing that we could have visited the Philippe Cousteau Anchor Museum. The open-air museum, on the west end of the beach, would have taken us off the Camino, but would have been con-venient if staying at the beach.

When we stopped for another break, this one alongside the road, all we had left in our backpacks were some potato chips, so that's what we ate. An old, fluffy-coated white dog came over to get a handout, so he got some broken chips and then he lay down in front of us like he had adopted us. I was relieved that he didn't try to follow us when we walked on.

After Salinas, we climbed to the neighborhood of Barrio El Cuete, proceeded through San Martin de Laspra, the Barrio de las Cruz, and descended into La Ventaniella Santiago de Monte. At first we enjoyed walking downhill along dirt paths lined with eucalyptus, but after a while we wanted some variety. We found some with the ascents ahead.

We approached *El Castillo de San Martin,* The castle and its site have a lengthy history. It's believed that it was occupied during the First (VII-VI BCE) and Second Iron Ages. It was a stronghold during the Roman occupation and also occupied in medieval times.

Though the many trees on the grounds prevented clear views, from the roadway we could see the castle's square tower and one of the stone walls, topped by pointed stones, that surrounded the castle and also extended down to the shore of the Ria de Nalón. Because it was situated on a promontory overlooking this important waterway, the inhabitants of the castle would have had good views up and down the river, providing a good defensive position.

Although the guidebook again said the waymarking was poor through this area, and had lots of backtracking because of mining operations or road construction, we didn't find too much difficulty. Of course, construction projects can cause problems, but the location of those problems changes over time.

We reached Soto del Barco about two o'clock. With a population of only 4,000, we didn't expect to find a four-star hotel. Originally its site, the highest point of the town, was occupied by a chapel built to honor Mary Magdalena. In the mid-eighth century, the Palacio de Magdalena was built and through the centuries was the home of a number of noblemen. In 2007, the Hotel Palacio de Magdalena opened its doors to the public and was now a four-star hotel.

10/1/15

It was fun to splurge! I think it's fun to use the range of accommodations as we do. Sometimes we splurge on a four-star, more often we save money with the clean, but less fancy two-stars hostals.

After we showered and changed clothes, we went out to find a meal. We went in a cafeteria and soon found out that a cafeteria here isn't like the ones we had in high school; we didn't pick up awkwardly-sized trays and slide them along a long steel counter as we chose dishes. Instead this cafeteria was a small room with simple furnishings where the server brought our choices from their Menú del Día. We had the fish soup and bacalao—both good, simply prepared food.

We both feel that way too much food is served, but a large mid-day meal, followed by a lighter meal at dinnertime is the custom in much of the country. I can see how it would work well for those taking the afternoon siesta, but it doesn't work well for us when we plan to keep hiking some distance.

We took a short walk, only two blocks, down the street to see the commercial district. The Camino here passes along the outskirts of town, so we saw only two restaurant-bars, a tiny grocery, and a handful of residents.

Soto del Barco is on the Ria de Nalón. Its location provided access to the bay, which allowed many emigrants to sail to the Americas. There are several attractive Casas Indianas in town that were constructed by those who returned. After our short visit to the downtown, we came back to read through the siesta.

I felt rested and strong when we started out and, for the most part, this was a great hiking day with perfect weather. What a bummer that my back is now acting up—sending messages, zapping me, letting me know that it could go out with the slightest wrong movement. I am wondering if I can continue to hike and if so, can I carry my pack.

We looked at a couple of bus routes and schedules, trying to see if there was a local service that could take my baggage ahead if need be. We didn't find any information, but I'm sure our hosts wherever we stay could arrange something for us. For now, we will just continue to play it day-by-day.

Our hotel room has windows facing east and, for once, no street or other lights shining in from that direction. I am leaving the curtains open so that we will be awakened by a nice sunrise tomorrow.

Friday, October 2, 2015
Soto del Barco to Soto de Luiña, 12.09 miles/19.5 km

THIS MORNING WE awakened at our usual time on this trip, 7:00 a.m. I glanced toward the windows and then thought, "You dummy, around here the sun isn't even up until after 8 a.m.!" The stars looked pretty good, though.

It started to sprinkle just after we set out, so we put on our rain gear. That made the rain stop, and we had a nice day weather-wise. Once again we encountered highway construction projects; it served as a reminder to double-check guidebook information online to be sure it was current.

We crossed the Ria de San Esteban and hiked through Muros de Nalón, then El Pito. In El Pito, we passed *Quinta de Selgas*, but found that tours of the palace and gardens were not available. We were a few days beyond their season. According to various sources, much of the original décor remains including period furniture and tapestries. There's important work by Goya, El Greco, Luca Giordano, Corrado Giaquinto, and Vicente Carducho on display. The 90,000 square-meter gardens are among the most important in Spain.

Most of our hiking day was on or near the N-632, N-632A, N-634 A, and N-634 highways that have become so familiar to us. Our day's stopping point, Soto de Luiña, has been on the pilgrimage route for a long time, and the building that houses the small town's library, assembly hall, and museum was formerly a pilgrim hospice.

We had thought with would do a bit less than twelve miles today, but it turned into thirteen-and-a-half because we took one wrong turn, and because of the construction and related detours. It made for a long day with many ups and downs. We didn't reach our hotel until after 4 p.m. and all I wanted to do was flop on the bed. Luckily it was a comfy one; they aren't all!

The Casa Vieja del Sastre, which according to their website, "is the result of the renovation of a traditional Asturian house built in 1890. The site is rich in history, it served as home of a wealthy family, priest's house, headquarters of the Guardia Civil, prison during the war, tailor's shop for over forty years and guest house." On a more practical level, pilgrims can receive a fifteen- percent discount if they have the Pilgrim Passport; it never hurts to ask.)

10/2/15

Checking into our hostel or hotel every day is almost always interesting—usually in a good way. Unlike the decor of rooms in a hotel chain, these places are all different.

The Casa Viejo del Sastre is one of my favorites so far; it shows a woman's touch. The bedroom walls are a muted tangerine, the spread is a soft moss-green, the linen curtains are crisp and white, and the floors are beautifully varnished. The bedroom opens to a small, enclosed, sitting room with rocking chairs and a clay-colored tile floor.

Throughout the hotel, preserved from its time as a tailors' shop, are old Singer treadle sewing machines, dress forms, and prints of fashionably dressed men and woman from the '40s.

When my back hurt yesterday, I worried that I would have to taxi ahead today, but with the help of ibuprofen and Ralph, I was able to do the walk. I hate having to take large doses of ibuprofen, but sometimes I must. That means, however, that I also often have to take Prilosec to protect my stomach. Crazy-making!

Even more helpful than the ibuprofen, was that Ralph took more of my baggage. He's now carrying my extra clothes and sandals and I'm carrying my raingear, our medications and toiletries, my writing papers, my paperback book, and my sleeping bag. We

are in agreement that the last thing that we need is for
my back to go out. Ralph's unflappable way of dealing
with things continues to amaze me. How was I so
lucky!

Saturday, October 3, 2015
Soto de Luiña to Cadavedo, 14 miles/22.5 km

THE DAY STARTED out with us walking along the quiet highway
N-634 and into Novellana, but then we turned off the road and
onto a footpath across a forested hillside and into Castapieras.
"Turn R, along the road toward the beach. Look carefully for a
small purple arrow spray-painted on the road 300 meters later,"
read the guidebook. We made the turn, kept looking for a purple
arrow, but couldn't find one. We spotted a yellow arrow (the more
frequent Camino marking), but stopped to look around before
blindly following it. The guidebook had mentioned, "[turn] before
a white house on the left," and sure enough, far down the road,
we saw a woman standing in front of a white house—she pointed the way. What were the odds that someone would be there to
show our direction?, I wondered. We turned onto a new footpath.

As we continued along, however, we found the guidebook 's
description of this part of the trail didn't do it justice; there were
both more challenges and beauty this day than expected. The
book hadn't mentioned that the footpath would lead us down
through a eucalyptus forest and into a canyon, across a small
stream, almost to a beach, and then up the other side: twice.
This was followed, with minor variations, several times. It was
a bit frustrating that the trail didn't take us out to the water; it
retrospect, we should have gone off trail to one of the beaches.
The highlight, however, was being off-road and seeing the mixed
forest of chestnuts and other trees.

We took our mid-day break in Santa Marina. At the bar, a
woman in biking clothes with curly red hair caught my attention; (I have a soft spot for redheads—both my son Scott and my
granddaughter Madison have red hair.) Jackie introduced herself
and Nicolás, and told us that they were riding the Camino. They

looked to be in their fifties. Even if I hadn't noticed her hair, I would have soon noticed her because of her outgoing, bubbly personality. She asked where we were from and then explained that she was part-time French, part-time American and currently lived in Los Angeles. Saying goodbye to them, we didn't expect to see them again given our different modes of travel.

We began to see hunters, in their neon green or orange vests, roaming the trail with their dogs. We had no idea what they would find because we had seen very little wildlife on the Norte. We'd seen only small creatures: frogs flattened on the road, and dozens of fat slugs and small lizards. This day we saw gopher mounds, which Ralph insisted I record in my notes because it was a first for this trip. Ah, the excitement of the hiking life!

We saw two tiny snakes. We couldn't identify, but I was delighted to get a good photo of one before it slithered away.

After we returned home, Ralph looked online to try to figure out what species the snake belonged to—it turned out to be a Cantabrian Asp. I also ran across a 2012 post (on Ivar's Camino forum) by Rebekah Scott. Rebekah and her husband Paddy own a home that they call the Peaceable Kingdom. It's in tiny Moratinos along the Camino Francés. Rebekah wrote, "A Swiss hospitalera this week in Otur (just outside of Luarca) was bitten by a poisonous snake while gardening. She's been released from hospital and will return home to Basel next week." Rebekah continued, "And the very same day I see this news item: a Czech pilgrim was bitten by a viper last week near Llanes! These are the very first reports I have heard of snakebites on any Camino . . . . and on the same day. No reason to run away screaming, but be careful out there, people!"

Our asps were not aggressive. The only aggressive snake that we have encountered on any Camino was in France. Ralph and I stopped alongside a canal to see if there were any frogs. A six-foot-long snake rose straight up from the embankment in a very threatening manner. Luckily for us, it was only ill-tempered, not poisonous. Of course, it could have caused a heart attack for one of us!

We arrived at out lodgings in the Hotel Astur Regal. "Regal" might be a big of exaggeration, but it was very clean, modern, comfortable, and only a few hundred yards from a beach. Some called it Cadavedo Beach, but it was also known as *La Ribeirona* on tourist maps. It was 440-yard/meters long, shell-shaped dark-sand-and-pebble beach, popular for surfing, but not swimming because of the strong wind and heavy waves. Unlike many area beaches, this one had toilets, a beach bar, picnic area, and lifeguard. From our hotel window we could see cows in a pasture, and beyond them we the bay and rocky cliffs lining the shore.

We saw Jackie and Nicolás again at dinner in the hotel and we stopped by their table to say hello on our way back to our room. Catching up on my journal entries and checking for email messages was on my agenda.

10/3/15

As we walked today through peaceful farming villages, I thought about the distances we hike each day and our pace. We don't hike very fast; more accurately, I do not hike very fast. Even when Ralph takes on some of my belongings, he often has to stop or slow down in order to stay with me—and of course my stopping to take photos takes up time. I'm often frustrated by my pace, but I don't want to give up the *experience* of taking photos—really taking the time to observe—nor the pleasure of taking the images home with me.

In cities, towns, and near farmhouses, I often photograph old doors, cobwebs in windows, falling down buildings, and collapsing roofs. Today Ralph joked that anyone looking at my collection of photos would think that Spain is all in ruins. This is not true, of course, I just like focusing on photos that show things with a history or have a bit of mystery attached to them. I like to think about who lives there, or did live there. What were their dreams when they built what is now an abandoned farmhouse? How many men did it take to build what is now a crumbling stone wall? What happened to the family that once celebrated birthdays and holidays in the old house that is now sagging and surrounded by overgrown vines and shrubs.

From: Susan
To: Andrea and Terry

Today was supposed to be about twelve miles, and ended up closer to fourteen; as you know, those extras are sure hard at the end of the hiking day. Sometimes the guidebook has us road-walking whereas the Camino arrows point another direction. Confusing!

I thought the terrain today was memorable—the gorgeous views out to sea rivaled those we saw in May along the shorelines of Bilbao and San Sebastián. We dropped into and out of canyons several times. The forests of chestnut and eucalyptus trees were gorgeous. At times the sun shone down through the leaves of the deciduous trees and I halfway expected gnomes to suddenly appear.

The track today was the most like the Pacific Crest Trail that we have seen. We found ourselves rock hopping across a stream, clambering over downed trees, and taking many PUDS (pointless ups and downs). Much of the bracken fern is turning brown as fall comes upon us, but the hydrangeas and fuchsias in the yards are still blooming.

This day went much better than Thursday, when I was ready to throw in the towel. Although the weather forecast for tomorrow is for rain, I am hoping that it is wrong again because some of the steep, dirt paths would be treacherous if soaking wet

You once mentioned there was an area with too much road walking for your taste . . . . . . I have come up with the theory that they put us on the road only if they can't come up with a harder, steeper, longer, rockier or wetter off-road track.

Love, Susan

Sunday, October 4, 2015
Cadavedo to Luarca, 9.5 miles/15.3 km

WE HAD MORE time to talk to Jackie this morning because she was in the hotel's dining room when we came down to eat. Nicolás was still in their room. We learned she was born in Paris, but had lived in Tahiti, Chile, U.S. and other places. I wondered what it would be like to live in such far flung places as a child.

When I was a kid, my family moved around a lot in the United States because my dad was in the service and later on because of his work. For me, moving a lot was a challenge: mainly because I was shy and I had to make new friends each time we moved. I vowed as an adult that I would not make my own children move as much. Some people probably have a different opinion about life on the move—that a child might learn to be more adaptable, and that learning other languages and about other cultures would be an asset. Apparently Jackie was one who had learned to be outgoing; whereas I stayed rather shy. After the fact, I wished that I had asked Jackie what her experience had been.

When Jackie had first mentioned they were riding the Camino, I thought she meant by motorcycle, but it turned out they were on electric bicycles, which allowed them to coast downhill and have motor assist when going uphill. They had started in Bilbao, 242 miles back. This was only their third day on the trail, and they expected to reach Santiago de Compostela in only two more days.

While we were walking, Ralph and I talked about was whether or not Jackie and Nicolás should receive the Compostela when they reach Santiago. I said no, they neither walked nor bicycled; they used motorized assist. A stickler for detail could figure out how much of the route would need to be pedaled and how much coasted. Ralph thought that since they had traveled more than two-hundred kilometers, they had earned it. He pointed out that many people had ridden in buses or taxis some of the time—including us on this trip. I wasn't sure I agreed with him—we'd walked hundreds of kilometers; we had only ridden a couple dozen. This discussion was all hypothetical of course, we didn't know if they would apply for the Compostela or not. Wouldn't this be a controversial question to throw out to a Camino forum? I thought.

I was very excited about reaching our destination today, the seaside town of Luarca, because Andrea had written previously to say, "We loved Luarca, probably because it has a port, a beach and markets for fresh food." Luarca, which was formerly a whaling port, was now indeed a picturesque town with dozens of colorful fishing boats in its small harbor. Some call it the *White City* because of its gracefulness and tidiness. A steep descent lead to the bridge across the Rio Negro that divided the town in two. It felt like a triumphant end to the day.

We were also very pleased with our room at the seafront hotel Villa de Luarca, which was built in 1906. It had retained the charm and romance of its early days—thick wooden beams and floors, quaint moldings, and vintage furnishings. The owner spoke minimal English, but was very charming and helpful. We decided to stay an extra day.

My niece, Karen, was vacationing near Nice, France, with her boyfriend, Andy. I was startled when her daily "joy and gratitude" email popped up.

From: Karen
To: Susan

Joy tonight sinking into a meditation after a harrowing experience involving escaping a flooding car. *Appreciated* the amazing French folk I flagged down who drove us all the way to our place through multiple flood zones as well as our hostess who drove Andy back to attempt to get the rental car out of the hole. *Satisfied* I am doing everything to calm my adrenalin-filled body and to be thankful to be warm and safe.

From: Susan
To: Karen:

Whoa, that sounds like a made for TV drama. Thank heavens you are okay and that help arrived when needed. It sounds like your ability to handle a crisis was tested and you went through it with flying colors. Of course, I imagine you would just as soon not have been put through all this.

I'd no idea it was flooding so terribly there. We have seen photos of flooding in southern Spain, but since the news is given in Spanish, we don't get much out of it.

Joy arriving in this charming town of Luarca, *satisfied* that we did well in the rain; *gratitude* that you are safe!

From: Susan
To: Andrea and Terry

Just had to tell you that we are in one of your favorite places on the Norte route, Luarca. It is wonderfully picturesque—I wonder if it was the boats and the harbor or the pastry shops that most pleased you ☺.

We did have to deal with a bit of rain to get here. No real problem, just the annoyance of taking off and putting back on the rain gear. As soon as we descended into town, the skies cleared and it's currently about twenty-six-degrees Celsius and quite balmy.

From: Susan
To: Joanne

Gads, my biggest problem today was walking for several hours in the rain and that wasn't all that bad because it was not very cold. Then I opened my email today to read that a close friend had to be re-hospitalized for sepsis following a surgery. Another message came from our niece who had to be rescued while traveling in France when their rental car got caught in flood waters.

And then the headlines about a mass murder that took place in Oregon. It seems so unreal that the fires continue in California, and it's so green over here that it's unbelievable. I did hear that there was recently a storm in the Sierras and more expected this weekend, maybe something good will come of that. This puts all of my problems in perspective!

Glad to hear the weather has cooled; definitely feels like fall here. It still amuses me that every hotel has a hair dryer in the bathroom, but the heaters aren't yet turned on. I imagine you remember from the years that you lived in England that they don't turn the heat on in the hotel rooms until it freezes, or so it seems.

From: Joanne
To: Susan

I remember about the cold winters in England. The schools in Bristol didn't turn on the heaters until November 1 and I remember our son Billy saying he was the only kid in his form (class) who had goose bumps on his knees (the school uniform included short trousers!).

From: Susan
To: Deborah

We are by the sea again in the quaint fishing village of Luarca. Can't say much about it yet, but we are staying two nights to investigate. All the precipitation here keeps it lush and colorful; lots of hydrangeas, dahlias, and vines are still flowering. Most of the apple-growing region of Asturias is now behind us, not too many days until we reach Galician lands.

Wish us luck with the weather so we stay drive

tomorrow while looking around. Fall has definitely arrived and I am wondering if they ever turn the heat on in the rooms. Being a Bay Area type, I am not used to having to wear my long underwear to bed.

Monday, October 5, 2015
Zero Day in Luarca.

WE FOUND OURSELVES dodging light rain as we made a trek out along the waterfront and climbed the hill to see the lighthouse, the Ermita de la Atalaya, and the cemetery. All of this was overlooking the sea. The lighthouse, which was no longer operational, wasn't open, but we were able to peek through the windows at the tiny interior. To my delight, the chapel was open and we were able to enter. It was tiny, but quite sweet and tranquil.

I thought I had seen some interesting, even wonderfully situated cemeteries before, but Luarca's—on a steep slope overlooking the bay—was the most beautiful I had ever seen. All the crosses, monuments, and gravesites were painted white or of natural stone; it was dazzling to behold in the sun. The gravesites and crypts were symmetrically lined up throughout the multiple tiers of the site. I imagined that the local residents were proud to say that the remains of Severo Ochoa, a native of this town and who in 1959 won the Nobel Prize in Physiology or Medicine with Arthur Kornberg, were here.

On the way back from the cemetery and the rest we passed several souvenir shops, restaurants, and taverns. Many of the restaurants looked inviting and we would have enjoyed some traditional Asturian dishes: the stews and soups as well as freshly caught fish and seafood. Andrea had written about enjoying, "*percebes*—goose barnacles that are a specialty of this coast. We used to knock small ones off our boat hull after long voyages at sea. They were good once we mastered the art of opening them (I broke two fingernails as a consequence.)" Regretfully Ralph and I weren't hungry yet and so we also missed out on another opportunity to visit the *chigres* and learn to drink cider.

Formerly Luarca was home to an unusual and popular

attraction, the *Museo de Calamar Gigante*. The Giant Squid Museum was said to have the world's largest collection of squid during its brief history. The museum, completed in 2010, cost more than two million euros. Unfortunately, that sum didn't cover the cost of building a concrete wall to protect the building in case of severe weather. Later that year, storms hit the museum and caused heavy damage. The museum was closed, then reopened in Spring 2011, but then closed again in Winter 2014, when the seawall was hit again by huge waves. In addition this storm caused more damage to the museum and destroyed most of the squid. To add insult to injury, there was a break-in and vandalism. In April 2014, the museum was closed until further notice.

10/5/15

Today's meals were better than average for these parts. Breakfast went beyond the usual tea and toast; we also had yogurt, cakes, juice, and fresh fruit. For lunch we had *Pimentos de Padrón* (Padrón peppers), some sort of braised, wilted vegetables (can't adequately describe, but good), and lightly breaded, thinly sliced beef with a mild-flavored blue cheese and cream sauce. Dinner was a multi-layered pastry with a delicately flavored pumpkin filling.

Three meals a day is too many when the servings are as large as they are. I'm not losing weight, but I am getting fitter. My leg is gaining strength. Even though today was a layover day, we still logged 14,000 steps.

I read online that flooding is extensive in Côte d'Azur and it was reported that seventeen people died of related causes. I hope Karen and Andy are doing okay now.

From: Susan
To: Scott

I was happy to get an email from Madison. I'm proud to have such a mature twelve-year-old granddaughter. She sent her message late at night during a break from doing homework—burning the midnight oil so to speak.

Ralph and I are doing fine. I think you'd like bicycling some of the northern coast, but we're not seeing as many cyclists, or anyone else for that matter, along this part of the trail. Not sure why, maybe because the weather is turning to fall or maybe because we are getting further away from the extensive beaches and tourist attractions of San Sebastián and Bilbao.

Our trail had a major split about fifty miles back and many folks went onto the other route, the Primitivo, which is shorter, but harder (especially for bikes!)

Love, Mom

Tuesday, October 6, 2015
Luarca to Navia, 13.3 miles/21.5 km

WE STARTED OUT from the hotel at 7:30 and ate at a nearby restaurant we had spotted the day before. We looked forward to having one of the breakfasts listed: American, Italian, French, and more. I happily ordered the American, and received a generous plate with two fried eggs, four slices of bacon, toast, and orange juice. It wasn't quite like home, but it was a nice change.

We hadn't gone ten steps before it started to sprinkle, so on went the rain gear. This did not put me in good spirits. We were looking at a long day and I could just imagine eight hours of walking in the rain. Not surprisingly since Luarca was on the water, our hike started with a climb. However, it was a relatively gradual one and went easily. Looking back toward the city, we saw a marvelous sunrise over the city's hills.

The rain continued on and off, but we were either on roads or dirt or rocky paths in reasonable condition. We ran into several other hikers, who all appeared to be in their fifties or sixties. Big excitement when we met up with a group of three women— Wendy and Linda from Ottawa and Anna from Denmark—who spoke English fluently.

We also met a foursome, three women and a man, from France who have been walking this route in stages over several years' time. Most French hikers who we have met on the Camino trails have been experienced, fit walkers and this quartet was no exception. After talking with us briefly, they took off and soon left us in the dust.

In the afternoon, we managed to miss a turn and had to retrace our steps a quarter-mile back to Villapedre. I wanted to see the Retablo of Santiago Matamoros (Saint James the Moor-Slayer) in the town's thirteenth century Iglesia de Santiago. Unfortunately, once again, the church's door was locked.

In the late 800s, according to the legend, Santiago Matamoros appeared on the battlefield at Clavijo to help the beleaguered Christians fight the Moors. The Muslims had demanded payment of a thousand virgins, which the Christian King Ramiro I, refused to pay. Following the cry, "Dios ayuda a Santiago!" (God save St. James!), a battle ensued with Saint James the Moor-Slayer leading the charge while mounted on a white horse and carrying a banner. It was claimed that five-thousand Moors were killed. This was during a time when fierce battles for control of the Asturian region were ongoing. Although most historians think that things did not happen in the exact manner legend claims, the story is a deeply-held icon within the Spanish culture.

Soon after continuing on, the Danish woman caught up with us again and I enjoyed chatting with her. Because most people choose the Camino Francés over the more difficult Northern routes, it always intrigued me why they chose this one—especially if it was their first Camino experience.

She said, "I chose the Norte because I didn't want to walk with the crowds of the Francés. I also prefer to hike alone during the day and meet up with people to talk with at night. The two Canadian women that you saw me with earlier weren't able to go as fast as I wanted to go because they were hurting." It appeared that I failed the speed test too, because when Ralph and I turned off to find a bar with a bathroom, Danish Woman went on ahead.

I thought the instructions in our guidebook were somewhat

amusing and wondered what we would find after tiny Piñera described, "… onto a footpath, which is badly overgrown and poorly marked. Look up the hill across the field to see small town of Villaoril. If the path is unclear, navigate as best you can to the village." The Camino del Norte has seen a lot of change over the last few years, and even though we had no problem finding our way into Villaoril, I can easily imagine that a while back it entailed a brief cross-country tromp.

This day went well for me. Perhaps finding a few new people to converse with, the rain being less constant than I had anticipated, the trail being very flat and in good shape, or because we were back on the coast, this was a wonderfully, enjoyable day. I was happy that I wasn't exhausted on arrival.

Our hotel, the Palacio Arias, was impressive; the stately mansion was first owned by Asturian Indalecio Garcia Arias and Coaña. He was one of the Indianos who emigrated to the New World. There, in Puerto Rico, he made his fortune in the coffee business, and then returned to Navia to stay.

The former palace has been modernized to allow guests. The grounds were well kept with mature trees, shrubs, flowers, and a grassy area with a splashing fountain. Five, wide steps took us up to the arched entrance and into the lobby where we were cordially greeted. Our guestroom was cheerful and large and the stylish bathroom had a wonderful shower.

Navia would be an exciting place to be in August—when it holds its internationally-known Estuary Swim and a number of other popular swimming events. Most of the swimmers are from Europe, but others come from around the world. The dates of the swim events are linked with festivities in honor of Nuestra Señora de la Barca and San Roque. Of course for a Camino hiker, it might be challenging to find accommodations when the city is abuzz with not only the athletic events, but also cultural and religious ones.

10/6/15
When Ralph and I talked tonight, we decided to

shorten tomorrow's hike into Ribadeo by taking a taxi a few miles out from here. Terry and Andrea told us that hiking across the bridge into the city would be a wonderful experience, and we didn't want to miss it. After Ribadeo, the trail leaves the coast and heads south another 165 miles until it joins the Camino Francés in Arzúa.

Reality has hit—we will not make it to Baamonde as we had hoped this trip. At this point, we are a full day behind our schedule, running out of time, and figure we'll probably get as far as Vilalba. This is all rather disappointing, but we hope we'll be able to come back another time to finish this trail and the Primitivo.

Ralph tried to make hotel reservations in Madrid before our flight home on October 15th. Most of the time, we've had no problem getting reservations for our next night's lodging, though for Saturday nights, we sometimes make them a couple of days ahead. This time he had a devil of a time getting anything. Apparently something is happening there on Oct. 13 and 14th. Could it be related to Columbus Day?

He finally found a *hospedaje* in the tiny town of Ajalvir, which is in the general direction of the airport, but twenty-six kilometers from Madrid.

We are very happy to be here on a quiet weeknight in our beautiful palace room. It's dreary outside and doesn't look very exciting for strolling. This is a good time for emails.

From: Susan
To: Deborah

I got a kick out of your term "Chauvinistic weather reporting" in reference to what France *doesn't* report about the weather in other countries. Maybe Spain has the same way of doing things, because I knew nothing about the flooding in France until my niece Karen and you told me.

We had a good hiking day, but even so, I always look forward to checking into a hotel and getting my warm shower. Thanks for writing; I enjoy your messages.

From: Susan
To: Karen
I assume you are again dry and joyful. I feel *joy* that the rain didn't last all day and I am warm and comfy. *Gratitude* that the trail was easy. *Appreciate* Ralph finding reservations ahead. *Satisfied* that we made good time.

Wednesday, October 7, 2015
Navia to Ribadeo, 11.5 miles/18.7 km

WE STARTED THE day with a taxi ride of 7.8 miles to Valdepares, thereby saving ourselves not only some distance, but also a bit of a climb. By riding instead of walking, we bypassed two towns, one of which was La Caridad. Unfortunately, we also missed the *Castro del Cabo Blanco,* an excavated Celtic settlement from the fourth-century BCE. Had it been closer to the trail, we might have visited the site. The views were said to be spectacular.

Our driver, Jose, was very interested in our trip and wanted to be sure we got off on the right foot, so he dropped us at the edge of town, instead of at the bar the guidebook had recommended. It took us a moment to get our bearings, but it turned out to be only a short distance to the bar and we were soon on our way.

The hiking was easy. However, two kilometers later in Porcia, we took a wrong turn and ended up heading for the longer coastal route. We didn't realize this for quite a while. Once we did, we had to figure out how to get on our preferred (the so-called official) route again. With all this, we lost an hour or so and several kilometers and probably broke even mileage-wise—the miles we gained from the cab ride, we lost when we got off track.

On the plus side, the weather was perfect: puffy cumulus

clouds, sun shining, not too warm. We stopped for a snack near Tol and then walked through the tiny fishing village of Figueras. Overlooking its harbor was the Palacio de los Pardo Donlebún, a national monument. The palace was built in the 1500s for the Sancho Pardo Donlebún family. Sancho Pardo was a seaman who took part in the Spanish Armada of 1588 and in other battles against British privateers and seafarers—including Francis Drake. Currently, the palace is privately opened and not open to tourists.

We were pretty focused on reaching Ribadeo. We looked forward to crossing the Eo estuary into the city on the *Puente de los Santos*, which links the autonomous communities of Asturias and Galicia. We found the modern, yet classic, design of the bridge very attractive.

I wished we had time to walk across the bridge on both sides, and there was a protected walkway on both sides, but because of the length of the bridge and the time required, time that we wanted to use for walking around Ribadeo's waterfront and city streets, we had to choose. We chose the east side in order to see the sparkling river, the marina, and the city—and the views were rewarding. The walk was better than one-third mile. If we'd crossed on the west side, we'd have seen the estuary's entrance into the dramatic sea.

Tourists are also drawn to Ribadeo because of the *Praia As Catedrais* (the Beach of the Cathedrals). It's about six miles west of town and is good for swimming at high tide, but even better visited at low tide when the Beach of the Cathedrals reveals its one-mile sandy stretch of shoreline as well as its amazing rock walls, arches, and caves.

We instead headed for our hotel, the Rolle. The proprietor didn't speak English and didn't really understand our version of Spanish very well. So he whipped out his smartphone and showed us how to use Google Translate with audio so we could converse. I thought it amusing that when a man spoke into the device, a woman's voice gave the translation. Before we went up to our room for the night, our host told us food would be put out for us at 7:30 the next morning. Until then, the door to exit would be locked. It made me wonder what would happen in case of fire.

Our room, again a two-star, was more than adequate. Wooden shutters covered the windows, the walls were of stone. The bathroom fixtures were sparkling white, and like every hotel room we had encountered so far, had a bidet. The shower was very modern, but it took us quite a while to figure out how to use it. That was another feature of European hotels—mysterious shower controls and no instruction manuals. However, we had quickly learned not to bump into temperature controls accidentally, because in general, the hot water temperatures were scalding.

10/7/15

All in all, I felt fine walking today and in general that's been true on recent days. I get tired, but I don't hurt. I've been able to significantly reduce my ibuprofen. However, most mornings I wake up with tight muscles throughout my lower body, and with sore legs and hips. Ralph massages my legs until I unkink, but I'd certainly like to know why this is happening.

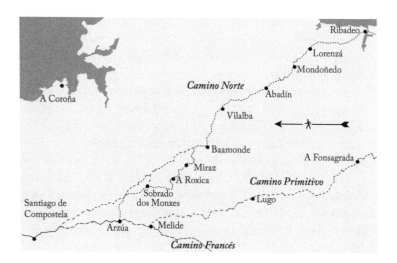

Thursday, October 8, 2015
Ribadeo to Lourenza, 10 miles on foot/16.2 km

LUCKILY, WHEN WE came down from our room, we found our breakfast laid out for us, and soon after an elderly gentleman, slightly rotund and balding, came by and unlocked the exit door for us.

The guidebook gave these directions to start the day: "From the bar…" A bar is not the usual landmark that I would use to give directions to our house. Ribadeo has a population of 10,000 so it can support much more than a bar. However, because they play an important role in Spain: a center of the community for socializing, a place not only to get a drink, but also coffee and pastries in the morning, the "menu of the day" midday, and dinner at night, everyone knows where they are.

The taxi let us out at Vilela, saving us seven miles; we passed through Olivar and then A Ponte de Arante, eased onto a dirt road that became a footpath, and then climbed steeply to Villamartin Pequeno. In the green valley, we watched as a farmer, with little success, tried to extricate his harvester from the deep mud. Work in the fields had ground to a stop as the workers waited for an even bigger piece of equipment to save the situation. I looked up the hill at the brightly painted houses of Villamartin Grande. I didn't want to climb yet another hill, but once underway, the ascent went quickly.

Even though we'd been seeing few people on the Camino over the last several days, we were still seeing some. When we stopped to eat our picnic lunch this day, who should show up but Italian Guy. We had last seen him three weeks back in Santillana making chicken sounds in the restaurant.

We also met Travois Guy, who was using a wheeled device to haul his pack up and down these considerable climbs. I supposed it was easier on his back, but it did not look easy overall. While we were staggering up yet another hill, we were passed by another pilgrim who I quickly named "Low-slung pack Guy" because oddly enough, he was wearing his backpack about two feet lower on his back than anyone else we had ever seen.

We continued to play leapfrog with the Canadian women, Wendy and Linda; generally we bumped into them when we stopped to eat or stay overnight. We'd also been seeing a couple from Austria. It had taken a while, but gradually we'd become acquainted with a few new faces and felt less alone. We proceeded through Gondán to end our day in Lourenza at the Hostal la Union. At dinner we talked briefly with a couple on trail bikes—he from North Carolina, she from Colorado. Colorado Woman said, "We have found ourselves pushing our bikes up many of the hills and slogging through the mud on the trails. Those who want to do the big miles, fifty kilometers or so daily, stick to the roads." In spite of it being a difficult trail for bicyclists, hundreds of hearty souls a year manage it.

Friday, October 9, 2015
Lourenza to Mondoñedo, 5.3 miles/8.5 km

THE TRAIL LEFT the coast two days ago. I expected the walk to become less interesting in the interior, but that was not the case. We'd begun to climb into the hills where we could enjoy seeing the autumn leaves around us. The wilder-looking open spaces were interspersed with tiny villages and farms; the terrain was not conducive to large-scale farming operations.

The houses changed as we moved farther inland and deeper into Galicia. The building materials generally came for what was available nearby; traditionally, the people have used rock and stone found close at hand. I enjoy seeing the craftsmanship that has gone into the slate tiled roofs, the *hórreos*, and the mortar-less stone walls.

Mondoñedo was in a valley near the end of the Cantabria Mountains. Its population was only about 4,500, but it appeared more prosperous than some of the other towns we had passed through. We came upon an elderly man and his wife harvesting enormous heads of butter lettuce and kale from their small vegetable garden. The combination of ample rain and good soil produced healthy crops.

THE MONDOÑEDO CATHEDRAL dates from the 1200s. Above the main entrance is a lovely Gothic rosette window, but there are also Romanesque and Baroque influences testifying to the many centuries through which the cathedral has survived. The wall paintings in the interior are beautiful and intriguing, but the scenes show both brutality and compassion. A group of four, entitled *Slaughter of the Holy Innocents,* caught my eye. According to St. Matthew's Gospel, after hearing from the Wise Men of the birth of Jesus (who would become king of the Jews) King Herod ordered that all boys in Bethlehem under the age of two should be killed.

It was not easy to look at such images. The best preserved was a scene with dark-skinned Moorish men with white turbans, and light-skinned knights dressed in tights, short chain mail shirts, and pointed helmets. There was a dark-skinned woman in a richly-colored scarlet dress—her ample breasts fully revealed, a swaddled baby at her feet.

A child in the scene clearly has been slaughtered. A second woman, in red dress and partially naked, crawls on hands and knees to flee the massacre. Swords are drawn on both sides. We see tears on the cheeks of the Moors, but in the center of the painting, one Moor is shown carefully easing an injured knight to the ground. On the left side, two women, one Moorish, the other light-skinned and wearing perhaps what is a nun's habit, appear to restrain a knight to prevent any further violence.

We passed the *Museo Das Zocas,* but it was closed— apparently permanently. At one point, the quaint museum displayed a vast collection of wooden clogs traditionally worn in this region. Most recently the owner, Alberto Geada, moved his collection to the Castillo (castle) De Castro, which is far off the trail to the north. Where the quaint museum will be permanently housed seems unsettled.

Our very short hiking day had some ups and downs, but wasn't very tiring. We checked into the Hotel Motero, where I had plenty of time to email friends. Life usually seems so much simpler here than at home.

We have learned about more flooding in Southern Spain and

France. The fatalities near Cannes, on the Côte d'Azur, have now been placed at nineteen.

From: Susan
To: Friends and family
Subject: Countdown from Spain

Well, after more than a month of a *timeless* (though when hiking sometimes more accurately termed *endless*) quality, we realized that our hiking trip here was ending for this year. We have started the process of taking bus, taxi, and plane so that next Monday we will reach Madrid area and spend two nights before flying home on the 15th. We have hiked 495.3 kilometers so far.

Meanwhile, we are enjoying a "ne-ro day" (near zero miles walked) in the city of Mondoñedo, which is large enough to have a cathedral, shops, multiple restaurants, and art studios. Yay!

Saturday, October 10, 2015
Mondoñedo to Abadín, 9.9 miles/16 km

When I looked out the window of our Mondoñedo hotel room, it was raining quite steadily, but we decided to wait until later to put on all of our gear. We went down at 8:00, but our hostess wasn't there. Even more disconcerting, the overhead lights weren't on and nothing was open. It wouldn't have mattered if we had left promptly—it wasn't yet daylight and we had a relatively short day planned—still, we wanted to eat. The hostess arrived about fifteen minutes later.

We ordered our usual tea, coffee, juice, and *tostada*. The first time I ordered a tostada I was quite surprised to be served toast— quite unlike the flat, crispy corn tortillas laden with shredded meat, cheese, refried beans, avocado, lettuce, and salsa filled dish we find in Mexican restaurants in the U.S.

When we went back to the room before checking out, Ralph put on his rain pants, but since the rain had stopped for the moment, I didn't bother. I decided to leave my camera out instead of burying it in my pack for protection from the elements.

The first part of the hike was on a minor highway with very little traffic. We climbed through the gently-rolling hills and a series of hamlets. Not only did the rain hold off, but the sun broke through. The mist rising out of the valley was quite lovely.

In tiny Lousada, I spotted a picnic table and plastic chairs set up in front of a farmhouse. On the table was a line of beverages: diet cola, Fanta, a beer, and a couple of other drinks.

"Se vende?" we asked the young boy who was sweeping the walkway near his front door.

"Si," he replied, and called to his mother to come help us.

"Three euros," said the enterprising woman. We could have purchased two sodas for a third that in a supermercado—but we were not at a market. Besides, we got to sit comfortably and enjoy the sandwiches that Ralph had purchased earlier.

While we were eating we enjoyed the antics of a pumpkin-colored kitten and a mixed breed dog who wanted handouts. Two chickens, who looked like they had Afros, were running around. I later determined they were of a breed known as Silver Polish.

The bicyclists from The States that we had met on Thursday, came by on their bicycles pedaling very slowly up the steep incline.

Colorado Woman quipped, "Making good time here." I had to laugh; none of us were making good time on this stretch of road.

The guidebook indicated that an even steeper climb, 2.2 kilometers long, was coming up, but after we finished the ascent we agreed that it didn't seem to be anywhere near that length and it wasn't any harder than many other sections had been. It was more remote: the forest a wonderful mix of eucalyptus, pine, chestnut, and oak. Looking across to the pastures was like seeing a huge patchwork quilt with shades of green, brown, tan, and gold. We were at last as far up as the wind turbines.

The final stretch was back to the paved road and then on good track. When we reached Fontan, we knew it was only five hundred meters until we reached Abadín, where we planned to stop. Once again, we ran into Wendy and Linda. This time they were coming towards us; they had turned back from Abadín.

That wasn't a good sign. They hadn't been able to find a place to stay in town, and they were tired and discouraged. None of us could figure out why this small town, without any obvious tourist attractions, would have "No Vacancy" signs posted.

I was relieved that we had a reservation. Because we knew finding a place to stay on a Saturday could be difficult, Ralph had asked the hostess from the night before to call for us. We entered the Pensión Niza via the bar. Half of the bar stools were occupied by middle-aged guys—two of whom were wearing camouflage gear. Once we found out that this was hunting season, we knew why these places were full this weekend.

Our room was graceless. The walls and ceiling were white; the wardrobe closet and night stands of Formica. The ceiling light fixture had three arms, only one of which had a light bulb that worked; that was the only source of bedroom light. The bedspread was some sort of shiny, silky comforter that didn't look very clean. The red vinyl-covered overstuffed chair had a ripped cushion.

The bathroom looked somewhat better because of its new fixtures—toilet, bidet, and basin. The bar of soap had been used before. I wasn't sure if that had been an oversight or the usual way of doing business, but it was pretty gross. The towels were thin enough to see through.

"Oh, well," I told myself, "at least we have a roof over our heads." Even though it was a disappointing place to spend the night, I convinced myself that I could put up with it for one night. I tried to keep in mind that, in general, we have stayed in much nicer places on this trip than usual.

The guidebook advised pilgrims to stock up on food in town because there weren't many places to buy food or groceries ahead. Ralph went to one of the small groceries to get supplies.

As usual, my worry about this day was a waste of energy. The weather forecast had given an eighty percent chance of rain, but what rain there had been came before we started and after we ended. And then, there had been the description of a long steep ascent at some point along the route—that we didn't even feel. All in all, this had been a pretty good hiking day.

10/10/15

It was time to make some new decisions. Once again, we are not going to get to Santiago—at least if we continue at our current pace. Partly this is because Ralph's spreadsheet of how far we would walk each day and where we would stop for the night was only a 'guesstimate.'

We like having some sense of where we will end up each day, but the reality is there are often unknown factors that determine what happens. Detours and alternate routes that affect the conditions and distances between places. Extra nights eating up time. Walking shorter days than anticipated. It didn't help that I wasn't at my best, physically speaking.

We don't want to jump on a bus and bypass any more of the Norte just to make it to Santiago this year. We can't make up for the lost day or two from our original plan, and I can't go any faster or longer than we already are.

We have decided to end our hike tomorrow in Vilalba. From there, we can take a bus to Lugo (which is, incidentally, on the Primitivo route.) Lugo is a city of almost 100,000 so it should have lots of things to see—including its Roman walls (a World Heritage site) that surround the old part of the city.

Other people might feel upset about stopping a hike short of the Santiago, but we have hiked so many Camino routes section-by-section over a couple of years that we are fairly philosophical about doing it once again. We have been to Santiago twice already; we are pretty sure we can get there on another trip.

Sunday, October 11, 2015
Abadín to Vilalba, 12.3 miles/19.8 km

ONCE AGAIN WE'D had the spooky experience of being locked in a hotel overnight. At 8:00 a.m. this morning, an old man came over to the pensión to let us out as arranged by the owner. Wendy and Linda showed up where we were eating across the street. Their albergue, which they had back-tracked to the previous day, had turned out to have spaces available and had been a good place to stay.

I told them that our room had been pretty awful. I was concerned about turning out the lights because I was afraid there might be bugs. The drawers in the nightstand were so filthy that I pulled them out of the cabinet and set them on the side table hoping that the housekeepers would take a hint and clean them. On top of that, the bed's bottom sheet was so narrow that Ralph and I kept taking turns tugging on it in order to keep some of it under us.

We started out in rain, which lasted until about 11:00. Just when we were getting rather tired of being wet, we came upon a restaurant that served *tortillas*. This was no ordinary Spanish omelet. To the usual ingredients of eggs and potatoes had been added carrots, peppers, and onion, which made the traditional dish moister and more flavorful.

We encountered a greater percentage of dirt track than usual—good going! The route was mostly flat, very little incline, and wound through forests and alongside farms. I knew I would miss the canopies of the fully-leafed trees. I photographed several beautiful red-capped mushrooms with white spots; this was perhaps the kind that Alice of *Alice in Wonderland* played with.

We weren't mushroom hunters and weren't about to taste unknown varieties. If it had been the *Amanita muscaria*, sampling it could have either poisoned or made us high.

Less dangerous to consume, but equally lovely were the small patches of delicately-colored lilac-purple crocus. The *Crocus sativa, the Autumn Crocus,* can be harvested for its most expensive parts: the three crimson-red filaments (stigma) from the pistil (the plant's ovary), which when dried become saffron. Saffron, which has been harvested for more than 3,500 years and used as a spice in many countries and cultures, is also used as a fabulous yellow dye.

Just when we wanted another rest stop, the Camino again

provided. We had come upon a farmhouse; across from it was a small shed with a wooden table inside. The woman of the household had set out wedges of the local cheese, chestnuts, a bag of small pastries, and fruit. Each item was priced at one euro, so we bought pastry and cheese. The cheese was reminiscent of a slightly salty wedge of Laughing Cow cheese, but I was delighted to have it. We sat on benches in the covered space and ate the fresh treats.

As we entered Vilalba, we knew we had walked our final Camino steps of the year, but we still had three days remaining before our flights home from Madrid. We felt the usual sense of relief at ending the day's hike, but also had a sense of exhilaration about the upcoming days. We looked forward to spending some of our extra time in Lugo.

We went by the Vilalba bus station to check on schedules, but there was no one in the building. A schedule was posted. We determined when buses to Lugo would depart the following day.

From the bus station, it was only a few blocks further along the main street to reach our hotel. The streets seemed rather quiet for a city of 15,000. Our host at the hotel, the Vila do Alba, was kind and friendly; he gave us our room key and pointed out the elevator. Wow! We rode to the top floor. What luxury!

At sunset, we noticed a lot of bird activity outside our sixth-floor window. Thousands of European Starlings had taken flight, a *murmuration*, gathering together and flying like a swirling and dancing cloud. The large, robin-sized, dark black birds began to separate into smaller flocks, to fly toward our building and up over the roof of the hotel, and then swoop down. As we continued to watch, they started to fly into a long row of shrubbery across the field below.

The birds also had attracted the attention of an elderly man walking his two dogs on a dirt path alongside the shrubbery. One of the dogs grew agitated by the movement and squawking of the birds and took off running. The man's calling to it did no good. The second dog stayed calm and with his owner the entire time I watched, but the runaway dog remained elusive. I wondered if the dog would return before it became too dark for the trio to find its way home, but when the racket of the birds stopped at sunset, he trotted back.

We left for dinner with a few recommendations from our host. We tried to follow his directions down a side street, but the blocks were irregular and we couldn't find the places he had mentioned. We continued on our own and eventually found ourselves in the parking lot of the bus station. There were several semi-trucks and trailers there for the night, but no restaurants. After circling past the hotel again, we succeeded in finding a place to eat. Dessert was excellent—*flan casero. Casero* (homemade) is almost always best).

10/11/2015

Dinner tonight was a celebration of sorts. I was gratified to see that the day's hike, plus the extra walking around town, had netted me 40,000 steps. More importantly, we were happy and relieved that we had made it this far. It has not been easy—especially for me when it has been painful. Sometimes I question whether it is even rational to keep doing something so difficult when stopping would end the problem.

We know we can't do this forever—or at least assume we can't. Other people seem to be perfectly happy without long-distance hiking—they go on cruises or lie on the beach or play bridge. We've enjoyed doing adventurous things before: kayaking at home and elsewhere; snorkeling in Hawaii and the Caribbean; and guided adventure trips to Africa and Galapagos. Why do we find it so difficult to consider ending our hiking days?

When we talk about resuming the Norte next year and adding in the Primitivo, we generally stay optimistic about the prospects, but we both know that this could be a crossroads—that my leg condition could get even worse and we would have to give up these trips that we love.

Cantabrian Viper

Interlude 2

Between Caminos

Spain and California, Fall and Winter 2015-16

Monday, October 12, 2015
Bus from Vilalba to Lugo

We left our hotel in Vilalba and walked the two blocks to the bus station. Again there was no one at a ticket window, but others in the waiting room told us that we would pay for our tickets when we boarded. Our plan was to stay overnight in Lugo, and then continue on to Madrid. Ralph had arranged for a ride to Madrid through a *blablacar.com,* a service that matched up drivers and wannabe riders. The driver Ralph had selected was to pick us up in front of Lugo's bus station on the next day. We then had accommodations outside of Madrid for the two nights before our departure flight on October 15th.

The bus ride to Lugo was not very exciting, but our hotel was quite nice—a three-star. I wasn't sure, but I thought this was the first hotel this trip with a functioning heating and A/C system. It sure made sitting and reading relaxing, and as a bonus, our laundry dried quickly.

Our location was just a couple of blocks from both the bus station and the old walled city. When we walked through one of the gates to visit the old part, we had no idea what we'd find. We entered the Saint Mary's Cathedral (more commonly called the Lugo Cathedral). While in the sanctuary, we heard singing in the distance and followed the sounds expecting to find a choir rehearsing for a Sunday Mass. Instead, the sounds let us back outside.

In the Plaza Major, a group, the Costa Dorada, was playing. Two women in short-skirted costumes were dancing and singing onstage backed by male singers and an small orchestra. The melodies ranged from *The Bullfighter's Song* (the spirited music you'd expect to hear at a bullfight as a matador entered the ring) to *Volare* ("Nel blu dipinto di blu") an Italian tune popularized in the U.S. by Dean Martin in the 1950s. The music was contagious and it wasn't long before people in the audience were dancing—individuals, couples, and in circles formed by adults and young kids joining hands.

On a second stage, another group was playing traditional Celtic music. All were men with the exception of one woman playing bagpipes. Most of the musicians were vocalists; some were percussionists. Strange though the instruments were to us, we still enjoyed hearing them.

We stopped to eat at one of the several restaurants. An accordionist sat nearby and added to the gaiety. We looked through many festival booths with vendors in costumes typical of the mid-1700s, when Spain was the world's largest empire. On this day the craftsmen and women were selling pottery, soaps, woven scarves, cheeses, baked goods and more. We watched the potters, blacksmiths, and weavers demonstrating their crafts.

Less traditional was the midway crowded with families trying the games of chance, entering sideshows, and kiddie rides . . .

On the outskirts, we found a row of eateries where long lines had formed to have *pulpo*. With their broad, sharp knives, the chefs quickly chopped the octopus into bit-sized pieces before throwing them into huge bubbling vats of oil.

Later, we learned that the *Fiestas de San Froilán de Lugo* is the city's biggest festival, and held annually in early October. In fact, all Spanish towns have a *fiesta or feria* (festival) around the time of the 'name' day of their patron saint. Probably the best known to pilgrims is Pamplona's *Feria de San Fermin*, which Ernest Hemingway brought to international attention with *The*

Sun Also Rises.

Tuesday, October 13, 2015
Car-share ride from Lugo to Madrid
Taxi to Ajavir

TODAY WAS AN adventure of a different kind. Our ride-share driver, Ruben, was supposed to pick us up near the taxi stand in front of the autobus station. Ralph had read the reviews about our driver beforehand and they were positive. Even so, we crossed our fingers and hoped Ruben showed up.

As 9:30 a.m. came and went, we began to feel a bit anxious, but the website had said to give a fifteen-minute leeway. Sure enough at 9:35, a young woman approached. She asked Ralph if he was the person who had arranged a ride and then introduced herself as Alicia. She explained that Ruben had found difficulty driving directly to the front of the bus station because barriers from the fiesta were still blocking access.

We climbed in Ruben's Audi A3 hatchback, and took off. My main worry had not been whether or not Ruben would show up, it was would we stop for potty breaks. That kept me stressed for about an hour. Then, at the two-hour point, the young woman asked if we minded a fifteen-minute break. Perfect! I hadn't realized until that moment that there were frequently "all-service stations" on both sides of the highway. They had food, restrooms, and gas stations; some had motels. I wished the U.S. had these predictable stops along our major highways.

After the break, Ruben and Alicia switched places so that she could drive. A couple of hours later, they switched again. Both were good drivers, never giving me a moment of concern.

And then, without notice, Ruben turned onto a secondary road. He entered a small town and pulled into a parking lot. Just as we were wondering what would happen next—whether we should be concerned—both he and Alicia got out, opened the hatchback to get something, opened the hood—and proceeded to add oil.

We continued on with no further surprises and arrived at

Madrid's Atocha station just after 3:00 as scheduled. The cost was fifty-five euros, which was more expensive than a bus, but faster.

From Atocha, we caught a taxi to take us to the small town of Ajavir where Ralph had made reservations when he found that everything in Madrid was booked. At least we were only eleven miles from the Barajas airport.

The Hospederia de Antonio was nice enough, and clean, and there were several bars and restaurants nearby. The problem was we were in the middle of nowhere with a day to kill. It seemed a waste of money to take a taxi back and forth into Madrid, and a waste of time to take a bus. So, we decided we would walk over to a slightly larger town, Daganzo de Arriba, the next day so that we wouldn't go stir crazy and we'd get some exercise.

Thursday, October 15, 2015
Flights from Madrid to San Francisco

WITH HOURS OF free time during the flights, I was able to write in my journal.

10/15/15

I'm ready to be heading home—the days are getting shorter and it feels like the holidays are almost upon us. It feels strange not to have plans to rush out to see Mom as soon as we get home. It's often been difficult to drag my jet-lagged self out of bed to see her the morning after we returned home from a trip, but it's sad to realize that she will not be there waiting for me.

Mom never understood my passion for hiking, but she always looked forward to my visits when I returned home. Other people have such busy lives they hardly notice when we're gone.

Initially when Mom moved into the assisted living facility, I had encouraged her to get involved in the facility's programs, but few of their activities interested her. Her natural reserve, her hearing and memory loss made it difficult for her to form new friendships. Her calendar pages in recent years have largely been empty except for family visits, and medical and hair appointments. I often felt sad that she had outlived her friends and most of our family—it seemed so unfair that her last years had become increasingly lonely.

During the last few years, she became increasingly dependent on me for emotional support. In turn, I often felt guilty taking time for the myself, the rest of our family, for friends, for travel, and all of our other activities. At the same time, it feels weird to be the new matriarch of our family and to have lost someone who felt that I was wonderful just for being me.

10/16/15
Home

As USUAL, WE hit the ground running. I started working on this book; I blogged for *Examiner.com* (now defunct) about local hiking. We resumed driving our grandkids, Madison and Logan, to school. I returned to my once-a-week volunteer work at a local elementary school. We caught up on the stacks of mail and tried to make our way through hundreds of emails. We saw friends and family at birthday parties, picnics, and dinners. We went to house concerts and other venues for live music, danced Zydeco-style, went to art exhibits.... I tried to take back the yard from the prolific weeds.

With the idea of returning to Spain to finish the last five days of the Norte and to walk the Primitivo never far from our thoughts, we tried to maintain our level of trail fitness. Ralph continued to carry his backpack whenever he went out to hike. On January 1, we went on our traditional hike, this time at Point Reyes National Seashore, with friends to celebrate the New Years 2016. I resumed my search for identifying and solving my physical problems. I joined a Pilates class and tried swimming for exercise.

Then, in late December, we had a breakthrough of sorts—an MRI showed that I had a small cyst sitting close to my vertebrae.

What was happening, in non-technical terms, was that the cyst was irritating the spinal nerves in my L1 and L2 (lumbar region/ lower back), which is a common location of back problems.

In January, I met with my doctor to discuss options. He stated the cyst would not grow or become cancerous; surgery was not recommended. He suggested a lumbar steroid injection. This was a bit scary (we were talking about my spine for heaven's sake), but the procedure, two weeks later, didn't hurt a bit. However, it also was ineffective—the relief from pain didn't last beyond the time it took for the sedative to wear off.

In February, we tried again—this time with two injections— one on each side of my spine. This time it worked. We held our collective breaths, not knowing how long the injections would be work, but once again I was able to wake up pain-free. I was able to steadily increase my mileage, and level of difficulty, of my hikes.

We made airline reservation to return to Spain. Even with our increased optimism, however, Ralph and I discussed what we would do if things went south. Ralph never agreed to it, but I came up with my Plan B. My thought was if my physical problems returned, Ralph would walk as planned and I would figure out how to get myself to the day's destination by taxi, bus, or other means. I figured finding rides each day would take some effort to arrange, and when I got to the next town, I would spend my spare time reading, writing, or poking around the place.

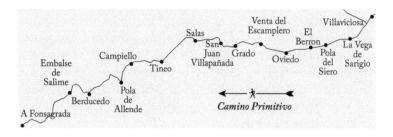

4 • Primitivo All the Way!

Camino Primitivo, Spring 2016

An early-morning walk is a blessing for the whole day.
~Henry David Thoreau

In May 2016, we returned to Spain with our two hiking goals—to walk all of the Primitivo route and to complete the remainder of the Norte. I was feeling pretty confident about my hiking abilities—a stark change from the despair I had felt only a few months previously. I attributed most of the pain reduction to the lumbar injections.

As mentioned previously, the Primitivo route is the oldest Camino route and took the pilgrims through the mountains of Asturias to avoid the Moors who controlled most of Spain during the ninth century.

Wednesday, May 11, 2016
Flights from San Jose, taxi from Asturias to Villaviciosa

TRADITIONALLY, THE PRIMITIVO route begins in Oviedo, but we wanted to start earlier, in Villaviciosa, near where the Norte and Primitivo split. (The actual split is in tiny Casquita, less than two kilometers after Villaviciosa.) The previous year we had walked past the trail markers to continue straight ahead along the coast on the Camino del Norte. This year we wanted to follow the Camino markings pointing southwest onto the Primitivo.

Reaching the start of our Primitivo walk was a bit

complicated—as most Camino starts seem to be. First were two flights—one from the S.F. Bay Area to Madrid and the second on to Asturias. Then from the Asturias' airport, we took a forty-five-minute taxi ride (seventy-eight euros) to Villaviciosa. We knew there were buses, including the ALSA line, available from the airport at considerable savings, but that would have involved a much longer travel time.

Our flights had gone well, but even with our business class accommodations, I'd slept only an hour or two in flight. Ralph had dozed off and on, but we were both exhausted. We just wanted to get to our hotel as quickly as possible.

We returned to the Carlos I because we had stayed there in October and liked it. The hosts were welcoming; the room was clean and relatively inexpensive. When we asked about breakfast, the hotel manager, a pleasant woman in her fifties, informed us that service began 9:00. That would have been too late for us, so she offered to put together a tray of food for us to eat in the morning.

We took a short nap—careful not to overdo in order to ease into the time change. After our rest, we went out to explore beyond our hotel. Beautiful sunny, blue skies and temperatures in the 50s to 60s seemed like good omens for our hikes to come.

While walking back to the Carlos, we saw a couple of guys across the street wearing backpacks. We assumed they were Camino hikers, but we couldn't be sure. On the Camino Francés, there would have been no doubt—anyone seen late in the day, with a backpack and limping, was on the pilgrimage route.

Our walk around town was in large part to make sure we were physically tired enough to sleep at our new bedtime. Since we had walked a lot in Madrid's airport while we transferred from one flight to another, and then around Villaviciosa sightseeing, I had exceeded my 10,000; I hoped for a good night's sleep.

Later, while looking at travel sites online, I found that there was more to Villaviciosa than places for pilgrims to eat and sleep. If we had come as tourists, we'd likely have headed for the beach to watch the surfers, and to see some of the local wildlife. Asturias's abundant rainfall creates conditions that attract different birds than are found in the drier interior. Birdwatchers have spotted such species as the Spanish Imperial Eagle, Great Bustard, and European Eagle-Owl. There are also grizzlies in the Cantabrian and surrounding regions. There are only about 130 bears remaining, so the odds are very low, but they are occasionally seen in the mountains.

Thursday, May 12, 2016
Villaviciosa to La Vega de Sariego, 10.7 miles/17.3 km

BEFORE STARTING OUT, we ate the breakfast Carlos I had set out in our room the night before: bread, jam, butter, and juice as well as a thermos of warm water for tea and coffee. We were happy to be out the door at 7:40. No sooner had we started out than it started to sprinkle.

It was exciting to once again pass the intersection of the Norte and Primitivo trails and to consider how much had happened since we had been at that point the previous fall. I felt tremendous relief and joy that I was getting my life back.

At a rest area we met a French woman close to us in age. Her home was a small village near Vézelay (the start of another French Camino route), and she had walked several other Caminos. She was all set to take this day's alternate route, which was higher and steeper, but also shorter than the way we planned to go. By the rate at which she took off to start, I judged we could not have kept up with her.

The first half of the day was moderate with ups and downs. Our guidebook had a listing for a bar located across from the monastery in Valdediós. We hoped to stop for lunch, but the place was locked up. However, we could see someone was out back burning what looked like tree trimmings and trash. We waited a bit, not certain what to do, when a middle-aged man from the village came walking along and called to the man in the field. It appeared that the bar's owner could ignore us, but not his neighbor. After a brief exchange with the villager, the owner indicated that we should meet him at the entrance to the bar. Still in his work clothes, he let us in and served us beers and then whipped up a fried-egg bocadillo. It was warm, whereas I was cold, so I was happy to have it. When we finished eating, the owner locked the bar back up and returned to his tasks in the back field.

We crossed the street to see the monastery and church. The Holy Savior of Valdediós, a Roman Catholic pre-Romanesque church, was consecrated in 893. There was an albergue within the monastery, so we stopped by to see it. Greeting us at the entrance was the villager who had helped us get lunch. It was three euros to take a tour. I felt a bit guilty not paying the fee and taking the tour, but we didn't want to take the time. Instead we took a few photos of the beautiful church in its tranquil meadow setting, and went on our way.

The trail began to climb. It seemed as if every time we climbed a bit more the rain came down harder. We met a continual series of "false summits" (places where a rise ahead looks like the summit, but isn't). I felt discouraged by my slow pace, but Ralph said that it was a hard climb for him too. When we finally got over the hills, we found a gentle descent.

Our route was along both paved, secondary roads and dirt track. The dirt sections were barely wet, rather than muddy as I expected. Even so, our trail runners became soaked. We weren't worried; we knew they would dry quickly.

The guidebook indicated there would be a gas station, with limited groceries, at an intersection at Alto de la Campa. We looked forward to reaching it to buy snacks, but found everything closed with no sign of opening any time soon. That was disappointing, but we had a few energy bars in reserve and weren't desperate. A couple of kilometers farther, we passed an establishment that served *desayuno* (breakfast), the pilgrim menu, and more. We weren't hungry enough for a meal; we were more anxious to reach our night's albergue.

The rain continued, becoming heavier at times, until we reached La Vega de Sariego. We located the *mercado* that we had read would have a key to our albergue. A sign on the market's door indicated they were open 11 a.m.-2 p.m. and again 4:30 p.m. until late. It was 2:30.

We were tired; I needed to get out of my wet things. Ralph walked another block toward the center of town and found the two-story albergue, but it was locked. Undaunted, he went around back. An elderly woman was working outside of a second building. She led Ralph back to the albergue and let him in with her key. There was no spare one to leave with us, so they blocked the door open while Ralph ran back to get me.

Inside were three rooms, each with four or six beds. I flopped down on one. Ralph held me while I had a good cry to let out my feelings of fatigue and frustration. Maybe it wasn't unusual to be exhausted the day after traveling across eight time zones.

We unpacked, took our showers, and enjoyed having the place to ourselves for a couple of hours. I was delighted that the heater was working and the room was warm, but apparently the system was on a timer because it went off after a while. A bit later, a few more people came in and unpacked in the second room. We waited until everyone else had settled, and then breathed a sign of relief when we knew we'd have our room all to ourselves.

There was an arrangement between the albergue and two nearby bars—dinner was to be served at one of the bars at 7 p.m., so at the appointed time, we went out to find the open one.

Friday, May 13, 2016
La Vega de Sariego to El Berrón, 8.5 miles/13.7 km

THE WEATHER LOOKED promising. We set out in good spirits. The apple trees were covered with pale, pink blossoms. Many of the homes near Aramanti, unlike many elsewhere that were painted in neutral colors, or constructed of stone, were bright blue.

Just beyond Aramanti we had to choose between walking through six-inch deep, muddy water in the ruts of the gravel roadway or attempting to balance while on the soaking-wet vegetation growing alongside the trail. We went for the latter and ended up wet, but not muddy. We liked these little challenges.

An unexpected highlight of the day was the *Puente Medieval de Recuna*—an ancient, arched stone bridge over a narrow river of the same name.

We wished for more signage just after the bridge when we came to a restful-looking park with picnic tables. We had come in on asphalt, but it wasn't clear if we were to continue on the pavement or follow the dirt paths alongside the river. We decided the paths were probably from park visitors going down to the rushing water, rather than from Camino hikers on the way. Indeed staying on the paved way was the correct choice.

The waymarking was said to be poor toward the end of this hiking day, but for the most part, we found it very good. We concluded that it had been a good day—the temperatures in the sixties, the scenery delightful.

5/13/16

We saw only one other person on the trail today. He was in a rush, so all we learned about him with that he was from Germany.

Our dinner tonight was good, but turned into a splurge—a seventy-five euros tab. We had broth with large, succulent prawns and clams; a huge platter of sliced beef; an almond-paste pasta, and vino tinto. I noted that this was one of the restaurants that charges extra for the bread. I understand that restaurants don't like to throw away uneaten bread, but I for the price we paid, I thought it should be included.

We are looking forward to arriving in Oviedo. With its population of 220,000, it's one of the very few large cities along the Primitivo. King Alfonso II is credited with establishing the capital of Asturias and I expect the cathedral will be spectacular.

I'm also excited about reaching Oviedo because we are planning to see Helena, a friend we met on the Camino Francés years ago. She now lives in Spain and it will be interesting to find out what she is working on now; her project back then was helping mark the Camino route out of Porto. It'll be fun to have an insider's tour with her.

Saturday, May 14, 2016
El Berrón to Oviedo, 8.4 miles/13.5 km

TODAY STARTED WELL. First we saw a garden display of calla lilies as we were leaving town, then we went through wooded areas and farms. We met a trio of pilgrims at lunchtime; they were Catalan and had started along the Norte in Santillana del Mar . . .Colloto, three miles before Oviedo, had many upscale shops and people dressed accordingly. Many of the restaurants seemed to cater to the more well-healed. Our lunch spot wasn't trendy, but we found that it served a very good tortilla. Usually when we order the omelet, we get a pie-shaped wedge; here we got a whole pie. We tried, but one-half was our limit. The waiter asked if we wanted to take it with us, but we told him we couldn't—too heavy to carry. It had also been a bargain: two beers, a soda, and the omelet for fifteen euros.

We reached Oviedo and our pensión. It had been a shorter walking day, but it was all on hard surfaces. The Hostal Fidalgo fit our basic requirements for accommodations in a larger city: e reasonably close to the trail, in a good part of town, and preferably near the sights as well as some places to eat.

The Fidalgo wasn't fancy, but it was clean, shiny and bright—made cheerful with a floral coverlet. Once again, we ended up with twin beds. We prefer a *cama matrimonial* (double bed) but that's not always available, and no big deal. We were on the fourth floor, with multiple keys to get in, which was also typical. We paid thirty-five euros; the nine euros additional over what we had paid for lodging the night before was well worth the extra.

We decided to take a Zero Day. It was very early in the hike to take a day off, but there were only two major cities on this route—Oviedo and Lugo—so there would be more to see here than in most places we'd go through.

After we got settled in, cleaned up, and did some looking around near our pensión, I emailed Helena and arranged to meet her for sidra the following night. She emailed back with a recommendation that we take a hike to a nearby hilltop for the views, so we went back out and headed for the tourist bureau to get maps. Turismo Guy, a rather portly fellow, suggested we take a direct bus because the final part of the walk was very steep. His caution made me wonder if we should take it a bit easier after our day's hike and in-town sightseeing. We decided to put the climb off until the following day and instead visited the city's cathedral.

ONE OF THE major treasures within the impressive Cathedral of San Salvador is the *Sudarium* (Shroud) of Oviedo. We were not able to see it because it is only displayed to the public on Good Friday, the Feast of the Triumph of the Cross on September 14, and on the last of day of the feasts, September 21.

The *Sudarium* (Shroud) of Oviedo is possibly as important to Catholics as the Shroud of Turin. It is a blood-stained piece of cloth believed to have covered the face of Jesus at his burial. It is thought that the Sudarium was carried from Jerusalem to Africa in the 600s, and then carried in a wooden box to the mountains of northern Spain when the Christians were fleeing the Muslim armies in the 700s. It was then placed in the *Arca Santa,* an elaborately decorated metal chest, to be protected within the *Cámara Santa,* a small chapel, built by King Alfonso II in 840 AD.

Questions of the authenticity of both the Shroud of Turin and of the Sudarium of Oviedo have been the subject of much debate by scientists and lay people for hundreds of years. It was common for imitations of religious objects to be created and sold during the Middle Ages—just as fake arrowheads and diamonds are sold now. However, the Sudarium of Oviedo has been studied by scientists. DNA indicates the 24-inch x 34-inch piece of muslin dates back to at least 700 AD, and there is some question about whether or not other stains on the cloth may have contaminated the sample.

Other interesting findings have surfaced. For example, Avinoam Danin, a botanist at the Hebrew University of Jerusalem, studied the Shroud of Turin and reported at a scientific conference in 1999 that he had detected pollen grains from plants that are found only in and around Jerusalem. Scientific studies of the Sudarium have also revealed pollen grains from the same species of plant. This suggests that the Shroud of Turin and the

Sudarium are both from the Middle East, and the Shroud is at least as old as the Sudarium.

9/14/16

We happened to be near the cathedral just as a wedding ended; the guests were gathered awaiting the bride and groom to come out of the church. Everyone was dressed beautifully. It seemed incongruous that several guests were holding what appeared to be long rolled-up tubes of cardboard and paper.

When the newlyweds came outside, the tubes became giant poppers—blasting large red pieces of confetti at the nuptial pair.

In the center of town, we found a number of new open-air sculptures. I was surprised to see a life-sized bronze statue of Woody Allen. I later found out that Allen's work is highly regarded in the region. In 2003 he was awarded the 'Prince of Asturias Award for the Arts.' In 2008, he returned to direct his film *Vicky Cristina Barcelona* in Oviedo. Allen described this city as "delicious…exotic…lovely…like a fairytale."

We found Oviedo especially charming at twilight. When we went out to find a dinner spot, we stumbled upon a festive street, Gascona, which is the boulevard of cider in Oviedo. Our way was lit by neon signs shaped like men pouring sidra from bottle to glass. Couples strolled hand-in-hand along the pedestrian-only avenue; friends celebrated at sidewalk tables next to the multiple places to taste the hard cider. It was fun to be back in cider country!

From: Susan:
To: Friends and family
Subject: Hola from Oviedo, Spain,

Just letting you know that we are alive and well on the Camino Norte. We are in a major city, Oviedo, for two nights. Going to meet a friend from a prior

Camino tomorrow for *sidra* (hard cider).

Our walk is going well and on schedule. First day was forecast as nice, but rained the entire day. Last two days rain was forecast, but didn't happen. This apparently is par for the course here.

More later!

I appreciated hearing from my newest daughter-in-law and emailed back.

From: Susan:
To: Diana
Subject: Food in Oviedo

Before I forget and because I know you like Brie: a sandwich of rustic bread with slices of baked apple, slices of Brie, (bacon optional), lettuce, and a bit of some kind of sweet jam or jelly. We need to try this at home!

Looking forward to tapas for dinner tonight. This is not Basque Country, but tapas are enjoyed in many regions. We are also not far from the Rioja, an important wine region, so we are enjoying the wines, too.

Must go now; we hear bagpipes over toward the central plaza and we see people in costume, so must check that out.

Love,
Susan

Sunday, May 15, 2016
Zero Day in Oviedo.

THIS MORNING WE made a steep climb and walked about two miles to two historic churches on a hill that overlooks Oviedo. Swirling fog hid the city and more distant views, but gave the ninth-century *Santa Maria del Naranco* a timeless aura. It was part of a palace complex built under the direction of Ramiro I.

The first thing we saw was three, gracefully arched windows on the south side of the handsome stone building. The lush green expanse of lawn added to the ageless quality of the setting.

A flight of stone steps led to the small door on the east side, but that entrance was closed off. Only a few people were on the premises when we arrived, but we had taken hardly any photographs of the building when a tour group arrived. Their guide led them to the north side entrance. We followed them to the door—hoping to take a peek when they went indoors. The brusque guide spoke only Spanish, but it was very clear that we were not going to be let inside with her paying customers.

Only a short distance further up the road was a smaller church, the *San Miguel de Lillo*. This a well-preserved, compact stone church was proclaimed by UNESCO to be a fine example of ninth century, Pre-Romanesque architecture.

Most people came to the sites by car or bus as part of a tour. Tickets were purchased back in Oviedo. Though it would be interesting to see the interiors, I was grateful to Helena for suggesting we make our visit on foot. Walking was worth the effort because it gave us time to slowly shift from one century to another.

The day got even better; we met up with Helena. Ten years ago we met her when we were all going through Astorga on the Camino Frances. She was from Portugal, and through emails afterwards, she convinced us that we should see her country and walk the Camino Portugués from Porto (which we did in 2007) . . .

Our attractive, compassionate friend showed us around old-town Oviedo. We walked along Calle Jovellanos, which is filled with wine bars much the same as the street of Gascon is packed with sidrerias. In one of her favorites, we watched our waiter pour our sidra with typical flamboyance.

Since Helena had moved to Oviedo, she had taken on a couple of challenges related to the Camino. One was to convince more residents and businesses to provide services for those making their pilgrimage on the Primitivo. Another was to help establish a pilgrim albergue in Grado—approximately twenty-five kilometers ahead of us. It was sad to say goodbye, especially not knowing if we would ever see her again. We appreciated her making time to see us in the midst of her many deeds for the benefit of pilgrims.

Monday, May 16, 2016
Oviedo to Venta del Escamplero, 7.4 miles/11.9 km

WE SAW A couple of pieces of unique artwork during today's hike. The first was on the outskirts of Oviedo: a bronze statue of a pilgrim entitled *Santiago Peregrino*. The piece was created in 2009 by the prominent artist, Pilar Fernandez Carballedo, a resident of Oviedo. The statue, translated to English, reads, "As testimony to the first pilgrimage road to Santiago—Monarch Astul Alfonso II the Chaste."

Many people have commented that it is hard to find the way out of Oviedo. Indeed, there were few yellow arrows, but we found brass scallop shells embedded in the sidewalks whenever we needed to change direction. Reading the shells correctly, by going as the base of the shell directs, was important (this would reverse in Galicia.)

Leaving the city we entered the countryside with its rolling hills. We went onto a dirt lane, which narrowed to a path. One descent in particular wasn't a problem for us on foot, but a hand-made sign, with a drawing of a bicyclist flying over the handlebars, and the message "Bajada pelgrosa (surcos)" warned riders of the dangerous ruts in the dirt track ahead.

Back we went again onto a road and followed it to cross the Ponte de Gallegos. The large, modern stone sculpture sitting aside the thirteenth-century Galician bridge provided an interesting contrast. Another sculpture, unlabeled, was a life-sized outline of a pilgrim, with staff and gourd, constructed of iron rods.

We spent the night at the Albergue de Peregrinos in Venta del Escamplero. We were lucky to have had a short day and have arrived early because there were only eleven sets of bunk beds, and we managed to get bottom ones. Not only did the albergue fill, at least six people were turned away—four went on by taxi, two others left on foot. There didn't appear to be any other accommodations in this tiny town, and I felt for them.

Tuesday, May 17, 2016
Venta del Escamplero to San Juan de Villapañada
10.9 miles/17.4 km

THE CASA DE Dylsia in Valduno came up quickly, where we stopped for a mid-morning coffee and tea. Continuing on the highway, we crossed over train tracks and the *Puente de Pentaflora*, a gorgeous three-arched Romanesque stone bridge over the Rio Nalón. The river, 145 kilometers, was the largest and longest in Asturias. The amount of water flowing under the bridge was impressive; one would not want to fall in, at least not in the springtime.

We passed through the quiet hamlet of Peñaflor, population 261. This mountainous land held both small farms mostly populated by grazing cows, and open countryside. The pace of life was slow—at least compared to Oviedo's busy streets—old traditions and ways of doing things respected. In town, a handmade saddle had been hung over a wooden railing alongside a storage building. It appeared to be made of rawhide stretched to form a rounded foundation; onto that base had been stitched pieces of tanned leather and carpet for padding. It was well-worn from years of use—signs of thrift and ingenuity.

Grado, where Helena had expended much effort, was next up. It's known for its annual reenactment of the *The Battle at Peñaflor Bridge*, which in 1809, saw the French beat the Spanish and the English. In an earlier fight, *The Battle of Lutos* in 794, the Asturians battled the Moors.

In Grado we purchased chorizo, cheese, and bread for our dinner and breakfast because the Cicerone guide said there would be no food at the albergue ahead. When we arrived at the albergue San Juan de Villapañada, we found the hospitalero to be particularly helpful, and though we were glad to have our own food, we also had a taste of the lentil soup and Spanish omelet that one of the other pilgrims cooked and shared.

Wednesday, May 18, 2016
Villapañada to Salas, 10.9 miles/17.5 km

LAST NIGHT, AMAZINGLY, hardly anyone snored and when they did so, it was only briefly and lightly. My main concern was that I would disturb others by having to go out to pee as often as I did; I found it embarrassing to have to go out repeatedly. However, it didn't seem anyone else realized it. I didn't hear Ralph go out, and he went out as often as I did. This is one of the things about aging that I really hate.

This day's walk started with a continuation of the steady climb that had brought us from Grado to Villapañada. We were definitely now in the Cordillera Cantabria. There was no snow at our elevation this time of year, but it was slow going, and the downhill sections were worse than the uphill because of the unsure footing. One place was so muddy that my pole went into the gunk about four inches and was hard to pull back out. I was lucky the mud didn't go over the top of my trail runners.

The first place we expected to find food, five kilometers along at Doriaga, was closed. That was disappointing, but made up for by a working vending machine. A detour around bridge construction added a kilometer or two. Just before Cornellana, we came upon a little food shack where we got a beer and a juice drink from vending machines. We hadn't realized we were almost in town; there'd have been more selection at a bar, but the stop had been refreshing.

Further along, in Villazón, we found a table, bench, register, and another vending machine. Ralph and I shared a sandwich from our limited supplies. A villager told us that we had eight more kilometers to go to Salas. That was hard to hear because it was getting hot and I had thought we were farther along . . .

We came to a busy highway and had to run across—always a scary endeavor. When we entered a tunnel under the freeway, I prayed that we would see our stopping point for the day, Salas, when we came out on the other side. Thank heavens we did. The terrain and the heat had gotten to me and I really wanted to bail. I was worried about the longer and harder days ahead; I hoped

I would get stronger, but wondered how fast that could happen!

The entrance to Salas was through a beautiful stone archway into the old town. The castle and tower near the center of town was the home of the noble family of Valdes Salas, whose best known member was Fernando Valdes Salas (1483-1568). He was a powerful political and religious leader, recorded as a General Inquisitor during the Spanish Inquisition and as responsible for taking many lives on behalf of the Catholic Church. In 1559, he wrote a list of books that should be prohibited that included works by Eramus (humanist, priest and social critic) and San Juan de Avila (priest, writer calling for change within the aristocracy). Salas became Archbishop of Seville, and was credited as founding the University of Oviedo (though construction began after his death). He was buried in the Collegiate Church of Santa Maria Maggiore in Salas.

We arrived at the Hotel Castillo Valdés-Salas—a place with both charm and history. Our room had welcome romantic touches—a cherry armoire for the clothes, an old metal stand holding a porcelain washbasin, a mirror in the corner just for decoration. The bathroom was sparkling clean and spacious. I enjoyed the luxury of a good shower and washed all my clothes; I felt human once again.

From the second-floor balcony, we looked down on the covered inner courtyard. Paved with stone, furnished with slatted wooden tables and chairs, surrounded by pots of roses, geraniums, and calla lilies, it looked like an inviting place for guests to have a leisurely cup of coffee and snack.

I, however, was looking forward to a good dinner with anything but cheese and ham. Entering the hotel's dining room was a treat in itself—walls richly painted red or gold, the window wall looking out on an outer, cobbled courtyard bordered in part by a gray, stone wall softened with red, climbing roses.

Afterwards I sat down to check emails and found one from Suzie Rodrigues, a Bay Area friend. We shared several interests such as hiking, traveling, and writing. I also wanted to write in my journal.

From: Suzie
To: Susan

I envy you. I'd love to be using my body for days on end and letting my mind run free and undisciplined. Well, someday soon . . . . Meanwhile, enjoy it all and send a small thought about it to moi!

From: Susan
To: Suzie

These ten- (or more) mile hikes in the hills with a pack are killing me, but the weather is usually reasonable, the food is good, the other travelers are interesting. Have yet to meet anyone else from the U.S. Most are German or Spanish, one from Poland, Belgium, Japan, and so forth.

This trip is definitely not all peaches and cream. Today was difficult because we went eleven miles, but the good news is that most of it was along country lanes with wildflowers all along the way and songbirds in the beech trees lining the path.

Biggest decisions of our day were probably which sides of the mud puddles to walk along. I am happy to report no falling in yet.

Thursday, May 19, 2016
Salas to Tineo, 11.7 miles/18.9 km

WE WERE GETTING further into the mountainous regions and began to see snow in the distance. Of course with my navigational skills, I had no idea if we were headed toward any of it. (I later found out that we were not.)

It was a pleasant walk. The further up we climbed, the wilder it became. Brightly-colored wildflowers—the purple columbine and red-violet foxglove began to appear. I stopped frequently to take photos—which also provided opportunities to rest.

One house along the way brought us to a dead stop. The modest structure of brick and stucco had been made large by the fanciful decorations that had been applied to it. Scallops and mussels formed by small, colorful stones had been used to create large mosaics on the front wall. Between the front entrance and the nearest window was a scene of the Middle East. The three wise men on their camels passed palm trees to follow the bright star.

Beside that was a full-sized, stuffed manikin. Was it a replica of a pilgrim? We couldn't be sure—the figure wasn't wearing hiking clothes, but was carrying a hiking pole.... On the far end of the front wall was a second mosaic—along the bottom was a decorative pattern formed of shells; next up a row of topiary plants, also composed of shells; at the top, figures of two angels ascended to the heavens. The folk art extended beyond the religious themes, however, there were various wooden sculptures and assembles to enjoy.

When visiting cities, it was not unusual to find museums with interesting art collections, but the number of places along the Primitivo where individuals had created their work and put it out where it could be enjoyed by passersby was unique.

A bit further on, we came to another form of expression—a resting place for pilgrims. The unlikely combination of slatted bench made of pallets, trash can made from re-purposed plastic container, bright-red modern vending machine filled with soda, and old stone water fountain was a very imaginative and thoughtful construction . . .

The final piece of artwork I noted this day was a sundial. The Pilgrim Monument was placed in 2004, a Jacobean Holy Year. The dedication read in Latin, "Viator horam aspice et abi viam tuam," which translates to "Traveler (or Wayfarer) look at the hour and continue on your way." The work was a life-sized metal figure of a pilgrim standing on a bright blue platform. He was clad in the traditional cloak and three-sided hat and carrying the water gourd and hiking staff. Where the shadow of his staff fell indicated the time by shading one of the brass hour-markers.

After checking into our accommodations, I decided it was time for another round of correspondence.

From: Susan:
To: Friends and family
Subject: Week One on Camino Primitivo
Hola from Spain,

We've now completed our first week on the Camino Primitivo. It is through rugged countryside and much more challenging than the better known Camino Francés. It's the most difficult Camino we have attempted—both because of the mountainous terrain and the long distances between accommodations.

So far, we have averaged ten miles a day—110 kilometers. The entire Primitivo is 350 km. Ralph trained for all this, but I hadn't done much because of my leg problems. Luckily, the lumbar steroid/cortisone injections I had several weeks before this trip have helped a lot. I am having minimal pain and have not needed to take ibuprofen so far. My main problem is endurance, but so far so good.

The walking varies from along the edge of the minor highways (with no shoulders) or into the hills along varied paths. The wildflowers are abundant and beautiful: columbine, buttercups, foxglove, and dozens more I can't name. Everything is fresh and green and we see happy cows, sheep, chickens, horses, and goats. Joy hearing the songbirds as we walk through the forests.

The farms and villages are interesting; I like observing how people live in this rather harsh environment.

Hope all is well with you; we hear nothing of what is going on in the US, but that is probably a good thing considering the things that have gone on when we were on similar hikes (such as 9-11).

Happy trails,
Susan

From: Susan
To: Karen

Satisfied that I have not (yet) stepped deeply or fallen entirely into the mud. Appreciated the vending machine room with tables, sodas, candy and sandwiches when there was little else open serving midday foods. Gratitude for Ralph carrying almost all of my extra clothes.

AFTER I FINISHED my correspondence, we went down and had a most wonderful pilgrim menu: an *ensalada* mixta of various lettuces, white asparagus, carrots, hard-boiled eggs (all dressed lightly); salmon steak (a first), and flan. And of course bread and vino.

Friday, May 20, 2016
Tineo to Campiello, 7.8 miles/12.7 km

Our day's hike began by going downhill into the center of Tineo and then making about a thirty-minute ascent. That made for an easier start than the couple of hours of uphill yesterday!

We passed a unusual pilgrim. He was dressed in typical hiker fashion—zipoff hiking pants, scarf around his neck, floppy hat, and carrying a water bottle, hiking staff with scallop shell attached, and bedroll. He faced the direction we were going and was standing next to a sign reading, "Santiago 286 KM." He didn't speak to us, however, perhaps because he was standing on the other side of a chain link fence and appeared to be stuffed with straw.

Our wide, dirt trail led to the *Mirador de Letizia* where we looked across to Tineo's hillside apartments—in lovely muted tones of blue, rose, green, and mustard. The sunlight breaking through the high clouds warmed the red rooftops. The city seemed to be floating on one finger of land, the other sloping hillsides were covered with forest and farmland.

Pana, former miner, now one of the living legends of the Primitivo, was not at his outpost—the rough, stone shack known as *El Ultimo de Filipina*, when we passed by. We were sorry to have missed him because we had heard that we could have obtained a sello, shared a glass of water or wine, and heard Pana's tales of days in the labor movement in Spain and his ancestors' participation in the Philippines-American War in 1898.

We continued going in and out of forest. A slight breeze loosened the pink-tinged blossoms on a huge apple tree. We encountered some muddy passages, but most of the trail had dried since the last rain. Then we came to a peculiar section where previous walkers had created something of a passage, but where they had not, we had to shuffle through a carpet of dry leaves at least four inches deep. As there were many deciduous trees next to the trail, we wondered if extra leaves had been purposely dumped on the trail to absorb the rain.

Our day's stopping point, Campiello, was really just a wide spot in the road across from some kind of processing plant with what looked like corrugated metal silos. It seemed strange that there were two albergues here. It also seemed odd that both had well-stocked *tiendas* with not only pilgrim foods, but also paintbrushes, comic books, and boots. I was delighted to find a collapsible umbrella to replace the one I'd lost earlier. I also found a vending machine with sixteen buttons that allowed one to select a cup of café largo, café with leche, café cappuccino, as well as tea with limón, and hot chocolate. Modernization is coming to the Primitivo.

We turned to the Casa Ricardo, which had been had been open only a year. The owners had taken an old, rundown farmhouse and its outbuildings and remodeled them to create what was now a beautiful place. Our private room had been designed and decorated with both comfort and aesthetics in mind; I liked the colorful, stained glass window, the miniature clog shoe holding the soaps; the functional heater, and the shower with not only the usual handheld wand but also a decadent deluge.

As I was outside hanging out my laundry, a man came up to greet me and introduced himself as the hospitalero. As usual, I didn't catch his name, but I did register that he was from Portugal.

"Do you know Helena?" I asked. Considering that Portugal has a population of more than ten million, it would seem that the odds are long that any two residents would know each other, but when we consider the comparatively small number of people actively involved in Camino support, it seemed more likely.

"Yes, I know her," he answered and gave me a curious look. Small world, indeed! I think it hit both of us at once that we had corresponded via email previously.

"What's your name?," I asked.

"I'm Rui."

Ah, yes, Helena had introduced us online late last year. Both she and Rui were considering setting up an albergue (and indeed, in October of 2016, Helena Bernardo posted photos on Facebook about newly opened Albergue Villa de Grado.)

Since the time that Rui and I had touched bases earlier online, Rui had been exploring various business ventures. He explained that he had done some consulting on setting up the Casa Ricardo, and was now helping as a host. He was also beginning to lead group tours of Portugal and the Camino. Rui showed me around the dorm rooms of the pilgrim albergue; it was probably the most well-designed that I had ever seen, and spotless. The mattresses on the bunk beds were wrapped in bug-proof material and used disposable fitted sheets that were changed each day. There was a power outlet by each bed. The kitchen was huge and had not only sink and fridge, but also a microwave and a fancy coffee press. There were both washer and drier (coin operated) and even separate recycling containers for plastic, glass, metal, and paper.

5/20/16

Although this was a shorter day than some and should have been easier, my moods went up and down at least as much as the terrain. I go through moments of fatigue and frustration. I find it upsetting that I can't go very fast; I go less than 1.5 mph. But, at least I am doing this! I am trying to do some yoga stretches in the evenings, but sometimes that's hard to fit in.

Saturday, May 21, 2016
Campiello to Pola de Allande, 7.06 miles/11.4 km

ABOUT A MILE along, we came to tiny Borres. Shortly after, we had to make a choice between two routes. One route, the turn to the right, was the *Hospitales Route*. It went up into the mountains and above treeline. This was the official Camino route and was described as being very difficult, but with outstanding views and was highly recommended unless the weather was foggy or otherwise inclement. The Hospitales Route was named for the former hospitals—accommodations usually run by Catholic orders—to house, feed, even cloth pilgrims in medieval times. It took pilgrims past the stone ruins of the *Paradiella, Fanfaron,* and *Valparaiso* hospitals.

We chose the route that went straight ahead—to Pola de Allande—and tried not to focus on what we might have been missing on the Hospitales. The few buildings we saw along the way were built for the harsh weather of the region: walls of thick, rough planks of wood and heavy stones, handsome roofs of curved red tiles.

The Asturian granaries differed from those we'd seen in the Galician countryside. Here the *hórreos* were much larger and usually square, rather than narrow and long. Even so, they were skillfully constructed to hold the tremendous weight of stored grain.

Before and after Porciles, we crossed small streams on short, sturdily built bridges. We patiently waited at the side of the narrow road as a farmer herded his horned, brown cows toward us. Porciles itself was tiny, but the owner of the grocery had big aspirations. Out front stood a board with a painting of a full-sized pilgrim with a head-sized opening for selfie-toting live pilgrims. The signs for Jose Manuel Boto's bar, café, and shop offered "bocadillo, pizza, ice cream, tobacconist's [sic], souvenirs: shell, pins" and more. Further, it indicated, "I speak English" and all was "low price." Even though we didn't stop, Jose's place left me with happy feelings.

From: Susan
To: Melanie

After a week of becoming "broke to saddle," I am getting used to my pack again. Each year, the transition takes longer, but now I'm starting to enjoy the hiking part of it. So far the trail has been easier than I anticipated—not to say that I haven't had some difficult days. Sometimes the climbs seem to go on and on—taking a long time to make the ascent. It's more about stamina than technical ability.

I thought today would be challenging, and it did have some ups and downs, but nothing harder than the hill up to our house. I was very happy that it didn't rain. If it had, it would have been more risky.

Tonight's hotel is super; it overlooks a very pretty little river rushing by in what is a bustling little town. At dinner, we thoroughly appreciated our plump, amiable host who took great pride in serving the house specialties—Asturian *fabada* stew and croquettes—to us pilgrims. Who knew that white beans and chorizo could be so scrumptious, croquettes so delicately flavored!
Cheers,
Susan

Sunday, May 22, 2016
Pola de Allande to Berducedo, 10 miles/16 km

I LOOKED OUT the hotel window to check the weather. Broken skies were letting some sunlight through, but people on the street were carrying umbrellas. We pulled out our rain gear and covered our packs. We were excited and a bit anxious as we started out—we knew we had some steep ascents ahead. Soon out of town we were on dirt track, then a minor road, then on rocky trail. The cows on the other side of the rock walls seemed uninterested in our progress. We stepped carefully through a stream rushing across the trail.

It began to rain; the wind picked up. After Penaseita, the trail's steepness intensified. We no longer saw farm animals, nor homes, or trees. The wind grew stronger. We pulled out our fleece hats. Gusts of wind made each step more laborious than the last.

Nearing the summit, I began to wonder if the wind was going to become stronger than I was. The stinging rain became colder and colder. Then just as we went over the crest of the Cantabria range of mountains at Puerto de Palo (elevation 1146 m), we spotted a white-painted, rounded, concrete structure a short distance away. There was no identification, but looking for any shelter at that point, we went over to see what it was. Unbelievable! A warming hut!

It was unoccupied, heavily-graffitied and otherwise grubby, the fire not lit, but it was heaven to have benches to sit on, and shelter. I studied the graffiti with more care. The charcoal in the cold fireplace had been used to write the "I was here" and which date messages, but there were also several drawings that had taken considerable time and talent—a wooden-hulled sailing ship with billowing sails such as those used in the Spanish Armada, a knight and his steed in full armor. While we ate our lunch, I wondered how many lives this shelter had saved in inclement weather. It turned out to be our only break during the day,

When we ventured out again, we stopped to take the lay of the land; we saw where the Hospitales Route and our Pola de Allande rejoined. We didn't linger long because it began to hail. Even though the descent also was steep, the scrub-lined trail was easy to follow because many others had gone before us. I felt a sense of exhilaration that helped me float down the mountain and into town.

5/22/16

This was the hardest day so far, and longer than most, but for the most part, I loved it. Always I am grateful to come to our accommodations to find warm showers, a place to wash out my clothes, and a relatively comfortable bed. Our private room is like icing on the cake.

I remember on our 2001 Camino Francés hike many of the albergues' showers had limited hot water and sometimes it was used up by the time it was my turn. In California we have been living with drought conditions for a couple of years and I have kept my showers short. Here I feel that I can be a bit indulgent because water is in good supply.

From: Susan
To: Karen
    Joy reaching the summit of this trail while being hit with wind, rain, and hail. Satisfied I am feeling much stronger. Gratitude for the bridges that help us cross raging streams. Appreciate our warm showers and beds.

Monday, May 23, 2016
Berducedo to Embalse de Salime, Almost 9 miles/14.5 km

AFTER BREAKFAST AT the hostal, we asked the owner if she could provide sandwiches for later. "No *pan*," she replied, but she indicated that in the next little town, we would find bread in the *tienda*. The guidebook said that there were both a store and an albergue.

We started out with a climb and were soon looking down at green hillsides and fog sitting in the valleys. When we reached La Mesa, we found was a closed albergue and no tienda. We noticed two guys in a postage-stamp-size grassy area behind the albergue just getting out of their tents where they had camped for the night. They were the first pilgrim campers we had seen.

A group of Italian day hikers, younger than us, started up the hill with us. My competitive side kicked in and I was pleased that we were able to stay ahead of three of the six.

It was a long climb to the pass over the mountain—generally following a wide track composed of dirt and broken rock. An installation of modern windmills was not far away. The land became increasingly windswept and rugged. We came upon natural slate rock formations and nearby at Buspol we found a very large farm-house, fences, and the Capilla de Santa Marina—all beautifully constructed using considerable quantities of the finely-layered rock. The quaint chapel was closed, but we stopped to admire it. Some sources say the foundation was built in 1327. It was built to withstand the harsh weather of this region—of rough stone and with a slate roof. The front window's wooden frame and the door were sailor blue; the doorway partially rotted away.

Further along, we saw a circular wall of rock perched above the trail. It seemed impossible to reach the wall because of the steep terrain, even more precarious to build anything on the site. We wondered who had built it, what for, and how, but typically it would have been used for shelter in inclement weather.

Because there had been no businesses open, we sat and ate our remaining food—a chocolate bar and potato chips. Then we began a descent of almost six kilometers: most of it straight down the hill on the rocky path. It wasn't so steep as to be risky under ordinary conditions, but it did require watching every step. The previous day's rain probably acted in our favor, because the ground was a bit soft, but not slippery and we were on previous-ly worn trail.

Eventually we could see the Rio Navio, held back by the *Embalse de Salime*. When the dam (and the downstream hydro-electric power station), was constructed in 1954, most of the town and hundreds of farms were flooded, but a line of old buildings remained sitting above the water. They water would make the perfect setting for a mystery novel: multi-storied, bleached, and abandoned buildings with no one around except for the ghosts of the former construction workers.

Looking across, we knew the river had to be crossed: it seemed a long way down. The last kilometer went into deciduous forests, but I was too busy looking at my feet to much appreciate it. There were fewer wildflowers on the rugged hillside, probably because of the elevation. Instead we were seeing yellow gorse, heather in light and dark shades of pink, and a few yellow wildflowers.

When we reached the paved road, the AS-14, we turned left, but noticed to our right a woven-metal gate set in a stone wall.

Was it the entrance to the dungeon of a medieval castle? I wondered. A sign read, *"Mirador Sobre Salto de Salime,"* so we opened the mysterious-looking gate and went through a short rock tunnel to the covered viewpoint of the dam and old buildings. Photos taken, we continued on down the road to cross the bridge over the dam and walk on the edge of the highway to our lodgings.

Most other pilgrims continue another five kilometers up to Grandas de Salime, but our hotel, the Embalse de Salime, was pleasant. While we were sitting on the veranda, we met a young woman from southern Holland who had stopped to eat. I would have liked talking with her more, but she was continuing on.

I took advantage of the good weather to sit outside and write in my journal and look at emails.

5/23/16

Odds and ends before I forget: This was not my favorite hiking day, mostly because of its difficulty, but I am amazed that I did it and that my knees withstood the downhill section.

We again saw the Frenchman who was so kind to us at dinner a few days back. We see so few others on the trail that this has been a pretty lonely time, so I enjoy and greatly appreciate it whenever we find other travelers to talk to or when friends write from home.

From: Clem
To: Susan

Thanks for the recent "Friends and family" update of your whereabouts. John and I have a pretty good map of Spain and Pola de Allande is on there, and you have or will soon cross the Rio Navia.

From: Susan
To: Clem

You do have a good map! As a matter of fact we are now sitting on our hotel's veranda overlooking the river and dam that is on the Río Navia.

Today was a long uphill, and then down a mountain for three miles. When the trail was being constructed, someone forgot to mention the advantages of switchbacks over straight trails—maybe they are an American invention?

But I am now sitting in the sun enjoying the river, the abandoned buildings of Embalse de Salime, my hubby, and being showered and clean again. I am feeling pretty good about life!

How's folk dance? Any more trips coming up shortly?

Love, Susan

From: Karen
To: Susan

I wanna see photos of the "raging" stream you mentioned yesterday . . . .

From: Susan
To: Karen

Should I have said "roaring"? Today the river we see is calm; it has been dammed.

Gratitude for the sights along the trail—fog caught in the valleys, stone houses blending into the mountainsides, the sun. *Appreciate* Ralph for being such a champ at tackling this challenging trail. I don't know how he does it. *Satisfied* that I am feeling physically good, and strong. *Joy* beating a bunch of middle-aged Italian men up the hill. And they were carrying daypacks and at the bottom of the last hill, they had a car pick them up. Hee hee!

Happy trails, Susan

Tuesday, May 24, 2016
Embalse de Salime to Castro, 10.5 km/6.5 miles

As we followed the highway up to Grandas de Salime, we went through a small park. We finally had some wildlife sightings—two gray-brown creatures about sixteen inches (40 cm) long with shiny looking scales. We thought they were snakes, but when we sent a photo to a friend for identification, he helped us properly identify them. Dr. William Lidicker is Professor of Integrative Biology and Curator of Mammals Emeritus at UC Berkeley, so I was confident he would know who to contact for scientific questions.

Bill wrote, "I showed the photo of the 'snake' to two herpetologists in the Museum of Vertebrate Zoology, and they both immediately and independently said it was a "slow worm." The name is *Anguis fragilis*, and it is a legless lizard, not a snake. It has a widespread distribution all over Europe and as far east as Iran. It even occurs in Scandinavia, and is one of the very few reptiles that is found in the UK. If you find [another] one, pick it up, they are harmless to humans, and notice that it has eyelids and so it can close its eyes. That is an easy way to know that it is a lizard as snakes do not have eyelids.

"These critters are burrowers, but also forage in leaf litter as you found this one doing. Another interesting thing about this species is that it is viviparous, that is it does not lay eggs, but its babies are born already hatched and active."

After our exciting discovery of wildlife, we went on up the hillside. There, we made a stellar discovery—the *Ethnographic Museum of Grandas de Salime*, which centered on the daily life of rural Asturias in earlier times.

We usually are too impatient to wait for anything to open while on the trail, but this day I saw an opportunity to learn something about the history and culture of this region and so I was determined we would wait for the 11 a.m. opening. There weren't many people in the tiny café; pilgrims who'd stayed in town had left a couple of hours earlier. An old man rose from his table, tucked his newspaper under his arm, and slowly made his way across the quiet street. We sat nursing our hot beverages as we waited.

We entered the museum as soon as it opened and were greeted warmly. We headed on the stone walkway for the largest building nearby and looked through multiple rooms: an old-fashioned dental office with its huge drills, a tailor's shop, a classroom with slanted desks in apple-pie order; a gynecologist's office complete with examining table and frightening instruments; an old-time barber shop with all of the combs, scissors, brushes and razors laid out ready for use.

Picking a favorite room was difficult, but I most enjoyed seeing the *albarcas* (clogs). Most, at least those for working in the fields, were of birch and had wooden pegs on the sole to keep the farmer's feet dry and prevent slipping. The display showed how the clogs were made from start to finish. Each type had a unique form of decoration. Most had pointed toes; some had the toes turned up like an Italian gondola. These were utilitarian tools, but had been embellished with carved figures and patterns. Obviously they were cherished as much as Jimmy Choo's and Gucci's are in some circles these days.

The farmhouse was also a treat. As was typical here a century ago, one room served as both bedroom and dining room. A single bed, covered with a woven spread, sat in the corner. Nearby were a chair commode and hope chest. In the center of the room was a plainly-decorated, rectangular table with several straight-backed chairs. In the corner was a large-format camera on a wooden tripod that would have suited photographers in that era. The kitchen held a marble sink, dark, wooden-stained cupboards; and patterned counter tiles. The black-painted iron stove must have required a half-dozen strong workers to move into place.

Ralph was more interested in the small structure housing a hydraulically-powered mill. We watched the process whereby wheat was ground into flour . . .

We spent an hour on the grounds; we could have spent many-fold more, but we needed to continue on the trail. I thought this was the finest ethnocentric museum that I had ever visited.

In Castro, we stayed in the albergue, but managed to worm our way into the town's tiny café for meals. There were only three of the oilcloth-covered long tables and the harried staff would have preferred to send us elsewhere because we had no reservations, but a group of four Frenchmen, dressed in camouflage shirts, insisted we be allowed to join them at their table. The bright yellow and lime-green walls, the rich blue shutters, and the shelves filled with books and games made for a cheerful place and the conversations at our table and around us were lively.

Wednesday, May 25, 2016
Castro to Fonsagrada (or A Fonsagrada), 12.6 miles/20.2 km

WE WERE ON the trail early enough to see a wondrous daybreak with bright shafts of sunlight shining through the dark, massed clouds. Initially, we passed by small farms with healthy crops of kale or other large-leaved vegetables and plots of richly tilled soil ready for planting. We looked out at a fantastic panorama—range after range of hills—the tops of which stood above the fog that filled the valleys between them.

It was remote. We spent much of the day ascending towards rows of windmills high on the hills; we saw few other people. We came upon a stone marker that read *"Encuentro Asturias-Galicia"* and knew that we were on the final stretch of the route by leaving Asturias and entering Galicia. Many pilgrims had previously passed along this way—dozens of rocks had been placed on top of the marker. The high point here was Porto do Acebo at 3,380 feet (1,030 m).

As we passed into Galicia, we kept in mind the direction *most* of the stylized, scallop shell markers would now point would be opposite what it had been earlier. Pilgrims would go forward in the direction the open end of the rays pointed (just as you use your fingers to point) toward Santiago. We remained in the mountains where the homes were few, the windmills whirled, and the number of prickly, yellow-flowered gorse shrubs outnumbered the trees.

The name of the town A Fonsagrada, where we were headed,

came from *Fons Sacrata* (sacred fountain). According to legend, a poor widow with two children, helped St. James. He, in appreciation of her kindness, turned the water in the town's fountain to milk.

A Fonsagrada, as many rural Galician towns, has been challenged by a decreasing population (now approximately 4,000) as well as an aging one. None the less, the town holds a welcome-to-spring festival known as *Fiera of the Butelo of the Fonsagrada* in February. This fair is a gastronomic event honoring a local specialty, the mountain cured *butelo* (pork). In 2017, eleven tons of the meat were sold at the lively event. A Fonsagrada also holds a regional market-fair on the first and third Sunday of every month, and a larger festival in early September.

Because A Fonsagrada is the first town with overnight accommodations when entering Galicia on the Primitivo route, many pilgrims start their walk there. We didn't find it a particularly attractive town, but it has a lot of history and is only 160 kilometers from Santiago. Our overnight stay was at the private pensión Casa Manolo.

Thursday, May 26, 2016
A Fonsagrada to Cávado Baleira, 11.84 miles/ 19.1 km

WE CHEATED A bit today and took a taxi about five miles out of town. Although we have been doing ten- and twelve-mile days, I didn't think I could manage fifteen. The ride saved us from some climbing, but certainly not all. After leaving the taxi, we found a dirt path that paralleled the highway.

We were eager to see the ruins of a former pilgrim stop, the Hospital de Montouto. It was established in 1360 by Pedro I (The Cruel). The hospital not only tended the ill, but also as most "hospitals" of the day, helped feed, clothe, and house pilgrims in need.

We first saw the *capilla* (chapel) and then spent a half-hour walking around on stone walkways, peering into windows and other openings. Considering the exposed, hilltop setting, we were surprised by how many of the small buildings remained and the excellent condition in which we found them. We learned the original hospital had been moved to this location, rebuilt, and remained open until the early twentieth century.

We were intrigued by four huge rough rocks known as *As Pedras Dereitas*, which are said to date back to Neolithic times. The stones stood on end in a nearby field. Perhaps it was like a mini-Stonehenge and used by pagans who were known to have lived in the area before Christendom arrived on the scene.

If the upright stones had once supported a horizontal top stone, or cap, it could have been a dolmen. Dolmens, widely built throughout Europe and in some parts of Asia and Africa, are generally attributed to the Neolithic age. Though many scholars believe dolmens were used as tombs, evidence is sometimes lacking. Dolmens, because of their association with prehistoric cultures and religious practices, were often destroyed by Christians.

Lunch was at a unique stop:—a pilgrim-friendly bar called El Meson. Here the interior walls were decorated with an assortment of disparate items: an ornately carved wooden headboard from someone's old furnishings, toy cars, a bicycle, a shield topped by lightbulbs and crown, a sombrero.

Next up, in tiny Paradavella, we spotted a small *palloza*, a Gallegan round, stone hut with thatched roof. Palloza have been used as homes, shepherds' huts, and for grain storage in these remote areas even before Roman times. The sturdy, handsome pallozas have become increasing difficult to find; newer building materials can now be brought to the area on new highways. I saw another small building—this one with a slate roof—that was so beautifully constructed it had to be considered more than utilitarian; it was a work of art.

We made our way through another stretch of flooded path, but we were glad to be on dirt again. We knew that soon we would be dropping in elevation and leaving the remoteness of these farms.

In A Fontaneira we found a former hospital, now a bar, known as Casa Bortelon that which still welcomes pilgrims. We also came upon yet another marvelous palloza—this one with a thatched straw roof, the straw held in place by braided reeds and held several feet above the ground by the thick, weathered wooden pillars.

This area was home to musician Florencio Lopez Fernandez, born in Pin in 1914. Fernandez became blind as the result of smallpox. However, he went on to become a violinist and was known as the *o cego dos Vilares* (the blind man of Vilar). He was well-known in Galicia and Asturias, often playing for the Hemuñeira—a popular Galician dance. He died in 1986, but his traditional music is still treasured in this community.

When we reached Cávado Baleira and our accommodations at the Hotel and Parrillada Mondeda, we found the passageways lined with suitcases. Soon after, the staff was busy handling a twenty-person, French tour group checking in. There was much commotion in the hallways, and noise, as doors slammed behind the travelers as they settled into their rooms. I felt left out when the group took little notice of us, but I could understand they wanted to spend their vacation time talking in French with friends.

I settled down a bit when I checked my emails. It was especially nice to hear from Lorinda, who had been a wonderful friend for more than thirty years.

From: Susan
To: Lorinda

We see other people, but hardly anyone speaks English so it is difficult for me because I would like to go beyond "Where are you from?" "Where did you start?" and such.

Even so, Ralph and I are doing well. In fact, we are a day ahead of schedule because he numbered the dates wrong on our planning sheet.

I am looking forward to Lugo on Saturday and

Sunday; it may be quieter than it was last year when we visited at the end of our fall Camino, but since we will have a full day to look around, I am hoping that we can walk on the Roman wall that surrounds the city.

I'm also planning to get a massage. Somehow it seems incongruous to do something so decadent when I am over here beating up my body, but I think I can manage it!

From: Lorinda
To: Susan

My very dear adventurous friend(s) . . . . . . Trusting that you are well, and having fun. Meeting new people, nearly as wonderful as yourselves, sharing good times, and hearing their stories. Yes? Looking forward to your next update from this most rigorous of the pilgrim trails with your 80-year- old husband who defies everything we know about human aging!!

From: Susan
To: Joanne

These are hard days and I have shed many tears from fatigue and frustration, but even so I feel stronger and better each day. We are in beautiful, remote countryside, but luckily there is a warm bed and good food each day.

From: Susan
To: Karen

Joy anticipating having a short day ahead: maybe five miles? *Satisfied* we are making progress. *Gratitude* for trail maintenance. *Appreciate* the sunny skies ahead.

Friday, May 27, 2016
Cávado Baleira to Castroverde, 5 miles/8.8 km

About halfway through our walk, we came to the town of Vilabade. An old man wearing a red baseball cap, plaid woolen vest, and blue cardigan gestured to us as we passed his farmhouse and typical, dilapidated barn. We weren't sure what he wanted, but we followed him inside and saw that he had hundreds, if not thousands, of whittled pieces of folk art displayed on makeshift shelves filling the rustic workshop. Most were about three inches high: birds, farm implements, crosses. They were whimsical, and roughly carved, and as Ralph commented, " . . . .they demonstrate persistence." We bought a small, carved plow for one euro and were tickled to have the memento.

In the same small town, we found the Church de Santa Maria—and were pleasantly surprised it was open. I had read that inside the fifteenth century building was a statue of St. James the Moor-slayer—also known as Santiago Matamoros. (We had seen a similar display in the retablo of the thirteenth century Iglesia Villapedre on the Camino del Norte.)

On a more practical level, we also found a food truck. We'd often wondered why there were not more of them around, given the many places where no other food was readily available. Of course all of these services cropping up would inevitably change the nature of the Camino experience.

A pilgrim, wearing two packs—one on his back, a smaller one on his front, stopped us to compare information on lodgings ahead. We had the usual difficulty trying to converse in Spanish, but we learned that he was Juan and from Barcelona. He indicated he was having knee problems and he also would be stopping in Castroverde.

Castroverde has a population of maybe 3,000 these days, but its site has been occupied since the ninth century and had a pilgrim hospital in the thirteenth century. We also had time to take a few photos of a well-preserved stone tower—all that remains of the Lemos castle. Much more contemporary was a unique water fountain in city center. A shallow ten-foot-wide concrete basin filled with water held five concrete statues—children forming a circle, arms around each other, and huddled under a ribbed, brass umbrella.

Because we had a shorter than usual hike, I could enjoy catching up on correspondence.

From: Susan
To: Friends and family,

I hope all is well. This has been a harder week for us than last in terms of the miles required between accommodations and because of the terrain. When we went over the highest pass on the route, I couldn't help but think of what an undertaking it must have been for our friend Helena and her friends to do this route in the winter.

We have walked about 142 miles and have another 74 miles on this route. Then we will tackle the last part of the Norte, which we began last year.

We generally see few people on the trail except when they are passing us in the morning, and at mealtimes. Most are French, Spanish, or German. We see some people repeatedly, but because everyone hikes at a different speed and stops at stops different places, there hasn't been a lot of continuity.

Last night our hotel was busy with a tour group from France; they seem to be cherry-picking what they hike, but seem to be strong enough. They are, however, getting their baggage transported ahead each day, so they have an advantage.

We are staying in pensions for the most part and we were happy to find a working heater in a couple of them. This sort of thing makes me appreciate central heating all the more.

Probably our favorite time of day—besides our beers at the end—is morning. We are usually up high, looking down on fog flowing through the fields and over the farmhouses or villages below. When the sun sends shafts of light down onto the high points, it makes the mountainsides and forests glow. Simply beautiful!

We are doing fine, excited about reaching the major city of Lugo tomorrow, only about twelve miles from where we are tonight in Castroverde.

Love to all,
Susan and Ralph

Saturday, May 28, 2016
Castroverde to Lugo, 13.4 miles/21.6 km

BEING WELL OUT of the mountains, the walking was mostly downhill and much easier. Once again we started out seeing sheep grazing in green fields, some apple trees and ceramic Sidra dispensers. When it started to rain, we were happy to find another self-serve shelter.

It was impressive—newly constructed of sturdy beams, with wood-paneled walls on two sides, and a concrete floor. Thought had gone into the furnishings: a microwave, the counter with faucet for refilling bottles or rinsing out a cup, and several chairs and tables. We inspected the four stainless-steel vending machines—one with hot beverages, one with chips and candy, and one with sandwiches.

The fourth machine was all about the Camino—it offered cloth patches with the blue background and yellow arrow; scallop-shaped necklaces and Camino-themed jewelry; and scallop shells decorated with the red cross that is said to be the cross of Saint James, and with a cord for wearing around the neck. I had mixed feelings about the commercial aspect, but it wasn't much different than seeing the trinkets for sale in shops and bars. No doubt such vending machines help pay for the building and its contents, and we greatly appreciated there being a clean, convenient, comfortable shelter in which to sit and eat.

The rest of our walk into Lugo was easy. New paths of crushed gravel made the walking faster and easier. I had to admit that the new surfaces made our way easier, yet I saw it as another sign that the number of people on this trail was expected to increase.

It wasn't difficult to recognize Lugo, a city of approximately 99,000, when we approached it. As we left behind the countryside with its scattered houses and farms, we came closer and closer to huge rows of multi-storied apartments and condominiums. Most prevalent were block-shaped, eight- to ten-story buildings, painted white, gray, or subdued shades of pink and green.

An old, multi-arched train bridge spanned the wide River Miño. Grass and other vegetation came right up to the edge of the city where we were to enter through the gate known as Puerto de San Pedro, one of five, original Roman gates.

Being satisfied with our hotel, which was just outside one of the gates to the old town, took some mental adjustment. Our room, on first entry, felt like a cell. It had splotchy, white walls with absolutely no decorative art, and a ceiling light with a harsh light better suited to an interrogation. Yet I was happy that I could burrow under warm blankets and turn on a heater. I was also proud that we had completed a thirteen-mile day, and I was pleased to see that my Fitbit recorded more than 43,000 steps.

In the evening we ate at one of the restaurants on the Plaza Major. Ralph had a starter of melon and ham, which reminded me to investigate further the differences between hams. The quality of ham in Spain varies from good to fantastic. Iberian ham comes, no surprise, from Iberian pigs. The origin of Iberian ham is designated by appellations (meaning the Designation of Origin): the majority of ham is *DO Guijuelo*, the others are *DO Jamon de Huelva*; *DO Los Pedroches*; and *DO Dehesa de Estremadura*.

You can get anything from prepackaged slices to the finest, *El Jamón Ibérico*. This is the *Cerdo Ibérico*, or Black Iberian pig, which can weigh up to five hundred pounds. Though called the black pig, the pigs can also be red or gray; they do have a black hoof.

Iberico ham is graded by three levels of quality. The first level is the *normal*—the pigs have been raised on a diet of dry feed (fodder). The intermediate level is from an animal that has been fed a mixture of fodder, grass, and acorns. The highest level, *bellota* (acorn) identifies the animals that have been raised with more opportunity to free-range in oak forests where they can feed on acorns, in particular the gambel oak, and grass.

Iberian ham cutters such as Florencio Sandhilrian are highly paid. Sandhilrian is a celebrity *cortador de jamon Iberian* who brings his knowledge of a lifetime and a sharp set of knives with him when he cuts a leg of pig into thin slices. For an hour and a half's work, he can charge up to $4,000.

The Iberian pig is native to Spain and researchers believe it has lived on the peninsula since the Neolithic era. There's a legend that the making of ham was first discovered after a pig fell into a stream with a high concentration of salt and drowned. Shepherds found it, cooked it over a campfire, and found it delicious.

I am not a connoisseur of ham, but I am very intrigued by the manner in which the Iberian ham is obtained—the whole process is almost a symbiotic one—perhaps artificially arranged, but worthy of note. The fact that the highly-valued pig requires huge amounts of pastureland, populated with cork and other oak trees, on which to reach the desired level of perfection, seems a wonderful way to raise animals and to preserve the natural landscape.

Sunday, May 29, 2016
Zero Day in Lugo

LUGO WAS FOUNDED by the Celts, but the Romans established a military outpost there in 13 BCE. Its beautiful stone Roman wall was built in the third century and surrounds the old section—making Lugo the world's only city completely surrounded by ancient Roman walls. The wall was placed on UNESCO's World Heritage List in 2000 and declared, "the finest example of late Roman fortifications in western Europe."

The stone barrier was composed of two parallel walls, was two kilometers in length, and ranged from thirty-three to forty-nine feet high. The walkway atop the wall was about fourteen feet wide—enough perhaps for chariot races—and nowadays very popular with tourists. The walkway could be accessed from several ramps or staircases (some of which are the Roman originals). A parapet (the walls' additional height above the walkway) was installed to keep people from toppling off the elevated walkway.

We walked a short portion—looking at the old homes from a different perspective and out at greater Lugo and the surrounding area. Inside the wall were upscale shops and restaurants as well as several handsome public buildings, churches, and an important basilica.

In the morning, after running into Juan from Barcelona again, we went to the Lugo Cathedral (also known as St. Mary's). The basilica was being readied for a big event: the arrival of the visiting bishop. Everyone was busily moving about: the couple dozen nuns in their white robes, the many priests in their garb, the laypeople in their best suits arranging extra chairs, and the musicians arriving with their instruments.

A middle-aged woman approached us and asked if we were pilgrims. We weren't wearing our scallop shells or backpacks, but maybe the hiking clothes and trail runners gave us away. Perhaps it was obvious that we didn't have any idea what a special celebration was planned for this day. When we said we were indeed visiting pilgrims, our friendly guide explained what was going on, and that this church was special according to Catholic theology because it offered communion twenty-four hours a day.

At the back of the church was a huge float—the platform covered with a replica of the Last Supper with richly decorated figures of Jesus and his disciples. Several men were struggling to turn the heavy cart around so that it faced the sanctuary's wide doors to the outside rather than the church's interior.

The service began. Those seated in the center part of the sanctuary could see the ceremony well. Those of us who were behind the center partitions watched what was happening on one of several TV monitors. Most in the congregation were quite old, but considering the poor condition of many of the old houses, and the number of unoccupied buildings on the outskirts of the old town, maybe we shouldn't have been surprised. We stayed for a while, hoping to hear the chamber orchestra play, but eventually gave up our seats to others.

Later we returned to the Plaza Major just in time to watch the procession. A couple dozen, smartly-dressed, honored guests had lined up in the square, as had a band, to witness the bishop and the columns of nuns and priests as they came out from the church. They were followed by several other groups. First came women in their Sunday best carrying banners of their church-related auxiliaries. Then came the Celtic dancers and musicians in traditional costume: the women in white cotton dresses, woven black shawls with brightly-colored patterns, and wide brimmed hats trimmed with flowers; the men in loose-sleeved white shirts, black vests, gold-colored cummerbunds, knee-length black pants, white socks, and caps.

The weather was not cooperative. For a moment the skies would clear, then a shower would begin and all of the umbrellas would go up. After all the work of getting it into position, the big float bearing the Last Supper could not be brought out because of the threat of rain.

Having experienced one of this year's important religious ceremonies and the musical festival last year, we wondered what it would be like to be among those pilgrims that reached Lugo during the last two weeks of June. They would most likely be caught up in another festival here, the *Arde Lucus*, which recreates some of the scenes of Lugo in Roman or Castro (earlier Celtic) times. It would be crowded with up to a half-million visitors viewing or participating in military camps, marriage ceremonies, feasts, gladiator tournaments, and a reenactment of the burning of the walls during the Roman occupation complete with fireworks. Anyone planning to come for this event would be wise to make reservations ahead.

Back in our room after dinner, I recorded a few thoughts in my journal.

5/29/16

Except for a few open restaurants, old-town Lugo became a ghost town at night. Maybe this was because it was Sunday, but it made me realize that it would have been a big mistake if Ralph and I had attempted to follow my proposed Plan B for this trip. If he had continued hiking town to town, while I had nothing to do except make my way to the next village, I would have gone stir-crazy.

The towns have been only a few miles apart; it wouldn't have taken me much time to get from one to the other. I'd seldom have found anyone to talk to, and I could only read so much. Not only that, I wouldn't have had anything to read. I brought two paperbacks with me, but one was horribly violent and the second was boring. We've searched for new books in the shops, but even in Oviedo and Lugo we couldn't find any written in English.

Monday, May 30, 2016
Lugo to San Román da Retorta, 10.8 miles/17.4 km

IT WASN'T TOO difficult picking up the Camino coming out of Lugo. We were lucky enough to meet up with Juan as we walked through city center. He and Ralph compared trail descriptions and map apps before we went on together to the edge of town and crossed the wonderful, arched bridge over the River Miño.

Basically, to get back on the trail we had to watch for the brass scallop shells in the sidewalk and follow them rather than look for the (mostly) nonexistent yellow arrows on signposts or walls. We had a moderate ascent out of town. After a while, Juan went on ahead because he walked faster.

There were no large towns, but we found a bar conveniently located at our halfway point in Burgo do San Vicente, where we had beverages, Spanish tortilla, and toast. Toast had become more of a treat than usual; we were enjoying the way it was served around here: spread with juice from a fresh tomato, or even better, covered with tomato slices.

Most of the day was on paved, secondary roads; the new, wide-track decomposed rock; and a few of the obligatory muddy stretches—nothing terribly difficult.

Sometimes we were in forest, sometimes in more open areas with bright-yellow lupine and other wildflowers. We saw several pieces of functional, public art similar to that we saw in

Santander while on the Norte last year—tree stumps that had been chained-sawed to make a simple seat or carefully carved to look like an overstuffed chair.

We continued a half mile past San Román da Retorta to the Albergue O Candido. The building itself was a simple two-story stucco affair, but the front had been transformed by a mural of a completely different style of house. The superimposed house was mustard-yellow with a steely-gray roof. The second-story windows, which in reality were basic aluminum-framed ones, had been outlined with dark paint to look like dormer windows jutting out beneath a peaked roof. The edges of the mural had been painted to appear like stonework around the doors and corners of the house. The finishing touches were of a single tree standing alongside the make-believe house, and a forest in the background. Even before entering the private albergue, we knew this was a place that appreciated creativity.

Once inside, we were directed to a private room. Once we unpacked and freshened up, we came out to the large room that served as kitchen, living and dining rooms, to meet the other guests. Perhaps it should have come as no surprise, but it was— Juan of Barcelona had arrived. His knees were bothering him so much that he was reducing his mileage and speed.

The other guests weren't all pilgrims; some were, but others were tourists and musicians. We looked forward to an interesting and entertaining evening. One young man from Holland was carrying his guitar on the Camino. He told us he couldn't conceive of being several weeks without his music. In my mind, he became Guitar Kid. An older Spanish man in his sixties, I dubbed him Spanish Gentleman. Another older man, this one somewhat portly, who played violin—I thought of as Violin Guy.

Whether a case of different customs, but we were surprised, and thought it a bit rude, that Spanish Gentleman saw Guitar Kid's guitar, picked it up, and started strumming. It soon became apparent that Spanish Gentleman had talent; Guitar Kid looked somewhat intimidated.

Spanish Gentleman return the Kid's guitar, picked up his own, and the three peregrinos began playing for us. Violin Guy was a self-professed amateur, and it seemed when he and either of the guitarist played together, the instruments didn't harmonize. They mentioned that the violin and guitars were not tuned to the same frequency so it went much better when they played separately. Spanish Gentleman new his audience—when sang and played popular Spanish tunes, we could all join in. Violin Guy played lively Celtic tunes, but no one dared dance to them.

We retired to our room and I pulled out my journal to record some thoughts.

5/30/16

Entertaining though the music was and genial as our host is, I am not entirely happy with our accommodations. It's so cold that I have to wear my down jacket even when in the dining room. And though we have this tiny room to ourselves and a private bath, only a shower curtain separates our bedroom from the bathroom. There's no closet, and no bedside lamps (lamps seem to be a luxury item in these parts.)

And on top of that, I found a large insect partway embedded in my left hip. He was almost as big as a ladybug, though not as fat. I tried brushing it off with my hand, but when it didn't let go, Ralph pulled it out with tweezers. We know it wasn't a tick and suspect it was a bedbug, but Ralph crushed it before we could positively identify it. I washed the spot, put on Neosporin, and hope for the best.

I know that Ralph is unhappy that I am not pleased with the room. He was proud of himself for finding a private room, but the lack of privacy, lighting and the darned bug have put me in a foul mood. It just goes to show that distance we walk is not the only determining factor in how I feel about how a day went—after all, this was one of the shortest days in a while.

WE HAD ABOUT seventeen miles more on the Primitivo before it met the Camino Francés. There were now many more people on the trail; we were now within one hundred kilometers of Santiago. We'd read that when we joined the Francés, we'd be seeing hundreds a day—a big jump from the thirty or so we were now seeing.

Tuesday, May 31, 2016
San Román da Retorta to As Seixas, 8.3 miles/13.4 km

BREAKFAST WAS SELF-SERVE. The host had left, but he'd told everyone the previous evening to help themselves to whatever was set out.

The day's scenery was pleasant and similar to the previous one—with a few notable exceptions. One was the white-colored, rock outcroppings on a not too distant hill. The distinctive rocks were light, but the dirt around us was a more common, brownish color. We began to see hórreos that were both larger and more colorful than we had seen elsewhere. Elsewhere in Galicia, the corncribs were usually of wood, and left to naturally age. Here many were made from poured concrete blocks, then painted with bright, geometric patterns.

What appeared to be a natural spring bubbled into a rock fountain. Alongside was a concrete statue of St. James in front of which pilgrims had placed flowers and other small gifts.

Further along, posted on a tree was a handmade sign with a photo of a pet, a Labrador of some sort, and an accompanying message: "My name is 'Leon' and I am not a pilgrim dog, but a hospitalero dog. If I try to walk with you, don't let me do it. And if I insist please let the hospitalero in Ponte Ferreira know, or call the phone number that's in my collar. Thank you."

The municipal albergue in As Seixas was new, modern, well-designed, and one of the best we'd stayed in on this route. Thirty-four bunks divided between two sleeping rooms; we expected them to fill up.

5/31/16

Our friend Juan arrived at the albergue shortly after we did. I think he sensed that I was out of sorts last
night. He presented me with a red rosebud he had picked
along the way and said, "Rosa de la Camino." It was such
a very sweet gesture and I tried to keep in mind that
moods come and go.

Later, the three of us shared a bottle of wine
Ralph had purchased. When we first met Juan, we
could hardly communicate. He seemed reluctant to
spend much time with us because of the language
barrier, but after running into him time and again,
things seemed to have changed. Anyway, we all now
try harder to manage a bit of conversation.

Juan said he's seventy. I'm drawn to him because
he looks at the world much as I try to—stopping to
smell (and photograph) the roses. He stops in bars and
other businesses along the way, and quickly engages
the barkeep or owner in conversation—something I
wish I could do.

He reminds me a great deal of our good friend
Tom back home. Both of them have a real gift for
engaging with people—they take the time to converse
and quickly put others at ease.

Wednesday, June 1, 2016
As Seixas to Melide, 9.2 miles/14.8 km

WE SET OUT from our lovely, stone, municipal albergue bright
and early and climbed once again up to a row of windmills atop
a hill. A 'trail angel' had created an alcove in the wall of a building and in the recess were a couple of five-gallon water bottles
for pilgrims to use to refill their own bottles. A couple of scallop
shells were attached with strings just in case someone didn't have
their own drinking cup. Early pilgrims would have used their
shells in that fashion.

Mid-morning we came to Parrallada & Bar Carbaro. Several

backpacks were lined up outside the restaurant. We passed a corrugated-steel bus shelter. Someone in the distant past had tried to improve its looks—had painted it a bright blue, but it was now peeling. The utilitarian bench inside had been covered with flower-printed Contact paper.

We were happy to reach Melide, and to know we had joined the Camino Francés. We were now in the company of many. Melide is considered to be the place to try the pulpo; we looked for an appealing restaurant. I tried to eat it, but couldn't get past my squeamishness about eating something with suckers. An acquired taste perhaps?

Once again, I settled in to write emails.

From: Susan
To: Melanie

There have been many changes in and around the Camino culture and all signs point to increasing efforts to make the walks easier. It is unreal how many taxis we are seeing scurrying around to either carry people or their luggage onward.

My competitive side, much as I try to shut it down, does not enjoy being passed by others. There are many people half our age carrying daypacks because of their assist. I remind myself this is not a race or a competition. I try to keep the adage "to each his own" in mind.

Each person's pilgrimage will be different. Purists demand that every inch of the Camino be traveled on foot, bicycle, or horseback. Others believe that it is well within the spirit of the Camino to use support, and may take a bus or other transportation from place to place up to the hundred-kilometer point. Many people use a service to ship their backpacks ahead.

Some people think that only staying overnight at pilgrim hostels (the refugios) is of merit. Others opt for hotel accommodations (freeing up room in the albergues for those who arrive later) they (or tour companies) have arranged.

For the most part, the economy here is weak. We see many abandoned houses, and the farms are small and no longer profitable. As is the story in many rural areas around the world, the young people leave for the city to find jobs; the oldsters continue working in the fields, some still using traditional tools such as the sickle to cut the crops.

Having reached this point on our journey, I feel like a minor miracle happened for me. I've had no pain to speak of, just fatigue, and I think that is related to my heart condition. I think that taking the medications for both atrial fibrillation and atrial flutter limit my capacity for exercise. I can go slow and steady, but can't put forth great bursts of energy because my heart rate is so low and is unable to supply enough oxygen. If I try to go up stairs too fast, I feel the lack and get dizzy, but I can go up hills just fine because they are more gradual and I can pace myself.

It's seventy-five degrees today. Nice! I am planning to get a massage; I think that makes me as pampered as any I point fingers at!

Love, Susan

Thursday, June 2, 2016
Melide to Arzua, 8+ miles/13.6 km

AT THIS POINT, we were walking very short days; we were in no hurry. We saw few farms, but increasing numbers of small landholdings with a square pad for the square stucco house, and a square garden for the neat rows of vegetables. Every village had places to stay, and many enterprising food vendors. One of my favorites was the appropriately named *Pequeño Oasis*. This small, plywood, pop-up stand had a dozen hikers lined up for coffee and pastries. Certainly these services were needed for the growing number of pilgrims.

We arrived about noon in Arzua. Another milestone—those

coming in from the Camino del Norte now joined us on the Francés. Though this signified that our hike was nearing an end, we knew that we would see this town again in ten days after completing the Norte ourselves.

Our accommodations at the Hotel Suiza were a mile off the beaten track, so not the best for spending time in the small town to watch the parade of pilgrims going by, but they were comfortable. The internet connection was good and I sat in our second-story room to catch up on journaling.

6/2/16

I was happy whenever we left the wide roads for dirt trails—until I found there was usually a disgusting amount of discarded toilet paper lining the way. Understandably, some trash ends up along the trail accidentally—a piece of tissue that falls out when one is looking for a glove in a pocket, a T-shirt that falls off the back of a backpack, and so forth. But, toilet paper—there is no excuse. I have never understood the mentality of those who pay back the Camino's hospitality by trashing it.

There are individuals and groups are trying to do something about the toilet paper issue. Rebekah Scott, of the Peaceable Kingdom in Moratinos (along the Francés) and her merry band of 'Ditch-Pigs' have gone out annually for several years in order to collect litter. *moratinoslife.blogspot.com* and in Fall 2017, the APOC launched its 'Clean Camino' logo to help bring awareness to the issue of increasing litter along the Camino.

LOOKING AT EMAILS is usually more calming!

From: Susan
To: Karen

Joy seeing a lovely weathered hórreo with climbing roses on it. *Satisfied* that the turtle (me) can sometimes beat the hare (hotshots). *Appreciate* Ralph working hard to find private rooms instead of shared ones. *Gratitude* that he works hard to make things easier for me.

From: Melanie:
To: Susan

Congrats on hiking without pain! Let's hear it for well-placed cortisone shots. And on making good progress on the road. Is your heart OK??

It's sad to know that the Spanish economy is so depressed. I don't know what the unemployment rate is there now, but two-to-three years ago I think it was over twenty-five percent. All those abandoned houses tell of sorrow and loss, just like in this country.

Love, Melanie

Friday, June 3, 2016
Arzua to Santa Irene, 10.3 miles/16.6 km

GOING FROM THE quiet Primitivo route to this oft-crowded path was amazing; the atmosphere of the hike changed dramatically, but it wasn't unexpected. Now, instead of seeing a couple dozen people on the trail, we were seeing many dozen. We estimated that half the people doing this latter part carried only a daypack and had their luggage transported. This represented quite a change from our earliest trip on a Camino route, in 2001 on the Francés. At that time this assistance was if not rare, at least hidden.

There were still quiet passages through forests, but there were also places every couple of miles where crowds gathered for coffee, pastries, and such. School groups came by—music playing, wooden poles pounding, clowning around in typical kid manner. It didn't always appear they were having much of a religious or spiritual experience, but it was gratifying that at least they were outdoors and socializing. No doubt they would carry the memories of this unique walk with them for a long time.

From: Susan
To: Karen

Joy having conversations with other pilgrims over dinner: Swiss; Italian, Spanish; and Americanos! *Satisfied* that I got the whole group to sing happy birthday to a woman in our albergue. *Appreciate* that all could speak English—and were willing to! *Gratitude* for a lovely dinner.

Saturday, June 4, 2016
Santa Irene to Lavacolla, 4.7 miles/7.7 km

LINES FOR THE women's restrooms began to appear in some of the restaurants along the way. The closer to Santiago, the more we saw signs that indicated the bathrooms were for customers only. It didn't seem quite right to me. I reasoned that the businesses benefited from the surge of popularity of the Camino, and even if a particular individual didn't make a purchase at a particular place, the numbers should average out. People had to go to the bathroom somewhere; if the bars didn't allow people to use their facilities, people would go wherever they had to—even along the trail. Pilgrims weren't able to just hop in a car and drive elsewhere.

After joining the pack of pilgrims we were often amongst groups of adults with matching tee-shirts sporting slogans or affiliations. There were many who were new to the trail—walking only the last one-hundred kilometers to earn the Compostela—but many were also veteran walkers who had started in St. Jean Pied du Port or other starting points. The greater number of people seemed to encourage a more festive atmosphere. I was surprised at how many were limping; I wondered if they had prepared for the day-after-day challenge of the trail. Even so, most were still hurrying along with their blisters and knee braces, amidst much chatter and laughter.

I noticed yard art that had been inspired by objects that most people would otherwise toss in the trash. The artist had created a playful construction by setting up an eight-foot-tall wooden post and adding two horizontal wooden boards to serve as arms.

From them were suspended a collection of treasures—a dented metal pail; a handsaw; an empty, plastic, anti-freeze container; a watering can; a caulking tube; a rusty lantern; an old triangle that in earlier times probably called workers to dinner; and a set of dolls constructed of folded straws. The chickens pecking through the small patch of grass in the yard didn't seem too impressed.

The three-story, terracotta colored Hotel Garcas, was a comfortable place to spend our last night on the outskirts of Santiago.

Sunday, June 5, 2016
Lavacolla to Santiago de Compostela, 7.6 miles/12.3 km

WE PASSED A chain link fence with twigs placed in the shape of crosses; I remembered the first time we saw these along the Camino Francés and how uplifting it felt to know that so many other pilgrims had passed this way.

We walked through the outskirts of Santiago passing by Monte de Gozo. The barracks-type buildings that we walked through in 2001 seemed to still be in use, but the route no longer led us through it. There was no need for a map; one could simply follow one of the many groups of pilgrims making their way west.

I enjoyed several cement constructions including a giant hiking boot inscribed, "*Se hace al andar*," perhaps influenced by a quotation by Spanish poet, Antonio Machado, "Wanderer, your footsteps are the road, and nothing more; wanderer, there is no road, the road is made by walking."

When we reached the Plaza del Obradoiro, the expansive main plaza in front of the west façade of the cathedral, tears came to my eyes. I was really happy and very proud to be there, but I felt choked with emotion because of the serious doubts I'd had about my being able to do the walk. I thought about the cortisone injections that I had; I decided to email and thank my doctors . . .

There were few people in the plaza compared to the crowds we'd seen on earlier arrivals, but much depended on the time of day, season, and whether or not it was a day of special religious importance. Maybe a hundred pilgrims and other tourists were seated on the concrete plaza, or sitting on concrete benches near the parador, or posing for photos in front of the cathedral's double staircase, but in a space so large it seemed empty.

A tourist train sat in front of the cathedral. The motorized vehicle was supposed to bring to mind an old steam train. Behind the white, decorated engine were three, covered, open-air passenger cars. Understandably, some people need transit to see the city, but it was jarring to see something that looked like it belonged in a zoo sitting in front of the historical edifice.

There was no service underway so we entered the cathedral and performed several of the traditional rituals. We descended the steps to the small room below the floor of the altar and gazed at the small silver casket that is said to contain the relics of St. James. We walked behind the altar to climb the steps so I could hug the gilded statue of St. James.

We went to the pilgrim office, which we knew had moved to a more out-of-the-way location then when we were last here in 2008. The grounds were strangely quiet. We were met at the entrance gate by a man who checked our credentials before letting us on the premises. Once inside, we stood in line and waited until a lighted sign flashed to tell us which desk we should each go to. We were lucky our mid-afternoon visit involved only a five-minute wait; we had heard of an hour or longer wait times.

We decided to have dinner on the Plaza Quintana at one of several restaurants with tables inside and out. The weather was perfect for sitting outside under the shade of the large umbrellas, and for people-watching. A pair of women was enjoyed a tête-à-tête while their young children played nearby.

Music was coming from the Plaza de las Platerias. After we finished eating, we went over to the steps linking the two plazas and where a crowd of maybe three-hundred people had gathered and sat on the concrete steps to hear the orchestra's performance. They played many rousing Spanish tunes—none of which we recognized, but the crowd certainly did. No sooner did a number end, than the crowd would roar its approval and the next piece would begin.

Later, I wrote in my journal.

6/5/16

An incident occurred tonight that could easily have turned sour where we live; I was a bit nervous watching to see how it would play out here. While we were watching the orchestra, a man came up the steps, carrying his daughter on his shoulders. He bumped into another man. I didn't see how that happened, but I presumed that the daughter's leg hit the offended man. The angered man then hit the father. The father stopped—now angry too, but before more could take place, a third man intervened and calmed the dad down.

I also spotted Juan; he was seated just a few rows below where we were standing. I knew that we could easily catch him after the performance, and as the crowd thinned, he came up the stairs. When he saw us, he began fretting because his camera had failed as he was recording the program. We took his email address and promised to send him our recording.

We bade our final goodbyes. When he hugged me, he said, *"Me gusta usted."* I know his saying he liked me was said in friendship, nothing more, and it was heartwarming to have met such a sweet person. I

It is now 10:10 p.m. and finally dusk; dawn will be six o'clock or so.

Monday, June 6, 2016
Zero Day in Santiago de Compostela

OUR PENSIÓN, THE Suso on the Rua do Villar, was in the old town and not far from the cathedral. At first I was disappointed that we weren't staying in a fancier place—it seemed like a celebration was in order—but I changed my mind. The rooms were clean, contemporary, and just big enough—especially considering we'd spend most of our time exploring Santiago. The room looked out over a street with a few restaurants and shops, but it wasn't noisy. Our tariff was a reasonable sixty-two euros and included a private bath.

We went to the cathedral hoping to hear a musical performance (choir or otherwise) but services were underway, so we went for a stroll through neighborhoods and shopping districts we had not seen before.

Early afternoon, we met Cathy Seitchik Diaz on the main plaza. Cathy, who, like us, was in the northern California pilgrim chapter, had seen on Facebook that Ralph and I were arriving and had texted me about meeting. Cathy and her companion David had just finished the Camino Francés; she was feeling quite bubbly and enthusiastic about arriving in Santiago and was looking forward to meeting up with other pilgrims she had met during their walk.

Cathy had other plans for lunch, so Ralph and I hurried over to the popular Casa Manolo on the Plaza de Cervantes. The Manolo had already become our favorite restaurant in Santiago. Everything we had tried had been good—the starters such as *Pimentos de Padrón*, croquettes, and white asparagus with mayonnaise, and the entrées including salmon.

Later there was time to read and send a couple of emails:

From: Susan
To: Friends and family
Hi all,

We arrived in Santiago de Compostela yesterday afternoon and will be sightseeing today. This ends the Primitivo trail and part one of our hike. It was wonderful to be officially recognized at the pilgrim office with the Compostela and also the new certificate offered, the distance award. They recorded our distance as 391 km instead of the 347 km we thought it was, but I was happy to take the extra credit.

The entire procedure was more efficient than it used to be, but I felt like I was in a local office of the Department of Motor Vehicles and I wished that the process was less business-like. Considering 200,000 people now show up annually, I guess I should appreciate any attention.

It was a wonderful arrival—I found myself in tears because as many of you know, I've been dealing with leg problems quite a while. I haven't felt this well in two years!

We also ran into Juan. It's amazing with all the people here that you see anyone you know, but reunions happen all the time. He has been very helpful. Many times he scouted out a town and then told us the best place to eat and what was going on in—a definite advantage of speaking the local language. When we saw him yesterday, it was with some sadness. Would we ever see him again? I am sure you've had similar experiences with these bittersweet endings.

I know that tomorrow will be primary Election Day in California. I am very glad that we voted before we left and even happier that we have had very little news about the campaigns this last month.

So far so good! Take care. Thanks for writing.

Love,

Susan and Ralph

From: Melanie
To: Susan

It must be so special to make Camino friends that you see over and over again on the trail—and so nice to have someone scout out the best places for when you enter a new area.

From: Susan
To: Melanie

It's partly the shared experience thing. You are going through difficult, but special things that most people back home (or otherwise in your life) don't understand, or maybe don't want to hear about in such detail.

You've been backpacking, so you know there's a lot

of effort expended, but much of the time, there's little going on that would make a good movie. There are rewards: sunrises, alpine glow, wildflowers, waterfalls, and more, but not a lot of drama. So little things mean a lot: getting sweet emails from a very dear friend, having someone hand you a rose, having someone offer you a glass of sidra from their party as you pass by. Things that we take for granted at home: a hot shower, a comfortable bed, a heater that is operational are sometimes hard to come by when on the Camino, but hearing about my excitement about finding them is not exactly spellbinding to friends on my email list.

I had an interesting conversation with someone we met today. She commented that she was in her fifties. Then, after we gave her our ages, she said we were her new role models. That gave me pause: I prefer to be admired for my accomplishments irrespective of my age, *but* it was still a compliment!

Thank you so much for being my faithful and interesting correspondent; it has meant a lot.

From: Melanie
To: Susan

What a sweet email! It's been special for me too staying in touch as you've progressed along your route. And it's sweet to hear about the memorable moments that occur along the way: our friend Juan, him tipping you off where the good places to eat are, even the noisy kids. All the things that break up the silent, meditative, one foot after the other, journey.

Love,
Melanie

After my lengthy email time, we went for dinner at an Italian place, also on Rua do Villar, and had a fruit salad of oranges, apples, banana, rice, lettuces, kiwi, dates. How welcome and refreshing that was after many days of the more limited choices in small towns. We also shared a pizza, which was a welcome change from the meat, potatoes, and bread standards.

We had ended our Camino Primitivo walk, but had not ended our Camino hiking for the year. It felt very strange to be ending one Camino and going back to finish another journey, but we both desired the sense of completion. The next day, we planned to take a bus from Santiago back to Vilalba, where we left the Camino del Norte trail in 2015. We expected that walk would take five days. We would then bus back to Santiago.

We would not walk the Arzua to Santiago segment of the Camino Francés because we had just done so. Finally, we would fly home Tuesday, June 14th.

Warming Hut at Puerta de Palo

Heading down from Puerta de Palo

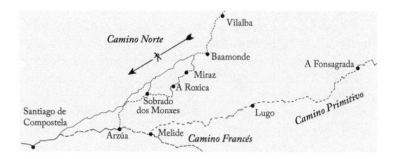

5 • The Third Time's the Charm

Camino del Norte, Spring 2016

Success seems to be largely a matter of hanging on after others have let go . . . . . .
~ William Feather

Tuesday, June 7, 2016
Bus from Santiago de Compostela to Vilalba

Our departure from Santiago was leisurely. We finished packing and then walked over to Plaza del Obradoiro to watch the pilgrims' arrivals and reunions in front of the cathedral before heading the mile or so to the Santiago bus station.

A group of six- and seven-year-old school children walked towards us, their teachers trying to keep the kids going single file. The kids were wearing dark brown cloaks and hats of the pilgrim style; it was obviously an adventure to be headed where we had just been in the center of old town.

As we walked through the commercial district, it felt strange to once again see people in business suits and tailored outfits rather than zip-off pants and quick-dry shirts. We took our time, but we still reached the bus station earlier than needed. At the ticket window of the Arriva line, a small sign indicated that the office would open about twenty minutes before departure time, but after waiting over an hour for the booth to open, we started

225

getting anxious. No employees in the terminal spoke English or understood our Spanish, including the woman in the information booth, but luckily we found a passenger who could help us. Good thing we asked—the booth wouldn't open; we were to go down a level to where the buses pulled in, find the correct one, and pay on the bus.

The comfortable ride took about ninety minutes with about half a dozen stops along the way. There weren't more than a dozen passengers onboard, so we wondered how the company could maintain the service and if bus companies were required to keep less popular routes open as a condition of licensing.

Because we had ended our 2015 walk on the Norte in Vilalba, we were now back in familiar territory. We walked the short distance from the small terminal to the center of town, and to the hotel, the Vila Do Alba, where we had stayed in the fall.

The manager, in his sixties, didn't remember us. He had probably seen hundreds of guests since we were there, but he was as friendly and helpful as we remembered. Once again we listened to his recommendations for restaurants and this time around we had better luck locating them than we did previously. Part of that may have been because this time of year it was still daylight at the dinner hour.

Dinner was excellent, but there was some confusion. When we were seated, the server told us the food choices, but didn't give us a printed menu. Most of the items were ones that we typically had seen on the pilgrim menus: the *Caldo Gallego* (white bean soup with sausage), salad mixta, pounded steak, the pork, *arroz con leche* (rice pudding) and so forth. So, we assumed that we were ordering from the inexpensive fixed-price menu. We were taken aback when we received a bill for forty euros rather than the usual twenty to twenty-four. We might have put up a fuss, but we let it go because the food was far better than usual and the prices were comparable to what we would have paid at home. We learned a lesson—ask the prices.

When Andrea and Terry were in this region in July of 2015, they emailed us their impressions.

From: Andrea
To: Susan

We are doing ok, have turned the corner from Ribadeo and now have only 120 km to go to Santiago, which is now just six walking days away. We have tried not to do more than 20 km daily but had to do 27.5 the other day, because accommodation is scarce at this stage. Actually it has been quite a logistical problem to sort out the day's walk so as to be sure of a bed at the end of it. However, we have managed with pensións and small hotels mostly which have not been too expensive and were reasonably comfortable.

It is still not easy for me to struggle up these steep hillsides in the sun with a heavy pack and we have met several walkers who say the terrain has been much harder than that of Camino Francés.

Today's walk was delightful, however, through woods and the countryside, and it was overcast until about 2 p.m. and we were almost there by then. We are in Vilalba tonight and tomorrow will go on to Baamonde.

We have been trying to eat when we arrive as there is not much food available in the evenings in these small towns, then to rest in the afternoon. Sadly, Wi-Fi is very limited; although all places say it is available it rarely works in the room and drops in and out. I guess that is a problem which isolated and smaller places suffer from in all countries, but it has made keeping in touch a tad harder for us.

We seem to have been winding our way around the ubiquitous A-8 expressway for weeks on end, and never seem to be out of sight of it really for long.

So many of the small villages are now shutting down without even a bar, as the traffic has been bypassed and their businesses cannot function profitably now. In fact Asturias and some of this province [Galicia] have been a mite depressing to walk through, as one can see people struggling under economic burdens and lots of lovely old buildings have just gone to rack and ruin as there is no money to fix them. Having said that, the people remain very warm and friendly, as ever and generally do their best under difficult circumstances.

Overall, we have enjoyed the Camino Del Norte though some days have been very hard and long. I am not sure whether it is just because I am older, but this time I think I shall be glad when the walk ends as I feel it has been very long. We have now walked for 30 days with six rest or play days, which is a good ratio and the daily rest has been very necessary for us to keep going. We are most certainly a lot fitter (though not slimmer I regret to say).

Things I have liked have been the proximity of the sea, and also, during the past week or two, meeting a few people of similar age, who are walking about the same pace, and staying in the same few hotels, etc. I have not enjoyed the amount of road walking or hard paved surface walking, today being a lovely exception.

We have seen mostly domestic animals, a few snakes (alive), zillions of chained up yapping dogs and bell-ringing cows and today a peacock and peahen. The humans have been varied both in age and nationality but we have had fun with an Italian couple and some Spaniards who disappear in a taxi (some people do it the hard way!) into Hilton-type hotels at the end of each day.

We send love to you both; take care of each other and enjoy every day.

Andrea and Terry

Wednesday, June 8, 2016
Vilalba to Baamonde, 12.2 miles/19.7 km

WE GOT UP a bit earlier than usual. We were out the door about 7:45, because we had a longer day and we expected it to be hotter than it had been. At first it felt good to be walking again. It was strange to go back to the slower pace of life of the Norte after so recently being on the Camino Francés. It was also much more pleasant to be seeing only a couple dozen people on the route.

I was comfortable wearing a short-sleeved blouse even though there was heavy fog. That lasted for a few hours, but when it burned off, it got increasingly hot and well into the 80s. Ralph used his umbrella some of the time—it makes a big difference in comfort level. We had yet to figure out a way that I could attach mine to my backpack so I could be hands-free to use my two hiking poles. (We have since figured this out: see "Packing" in Resources).

The trail was about fifty-fifty dirt track and paved roadways. It seemed perverse that whenever the temperature rose, we came to sections of heat-radiating pavement. We were lucky to find a couple of stops to cool off—once midway at a bar, the second in a freeway underpass. Pathetic as that may sound, the shade was welcome, there was no traffic, and there was a curb on which to sit.

Despite the discomfort of the heat, we stopped for a few moments after lunch to admire the *Ponte de Saa*, a Medieval bridge over the Rio Labrada.

A stork, his long legs keeping him dry in a partially, flooded field, was feeding in the tall grass. A bit later we saw a pair of the large birds in a nest high up on a post. Though storks now appear to be remaining in Spain year-round, rather than following their traditional migration route back to the Sub-Africa, we were still delighted to see signs of them nesting and raising their young.

We stopped when we first reached Baamonde and had beers. As often as the town's name had popped up in our information about the Norte, I was surprised to find that it wasn't larger than 6,000 people. Its popularity among pilgrims was largely because Santiago was only a hundred kilometers away; anyone wanting the compostela, could start here.

Though we saw less than a dozen pilgrims this day, we expected things to be different from here on out. The municipal hostel had ninety-four beds for handling the increase in numbers. We went on to the Hostel Ruta Esmeralda where we had reservations. There was a gas station and restaurant on one side of the property and a huge car and truck wash on the other. Given the location, and that there is plenty of room for truckers to park alongside the highway, we assumed truck drivers often stayed there. The room was okay; the shower was modern and good. Other than the albergue and the Esmeralda, there weren't many options.

6/8/16

I don't do well in heat, so for a time today it just seemed unbearable, and I didn't think I could continue on. Luckily the end came up earlier than I anticipated and the shower put things right again.

The place we stopped for cold beverages when we first reached town was right near the big albergue. A group of hikers, probably in their thirties, stood outside. They pretty much ignored us so I was glad we weren't staying there.

From: Susan
To: Karen:

Joy surviving twelve miles on a hot day with too much pavement and too little shade. *Appreciated* the shade of the freeway underpass. *Satisfied* that I walked faster than usual. *Gratitude* to friends and family who cheer me on.

From: Karen
To: Susan

Joy today being strong and able to participate more fully in the barre method class. *Appreciated* Laura getting me a big meeting with her company overlooking the bay. *Satisfied* I set boundaries today. *Grateful* for going to bed on time!

Thursday, June 9, 2016
Baamonde to Miraz, 9 miles/14.6 km

MY SLEEP HAD been restless because of the lingering heat. So, this day's start was not an auspicious one and then we had to walk alongside the flat highway. I was grateful there was a shoulder and that in this region cars move a bit away from us.

After two kilometers, we turned left onto a dirt track and went past an old, stone chapel dating from the fourteenth century. True to form, it wasn't open, but that rarely stops us from looking into windows. The trail climbed a bit and continued through a few small towns. We walked by several eucalyptus plantations young and old. It was a treat to see several patches of wildflowers again. One of our favorites, the purple-violet colored foxglove, seemed to grow everywhere.

Like many long-distance hikers, we were generally so focused on how many miles we had to hike and our destination for the day that we wouldn't venture far off the trail. This day, however, we were intrigued by colorful signs promoting an albergue that was only a bit off the trail. We had plenty of time to detour 150 meters.

The Witericus Café y Albergue Rural came into view. Golden California poppies spilled out of the planted areas and had popped up around the stone foundations of the buildings. I was reminded of our springtime hikes in the deserts of southern California and our parklands in the S.F. Bay Area.

We entered the tiny restaurant and lovely smells greeted us. On the glass shelves atop the counter was a beautiful selection of pastries. Deciding what to try was part of the fun; we each settled on a slice of *Torta de Santiago* (almond cake/pie of Saint James). Perfection: flavorful and with the perfect degree of moisture.

The interior's stone walls were decorated with Celtic ceramics and the region's traditional stirring music was playing. A wood stove sat in the corner. The owner Elena, and her father Pepe, were very hospitable and so I asked to see the sleeping room. It was, as Elena put it, "small with only nine beds, but peaceful." There were the typical bunk beds, one single, and two very clean bathrooms. I almost regretted that we couldn't spend the night in the albergue, but it was too early for us to stop, and we had accommodations ahead.

Next along the trail was the village of Seixon. We noticed a house surrounded by a plastered wall, which had been studded with several pieces of sculpted work. Through openings in the wall, we could see inside the enclosure to where a middle-aged craftsman sat surrounded by additional pieces large and small. If only we had been able to communicate in order to ask if we could look around at his workshop. Still, we had no intention of buying as we hadn't the means to carry anything home.

We stopped for lunch at the Bar Laguna, which was at a minor crossroads. When we arrived in Miraz to stay, we were surprised to see there were three albergues in close proximity to each other. As far as accommodations had gone so far, it often seemed like feast or famine, and the reasons for that were not often apparent to us.

The first place we came upon was the San Martin al Ernie, a pilgrim albergue run by the UK-based Confraternity of Saint James. Next was what appeared to be a private albergue, and then we came to the O Abrigo, a brand-new albergue, where we planned to stay.

The O Abrigo had two sleeping rooms with bunk beds: ten in one room, eighteen in the other. Ralph had made reservations for what turned out to be the one and only private room with bath. It was huge compared to the norm—even larger than our bedroom at home. Ralph was quite pleased with his coup; I was too, but I felt a bit embarrassed to have such a large space while the others were more crowded.

After we unpacked, we walked back to the San Martin albergue. The ladies who were volunteering as hospitaleros showed us around. It had the standard bunk beds, but a brighter and more spacious kitchen than most albergues, and some lovely, well-tended gardens (the English influence) with comfortable places to sit.

Kale was growing in the vegetable garden, which brought up a question that I'd had for a while, "Why do the people here let the plants flower and go to seed?" I asked.

The woman in charge of the garden answered, "Because every part of the kale can be used. The flowers and seeds can be used in salads, the leaves can be harvested as needed, and the stalks can be used as stakes for other crops that need support."

Our O Abrigo albergue didn't have a kitchen for pilgrims to use; it had a *taberna*. By four o'clock, we were sitting on its porch and people-watching. One table had five bicyclists; their road bikes leaned against a wall. Another table had five pilgrims who were conversing in Spanish. A single man was seated close by. A married couple, from Georgia, stopped by momentarily to talk, but then went up to shower and clean up. The few minutes' conversation was enough for us to know they were good story-tellers. I was happy to learn they were spending the night; we would be able to speak English again.

I heard the pitter-patter of animals coming down the lane next to us and turned to see a goat herd going by guided by three dogs and two old women. I regretted we would soon be out of farmland and no longer be seeing domestic livestock.

Georgia Couple came back down from their room and joined us for dinner. Justine and Michael, who we estimated were in their forties, had been hiking the Norte together for only a few days. However, she had started in Irún and traveled on her own until Michael arrived to join her on the trail.

Justine had met up with a trail angel even before she set foot on the Camino. She had arranged a stay at an albergue and for the host to pick her up at the train station in Irún. The host showed up, but unfortunately, Justine's luggage had been delayed on her flight from the U.S. The host assured Justine that when the luggage did show up, she'd deliver it to her wherever she was on the Norte.

Justine continued, "Not only did the luggage arrive and get delivered by my host, but she promised to stay in contact with me the entire time I'm on the trail just in case I need help."

After dinner, I was happy to have enough time and energy

to write in my journal.

6/9/16

Yesterday evening, I unexpectedly found twenty-five emails in my inbox from the third graders I worked with as a volunteer this year at Oakland's New Highland Elementary. Their messages were short and sweet—thanking me for reading to them, making cookies with them, and arranging field trips. Nothing beats being told how wonderful you are!

I enjoyed reading their messages, but I couldn't answer them because it was their last day of school. Their teacher, Tracy Dordell, had sent them on her smartphone. It was very considerate of her to put them up to it.

Michael mentioned a couple from Australia that they had met on the trail—sixty-year-olds Janette Murray-Wakelin and Alan Murray. When Janette was diagnosed with cancer in 2001, they were prompted them to make several changes in their lifestyle—including adopting a raw vegan diet. They also set an impressive goal—to run a marathon every day for a year. After reaching their goal in 2013, they had written a book, *Running out of Time,* and were working on documentary about the benefits they have found in their lifestyle changes.

I was surprised today when Justine told us she had completed about two-thirds of the Norte alone. I guess I need to consider what stereotypes I hold regarding women from southern states. Justine said sleeping with a roomful of men took a little getting used to, but there had been no issues. She's outgoing and an entertaining conversationalist, so it's no wonder she'd met many people along the way.

Her good luck reminded me of one of the many times we have been helped while hiking. We were on the Geneva to Le Puy route. Our French hosts were extremely kind, sharing not only their house, but also meals.

When we left their place the next morning, we inadvertently left behind some clothing. They knew where we were staying that night because they had called ahead for our reservations. When they found our items, they drove to the new place to return them. It was a complete surprise when they knocked on the door; we hadn't even had time to unpack and realize that anything was missing. We cherish these kinds of hiking experiences.

Thank goodness today was considerably cooler than yesterday. I much prefer temperatures in the seventies or lower. It helped that the cloud cover lasted most of the day. We also had a bit of rain, but not enough to put on our rain gear. It was a good hiking day!

Friday, June 10, 2016
Miraz to A Roxica, 6.7 miles/10.8 km

THIS WAS A *very* short day. We ate with Justine and Mike in the morning and then had to say goodbye. They, in contrast to our short hike, were going to go twenty-four kilometers because they were running out of time.

Just outside of town the trail climbed; we reached a barren area with rock outcropping interspersed with rough shrubs. The gray skies and drizzle added to the eerie feeling of isolation. There were signs that there had previously been a quarry operating here—we could see the drill marks in some of the huge stones.

Vegetation was primarily the colorful, yellow gorse. It's considered invasive in the western United States. It pushes out less aggressive plants, and no animals back home eat the prickly spikes. It's also considered an invasive in parts of South America, Australia, New Zealand, and Hawaii.

However, it is prized in many places. In fact, it's native to Spain and other parts of Europe. The flower, known as *chorima* in the Galician language, is considered the national flower of Galicia. In Ireland and Scotland it's frequently used as hedges to line the fields in their harsh climates. Many enjoy its bright yellow flowers that show up when there is little color otherwise.

There are several varieties, which bloom different times of year, which is the origin of the saying, "When gorse is out of blossom, kissing's out of fashion." It has many other uses: thorny cover for bird nests and shelter for animals such as the Dartmoor Ponies who live in semi-feral conditions, and for domesticated animals. In Scotland, it's crushed for winter feed for cattle.

Some people admire it because it's a survivor than can flourish in a variety of conditions. The problems seem to arise when it ends up in areas with more moderate climate because it has no natural predators and spreads very quickly.

We also saw eucalyptus, heather and bracken fern. Eucalyptus, originally from Australia, is also considered an invasive plant in California; it is highly flammable and difficult to eradicate. Yet, in Spain, we saw it being sold and planted in some areas, and signs suggesting people not buy it in others.

We hurried by an area where pine trees were being logged. The equipment was set up very close to the road and we watched with interest to see which way a tree the men were working on was going to fall before we proceeded. It fell, in the opposite direction, as we hiked by. We saw few animals—cows only in a couple of fields.

We went through a series of tiny towns with few houses. It was not until we were a few kilometers outside our destination of A Roxica that we found an inviting place to take a break in a covered bus stop. We were able to sit while we ate our prepackaged, chocolate-covered doughnuts.

Our albergue, the Casa Roxica, was "complete" at 4 p.m. I felt for any later arrivals because they would have no choice but to go back, which would be demoralizing, or forward another fourteen kilometers to the monastery in Sobrado de Monxes. Our sleeping room had five sets of bunk beds and one single. We were given disposable paper sheets and pillowcases—an increasingly common practice. While this may help, we didn't depend on the hostels' protective bedding against bedbugs; we sprayed our sleeping bags with Sawyer's Permethrin before we left home.

After we got ourselves settled, I hung my clothes outside to dry—optimistic that the rain showers were done for the day. One thing I was looking forward to at home was different clothes! I settled for writing in my journal.

6/10/16

Tonight we are sharing accommodations with several people, including an older couple, Waltraud and Altena-Höffken. They appear to be in their 70s. They started from their home in Germany in March and have walked probably 4,000 km this year. They do eight- to ten-mile days and have their baggage carried ahead. The fact that they have done similar distances year after year is very impressive. I'm not sure I want to devote that kind of time to walking long distances or to take that much time off from all of our other interests, but I am intrigued by those who make those kinds of life choices.

There's also a young German guy here. He's suffering from many blisters and a broken toe. He has taped his big toe to his second, and it appears to be healing well. With all that, he walks twenty- to thirty-mile days while wearing boots. All three speak English well, but when they are together they go back to speaking German.

Another group has come in: four hikers in their twenties and thirties. Three of them, friends from Michigan, started out together from west of Bilbao; the fourth, a woman from Switzerland, joined the trio a ways back.

FOR ONCE WE could join in the conversations because everyone spoke English. Our hostess set up a long table for us in the albergue's dining room and handed out the bowls and plates of food from the kitchen through a pass-through window. It was standard fare of salad, steak, boiled potatoes, and dessert—and it was tasty.

The trio from Michigan appeared very interested in our travels. Nothing like being treated like you have something of interest to say to others, rather than being ignored because you have reached a certain age. Alec, who was here in Spain for a year of study as well as walk, wanted to know all about our trips, and my books on Patagonia, the John Muir Trail, and so forth. One of the young women had some mountain-climbing experience and another played college volleyball. They were young, but they were accomplished.

Then, as we were almost finished, another young German arrived. He packed in the food like he hadn't eaten in days and had no qualms about asking for more. Not a word was said by our host about the latecomer's entrance. Young German Guy seemed to know just how to charm and flatter our host—she kept piling food on his plate. His claims seemed a bit exaggerated—I wasn't convinced that he had both walked 40 kilometers this day and had made many stops along the way to have beers with various acquaintances.

But, his tales were so ridiculous, he was funny. He related that when some of his drinking companions suggested he cut down the amount of his drinking, he quipped, "I tried stopping drinking once and it was the worst fifteen minutes of my life." It was a very entertaining evening.

We had seen and killed a cockroach when we arrived; that was enough to ignite my imagination. When we went to bed, I kept imagining that something was crawling on me. None were, no bites occurred, and bedtime went smoothly. All beds were taken, but everyone was quiet.

In fact the others were so quiet that I hated getting up to use the bathroom myself. The bathroom had an automatic light that went on when the door was opened sending a shaft of light onto one of the beds, and the door itself had a horrible squeak. I fretted, but it didn't help me not have to get up. I wondered if it should be mandatory that hosts spend a night in the bedrooms they offered before they could be licensed.

Saturday, June 11, 2016
A Roxica to Sobrado dos Monxes, 9 miles/14.5km

IN GENERAL THE Norte's route was adequately marked, but this day we came to a couple of problematical intersections. The first was a "T" with no arrows or other signs. It was unusual that the split was not marked; we wondered if someone had removed the sign.

When we came to a halt to try to figure out our next move, we were surprised to find Alec retracing her steps. She had tried going to the left on the paved road, but she hadn't gone very far in that direction because a dozen dogs were either lying in the street or standing up and barking and growling at her; she didn't want to wade through them.

Then she had turned right to follow some dirt tracks, but she found the path was not well worn and eventually came to a dead-end. We all agreed we needed to try the left turn again. Ralph and I started to lead the way through. We came upon not only the dogs, but also a couple of cats climbing out a window. While Ralph is comfortable around dogs, I get very nervous when passing them if they are not under their owner's control. (It hadn't help reduce my fears when I was bitten while on a hike back home.) I looked around at the nearby houses, trying to figure out if there was anyone around who could call the animals. Not seeing anyone, I decided to approach the house nearest the dogs.

An old woman came out, kicked one of the dogs, and asked in a not-too-welcoming manner what we wanted.

"Is this the Camino?" I asked. She nodded that we were going the right way.

WE CAME TO a man-made lake with a bird-blind and picnic tables, so we stopped for a while. Ribbiting frogs were everywhere; as we walked close to the shore, their green-striped bodies plopped into the water. We ran into a woman from Maryland who had just completed the Camino Francés.

"I'm now doing some of the things that I didn't slow down for when I was on the trail. I found a young local guide to take me bird watching. He is knowledgeable about the local birdlife," she said.

After arriving in Sobrado dos Monxes, we registered at a private albergue, the Lecer, then went next door to eat. We walked over to see the huge nearby monastery, which was built about 900 CE.

In 1142, it became part of the Cisterian order, which meant that it also became a pilgrim hospital. It has continued to welcome pilgrims throughout its history. Because we arrived mid-afternoon, the cloisters and albergue were closed to visitors, but pilgrims likely would occupy the 120 beds later in the day . . .

We followed the sound of music in the distance and came to a school. Crossing the parking lot to enter what was a cavernous multi-purpose room, we found an event just getting underway. People were starting to gather, women still bringing in casseroles. We weren't certain if we were crashing a private party or if it was a public event, but people smiled and looked welcoming. We weren't hungry, but I didn't want to miss the opportunity to take a photo of a sixty-inch-wide pan of paella—tended by a proud chef. We had hoped for live music, but when we saw that it was recorded, we decided to leave.

The town was small so heading back to the albergue to read and write in my journal made sense.

6/11/16

This albergue is interesting. The rooms are relatively small, but partitions have been placed around the twenty-plus beds to afford more privacy than most places have. There's a kitchen, in which I am presently sitting while writing this and watching several of the other pilgrims try to figure out where to hang their laundry. There seems to be a choice of hanging clothes to the side in this large room, but where the water would drip on the tile floor, or outside in an alley, where anyone walking by could carry it off.

Today's walk was short too, and there were no hard climbs. We reached the high point of the Norte, but it was a gradual climb to 710 meters—sort of anti-climactic. I guess it's considered unremarkable in these parts, too, because it isn't even marked. Probably eighty-to-ninety percent of today's walk was on hard surfaces. More cows and rounded rock formations. Things winding down here, only thirty miles to go on Norte.

From: Susan
To: Clem

We have been in such remote places much of the time on both of these Camino trails that without people to talk to, and friends like you who write, I would go bonkers. We can only walk so many hours a day, and can only eat so many times.

It feels unreal to be so close to heading home; thank you for all of your notes from the home front. We actually had three Americans in our albergue in A Roxica last night. Oh, to be 20 again and looking forward to so many adventures. They were interested, interesting, and enthusiastic. Much fun.

Cheers, Susan

Sunday, June 12, 2016
Sobrado dos Monxes to Arzua, 13.7 miles/22 km

WE WALKED QUIET roads of pavement or gravel until we reached Casanova, then followed a forest trail for about a kilometer, where we again found paved paths and roadways. The old stone cemetery in tiny Boimil, the San Miguel de Boimil, was well tended. Several of the old buildings lining the Rúa Gándara in Boimorto were in disrepair, but for the most part the town looked welcoming. There were baskets of flowers hanging from many houses, and playgrounds, a grocery store, pharmacy, and bar and restaurant.

WE REACHED ARZUA, which ended our Norte walk. We had come by the town just ten days earlier as we finished up the Primitivo

(May 11 to June 6, 2016) en route to Santiago. Now, we stayed in the Pension Rua, which was in a very convenient location—just steps from restaurants with outdoor seating where we went to sit and watch all the center's activity. It was a surreal experience to sit and watch hundreds of other pilgrims on the final stretch of the Francés as we were celebrating the completion of our long journeys.

Monday, June 13, 2016
Arzua to Santiago by bus

BECAUSE ONLY A few days earlier we had walked into Santiago at the end of the Primitivo walk, we chose to take a bus into the city after the end of our Norte walk.

We found the Hotel Restaurante Rua Villar, which was just steps from the cathedral and the Plaza de Praterias. Staying at the Rua Villar was a splurge, but was worth it to us because the hotel, converted from an eighteenth-century manor house, was beautiful and had excellent service. I loved the contrast between the dark heavy beams and the lightness provided by the central skylight. There was something about having one set of windows of our room opening to the interior's center corridor and another set opening to the outside that made me feel like I was in a splendid home rather than an impersonal hotel. On a more practical level, I loved playing with air conditioner controls that really worked. It all seemed perfect for our final day before flying home.

We paid one last visit to the Plaza del Obradoiro. Even though this was our fourth time in Santiago, I still found it difficult to figure out which building was which because the area occupied by the cathedral and the surrounding related buildings is huge. The cathedral soars above the city center "in a splendid jumble of moss-covered spires and statues" as the Lonely Planet's *Spain and Portugal's Best Trips* puts it.

A visit was due to the *Pazo de Xelmírez* or (The Gelmírez Palace), the former episcopal palace of the cathedral of Santiago de Compostela. It was built by Diego Gelmírez, archbishop of Santiago between 1120 and 1136. It's also on the north side of the cathedral off the Plaza del Obradoiro.

I VOWED THAT next time we reached Santiago, we would take the rooftop tour of the cathedral—said to be a highlight of the Santiago de Compostela experience. Tickets are required for the guided tours (most in Spanish only; check with the office for details) of the cathedral roof and an unguided visit to the permanent collection in the cathedral's museum. Tickets may be purchased at the cathedral, but may not be available at the time one wants to go; the safest bet is to order them online in advance.

Finally, we scurried around to buy a couple of gifts. I had been on the lookout for *El Juego de la Oca del Camino de Santiago* (Saint James Way's Goose Game) and found it at the gift shop associated with the cathedral. It's a very simple game played on a cardboard mat. What makes it unique is that the tokens or pieces that are moved around the board are cardboard characters in pilgrim garb: an equestrian, a monk, a bicyclist, and three hikers. A roll of the dice determines how many spaces the player's piece moves along the game board, which is decorated with stages of the Camino.

After our full day, I wanted to share our moment with my niece.

> **From:** Susan
> **To:** Karen:
> **Subject line:** Joy
> *Joy* finishing the second trail today. *Satisfied* I walked more than thirteen miles to do it. *Gratitude* to Ralph for endless support. *Appreciated* my good rain gear.

Monday, June 14, 2016
Flight from Santiago to home

REFLECTIONS FROM HOME

EVERY CAMINO BRINGS a different experience. Usually our walks have been on new routes because we enjoy the novelty, but whenever we return to familiar routes, we enjoy 'coming home.' There's no right or wrong—whether you do the same route time and again, or a different trail each time, there are always new adventures, new sights, and new takeaways.

I CONTINUE TO miss my mom. When I think about her, I reflect on the ways she made a difference in the world and without a lot of fanfare. In many ways she was a product of her time—women expected to stay in the background—but I often saw her work around societal dictates and quietly do things her way.

She and my dad did a lot of home remodeling when I was growing up. She was a frequent visitor to the local lumberyard where she would be the only woman in evidence. While the men were loading 2 x 4s into their pickups, Mom would stick them out the back of her Nash Metropolitan and cart them home.

The causes she supported—the regional music association, the hospital auxiliary, the heart and other health-related fund drives, took her not only to the country club for social events, but also door-to-door in working class neighborhoods soliciting support and donations.

I am grateful that she provided a role model of what a strong and determined woman can do in her later years. We watched with amazement when she, then in her eighties, designed her new home back in her birthplace of Pendleton, Oregon. Though she hired a contractor to do most of the construction, she built the fireplace mantel and all of the bookshelves, laid the flooring throughout the hall and den, and added the finishing touches to the window moldings. Then she proceeded to make all the curtains and dust ruffles for the beds.

I CONTINUE TO frequently exchange "gratitude messages" with our niece, Karen. Here is a sample of what I could send now related to our walks.

Joy being free to wander through forest and village on another continent. *Gratitude* for the people who provide us with lodging and food at the end of each day. *Appreciate* friends and family members who correspond with me when we are on the trail. *Satisfied* that I have gained confidence in my ability to prepare for and walk the Camino trails at my own pace.

Mom's family: her brothers Byron and Laurance; her father K.G., Vivien (my mom), her mother Margaret

Do you have the right gear?

Planning Your Camino — Resources

Thoughts come clearly while one walks.
~ Thomas Mann

When considering which Camino route you might hike, or when planning your trek, it can be helpful to compare the Norte, Primitivo, and Francés routes and to prepare accordingly.

Comparing the Norte, Primitivo, and Francés Routes

Just as there are significant differences between the north of Spain and the rest of the country: geography, climate, culture, economy, politics and more, there are many differences between the Norte, Primitivo, and Francés routes. Some of these differences may not directly affect hikers, but observing and understanding some of the distinctions will make visits richer.

Notably, there will be far fewer pilgrims on the northern routes. The trails (more so the Primitivo) are physically harder, the distances between accommodations greater. There are several, intertwined, reasons for this.

The geography is different—the Bay of Biscay of the Norte is in sharp contrast to the mountains of the Primitivo, and both are very different from the dry, flat meseta of the Francés. That affects not only the views that you will have when you travel through, it also affects transportation, industry, tourism, what crops can be grown, and how easily people can reach one another.

The weather of the north is different—with more precipitation. The growing seasons are shorter and the wilder landscape is more conducive to small farming than large-scale operations. The availability of certain crops affects the foods that are more commonly served. Therefore, in the north you are more likely to find pintxos, seafood, and hard cider rather than rice-heavy recipes such as paella.

The roots of the people of northern Spain are different from those of the south. The Norte begins in the heart of Basque country where the people speak *Euskara,* their own language, and often Spanish. Both the Norte and Primitivo travel through Asturias and Cantabria, where many celebrate Celtic heritage, and meet the Camino Francés in Galicia (with also has Celtic roots).

You'll even see that cultural differences are reflected in the kinds of sports and recreation enjoyed. Though many associate bullfighting and flamenco with this country, these activities are most often found from Madrid south. Along the Norte, in Basque Country, you'll find that soccer, surfing and fishing, as well as rural sports such as dragging weights, wood chopping, and other displays of strength are popular.

When you add in the different forms of architecture and even the different ways that the cities are laid out, you begin to realize how unique each Camino is.

We found the Norte and Primitivo routes were more about cultural and spiritual experiences than religious ones. The Norte route, particularly as it ran along the Bay of Biscay, was more oriented toward tourism than toward pilgrims. For example, although cosmopolitan Bilbao has the amazing Basilica of Begoña overlooking the old town, I suspected there were more visitors to the stunning architecture of the Guggenheim Museum than to the cathedral.

Along the Primitivo there were impressive churches and cathedrals to be sure—the *Basilica of San Julián de los Prados* in Oviedo; the pre-Romanesque church of *Santa María del Naranco* and the *San Miguel de Lillo* outside of Oviedo; and the *Catedral de Santa María* in Lugo. But because there were comparatively few large cities along the route, and most of the small chapels were closed unless a service is underway, there weren't the number of opportunities to join a pilgrim mass along the way that there were along the Camino Francés. For us, because we were not seeking a religious pilgrimage, these factors were not of concern, but they might be to others.

Though we noticed that accommodations for those traveling on foot were growing in number, the comparatively small number of people on the Norte compared to those on the Francés meant that there was less of an emphasis on pilgrims' needs. For us, the unique cultures of the Basque, Asturian, Cantabrian, and Galician autonomous communities were fascinating and the lands through which we passed were varied and beautiful. On some days the views along the Norte (as it turned inland) and Primitivo were similar to ones along the Francés, when there were tiny villages, and postage stamp-sized gardens, and muddy tracks, but the numerous beaches and rugged shorelines of the Norte were unique. And though there were mountain passes on the Francés, the time that route spent in the mountains was short compared to the many days that the Primitivo (in particular) and the Norte (somewhat) spent on higher ground.

DISTANCES AND TIME requirements

Distances: Roughly, the Norte is 512 miles, the Primitivo 240, and the Francés 500. However, figuring out the precise length of the northern routes, particularly the Primitivo, is more complicated than it is for the Camino Francés because there are more detours and alternatives.

Primitivo: When we reached the pilgrim office in Santiago, they recorded that we had walked 242 miles/391 km. However, the U.K.'s Confraternity of Saint James gives the mileage as 229 miles/370 km (shorter via Hospitales route), and our spreadsheet calculations (based on the Cicerone guidebook's mileages given) indicated we would walk approximately 216 miles/350 km from our starting point at Villaviciosa.

Norte: According to the American Pilgrims on the Camino, the Norte route from Irún to Santiago is 512 miles/825 km. According to our spreadsheet figures, based on the Cicerone guide, it was approximately 507 miles/817.5 km.

By comparison, the *Camino Francés* from St. Jean-Pied-de-Port, France to Santiago is generally given as nearly 500 miles/780 km.

Time: Roughly, the time required for the Camino Francés or Camino del Norte is five weeks; the Camino Primitivo, two. American Pilgrims estimates thirteen to fifteen walking days for the Primitivo from Oviedo to Santiago (allow a couple more if starting farther to the north), compared to thirty to thirty-five for the Camino Francés. What I've read on the Camino forum, suggests twenty-nine (low) to thirty-three (average). Because Ralph and I completed the route in stages and because I was dealing with a physical setback, we took considerably longer.

Figuring out how long it will take to walk a given Camino depends on several variables—your goals, how far you can walk per day with or without a pack, the length and difficulty of your route, the weather.

If you want to stay extra days in certain places or conversely you have time constraints, you might require more or less time to do the trail. If you have physical problems or become ill, you may need extra time. Many people find ways to save time or energy by bypassing portions of the trail (up until the last 100 kilometers) or by shipping baggage ahead.

WHEN TO GO: Weather and Events

Weather: As briefly mentioned earlier, the climate along the Norte route differs from that of the Camino Francés largely because of the north's marine influence. The weather is highly changeable—even the local people will tell you that predictions are only a best guess. You are much more likely to have stormy days than you would have on the Francés. The rain can be very heavy—fog and drizzle your constant companions.

Of course, that means that the grassy fields and hills are a lush deep green. In fact the coastal stretch along the Bay of Biscay, from the Basque community to the Cantabrian, is sometimes referred to as the Green Spain. You will continue to see this Atlantic marine influence as you enter Asturias and approach the Picos de Europa.

Both the Caminos Norte and Primitivo go into the interior mountains. Because they stay in the mountains for a greater distance, arguably they are more hazardous than the Francés for winter travel. A pilgrim making a winter-crossing of these routes faces several additional challenges over the Francés. More physical effort is required, the trails are more remote and less traveled, and there is a greater difficulty of route-finding when trails and waymarkings are hidden. In addition, there are fewer accommodations on the northern routes than on the Francés, and still fewer that stay open all year long.

Our northern hikes were in April-June and September-October. April was indeed very rainy, but not torrentially so; May and June had only a couple of days that were rainy enough to warrant putting on the raingear. Along the coast it was almost always humid. Temperatures were usually on the cool side—especially in the mornings and evenings. On the Primitivo, we encountered hail in June, but only at the highest elevation and short-lived. When the trail enters Galicia, the weather will be much like that of the Francés—usually more rainy than stony when not in the mountains.

At the other extreme, heat-wise, the Norte and Primitivo, rarely have the triple digit temperatures that the Francés can see in the interior (including the meseta). However, when humidity is added to the mix, hot weather can be enervating on the northern routes, too. One strategy for coping with the heat is to take advantage of the longer days—start early, rest mid-day, continue into evening.

And, if you want to swim on one of the gorgeous beaches along the Norte, the best time is generally in August when the average sea temperature is 21°C (71°F). Of course, that's also high season and when you will encounter the most vacationers. Accommodations will be more difficult to find and more expensive, but that situation improves as you move west.

As with most any route that takes one more than 500 miles across a land, the weather and climate along the Camino del Norte can vary widely. Generally, the best weather can be expected mid-May to early October. However, with climate change being what it is (changeable), one can't guarantee things will remain the same, but historic patterns can be informative.

Events: July 25th is Saint James Day and for the last two

weeks in July, the city of Santiago de Compostela celebrates its biggest festival of the year with cultural and religious celebrations. Many pilgrims time their Caminos to reach the city on that date. Other holidays and special events are frequently encountered on Camino trails and the northern routes are no exception.

In addition to religious holidays such as Easter and Christmas that are celebrated throughout the country, any community that is large enough to have a church will most likely have a patron saint and within a city, each neighborhood (barrio) will have its own fiesta (perhaps including bullfights). Any occasion may be cause for celebration—the wine harvest, the end of fishing season, a market day and these parties offer the opportunity to enjoy the local produce and other foods, beverages, music, dance, and crafts.

Parades may include a float with a replica of the Virgin Mary, or they may recreate scenes reflecting ancient rituals and Celtic influences. You may see the Galician *gaita* (or *gaita galega* in Galician), a traditional instrument of Galicia similar to the Scottish or Irish bagpipe, being played. You may also see children dressed in dark costumes of witches and warlocks in scenes reminiscent of the Dark Ages.

Whether you want to join in, or avoid spending time in places where celebrations are occurring, you can plan around the various holidays, fiestas, and bullfights that are likely to bring out large crowds. If you are making sleeping reservations, book ahead.

Another big, regional event that you might come upon is the Transhumance. In the Basque country, celebrants refer to the importance of the tradition—one that has been practiced for more than 6,000 years along now ancient paths. In the spring or early summer, the herders with their sheepdogs and guard dogs (protecting against wolves or bears) move their animals into the mountains where the grasses are green and plentiful after the winter's rain. In the fall, the animals are moved to lower elevations where the weather will be less severe. The distances that the sheep travel move can be up to 500 km between southern valleys and northern mountains, and can take several weeks.

There are more than 125,000 kilometers of drover roads in

Spain and Portugal linking together various regions. The Transhumance was a wide-spread practice during the Middle Ages. It died off in many regions, but has been revived in others such as Madrid. If you happen to be there in late October before or after your Camino, you might see the Feast of Transhumance. In 2015, more than 2,000 Merino sheep were herded by their pastors into the city-center streets as well as the Puerta de Sol. Supporters like to recognize the importance of livestock and their keepers. Distractors point to the disruption of blocking off many of the cities' major streets.

With all of these holidays, festivities, and special events in Spain, it's a good idea to check online before you make firm travel plans to see if there are unique celebrations that may affect your travels.

Finally, remember that August is a very busy time on the Norte because it's when most Spaniards and other Europeans take their long vacations.

Transportation to and from Norte and Primitivo Routes

On the various forums, you will find many suggestions on how to reach your starting point and how to return home after your Camino. The first thing to consider is whether you want to reach those points as directly and quickly as possible, or whether you want to spend time in Madrid, Barcelona, Paris, or elsewhere before setting out for your hike. We have been using the *Rome2Rio.com* website frequently for our connections.

Norte: To reach Irún (Spain) or Hendaye (France)—right across a narrow river from each other, you have a couple of good options—and they are not as complicated as they first appear. By air, you can fly into Biarritz, France and take a bus to the Biarritz train station (ten minutes) and then the train to Hendaye (twenty-five minutes) and start your adventure.

Alternatively, you can fly to San Sebastián's airport, which is northeast of the city. From the airport, you can take a bus for a couple of dollars into Irún's city center (or walk there in thirty to forty minutes.) Or, you can fly into Bilbao and backtrack to Irún from there. If you are traveling from the U.S., you can fly into London's Heathrow, and transfer to one of the low-cost carriers such as RyanAir.

If you are starting your trip from a major city such as Madrid, you can take either bus or train. From Madrid this will be under six hours; from Barcelona it will be six hours by train, seven by bus, to reach the train station in Irún.

Primitivo: Reaching Oviedo by bus isn't bad—it's a forty-five-minute bus ride from the Asturias airport. We wanted to reach Villaviciosa (near Sebrayo where the Primitivo and Norte split), so we flew to Madrid, then to Asturias airport and took a taxi on from there. There are buses (ALSA), but getting to Villaviciosa requires a ride of almost three hours and a transfer.

To get to one of those starting points from other cities along the Bay of Biscay, you may find a FEVE train connection.

Returning home from Santiago: Santiago has a local airport, Lavacolla. From there, you can find some of the low-cost carriers as well as the major airline, Iberia. If you have your Compostela, you may be able to get a pilgrim discount.

Alternately, you can take train, bus, or our wonderful find— *blablacar.com* to Madrid or another major city and fly from there . . .

PILGRIM STATISTICS

There may well be times on the northern routes that you will not see any other hikers during the day. You will definitely see more farm animals—cows, horses, and sheep—than people in the inland sections.

As the statistics kept by the *Oficina de Acogida de Peregrinos* (Pilgrim Office) in Santiago de Compostela indicate, the Camino de Santiago routes have seen a huge resurgence in travelers in the last several years and the numbers continue to rise.

The Pilgrim Office maintains records showing the number of Compostelas issued. Currently posted are records from 1986 to 2016. In 1986, there were 2,491 certificates issued, in 2016 there were 277,913 (on all routes).

Though many people are fine with the steadily increasing number of other pilgrims on the Camino Francés, many others prefer a less crowded experience. Also, many who have already walked the Francés route are interested in walking some of the other routes.

Percentage-wise, the most popular routes in 2016 were the Camino Francés (63.4%), Camino Portugués, Camino del Norte (6.2%), Via de la Plata (3.3%), and Camino Primitivo (4.4%). However, the statistics indicate changes in routes chosen over the last few years. The percentage of pilgrims on the Francés has dropped from its 2006 figure when it saw 82.1% of the total. The Portugués has seen the largest rise percentage-wise, jumping from 6.4% to 18.8%.

The Francés saw 176,115 certificates issued in 2016 (+4,000 over 2015). The Camino del Norte's numbers went up to 17,792 (+1,921 over 2015). The Primitivo went to 12,090 (+ 664 pilgrims over 2015.).

The figures above include all who have traveled a minimum of 100 km (60 miles) on foot, or 200 km (120 miles) by horseback *and who have registered* in the pilgrim office.

If you look further into the statistics, you'll see that 1993, 1999, 2004, and 2010 were Holy Years. The next such occurrence is 2021 and if history repeats itself, that year will again show a significant jump in the number of pilgrims heading to the Pilgrim Office.

Peter Robins, who lives in the UK and is also known as the Walking Pilgrim, maintained a website for several years that listed hundreds of Camino routes. (He has now passed that job over to GitHub. *pilgrimdb.github.io/alphalist.html*)

Robins gave his criterion for including a route on his list thusly: "Nor is there any real rule on how a 'pilgrimage route' differs from any other walking route. In general, pilgrimage routes are based on historical medieval roads, and visit towns, especially those with a shrine or other religious connections, whereas walking routes are pleasant walks in the country. In practice, some of those claimed as 'pilgrim roads' are just rebranded existing long-distance paths and have little to do with pilgrimage."

Robins states that we really have very little information about what these routes were. It seems reasonable, however, that as time went by, certain routes became increasingly used because of geography, weather, accommodations, and political realities (namely wars).

The Camino route, the Via Gebennensis, that Ralph and I took from Geneva, Switzerland to LePuy, France in 2011-12 is a prime example of what the Confraternity of St. James calls a "designer route." It was created in the 1990s to bridge the gap between Switzerland and LePuy and allow walkers to continue in route to Santiago on "quiet, waymarked forest tracks, old lanes, footpaths and minor roads."

Terrain and level of Difficulty; Route Finding

When we started considering walking the Camino del Norte and the Primitivo, I thought the routes would be mostly on dirt track, but a bit of research soon revealed that we probably would have a lot of road walking. Indeed it did involve much more than we preferred, but that said, there were also a lot of three-meter wide tracks that were more suitable for moving flocks of sheep from one place to another or for taking the occasional traveler on foot to Santiago.

There were places where we were forced to walk on the edge of the roadway, sometimes with no marked shoulder, but the traffic was usually light. As the Norte and Primitivo become more popular, there probably will be more routes moved away from traffic—as has already happened on the Camino Francés.

The Norte goes through several large cities along the coastal section: San Sebastián, Bilbao, Santander, and Gijón where you will be on city sidewalks getting through town. Some guidebooks suggest hopping on a bus just after Bilbao and in order to bypass the heavily industrial town of Portugalete (if you do, however, you will also bypass the fascinating transporter bridge and seeing the Basque mansions along the beach).

Because the Primitivo only goes through two large cities, Oviedo and Lugo, there is very little time that you are walking through industrial areas and suburban housing tracts.

It's pretty difficult to get reliable statistics on the question of proportions of pavement vs. dirt tracks on the Camino Francés, much less on the less taken northern routes. The Australian-based tour company RAW Travel gives these numbers: 505 km of paths and tracks, 203 km of quiet roads (mostly through small villages), and 90 km.... along main roads." *caminodesantiago.com.au*

Francis Tapon, in his *10 Reasons Why El Camino Santiago Sucks* wrote, "Only about 1% of El Camino is a narrow (1-meter wide) dirt trail; 99% is a road (either a dirt road, 2-track road, paved road with little traffic, or a busy highway). When Tapon's article was published, it provoked a lot of interest. There were millions of hits on his post and a fair number of readers took issue. Some felt moved to challenge Tapon's comments and sent in photos that they thought would support their arguments.

However, instead Tapon believes the photos support his original claim. Tapon commented on one photo sent to him that "...shows a wide road that 3-4 pilgrims could walk side-by-side on! Not a narrow trail that you see in the wilderness that is only good for single-file walking. When you search for images on El Camino, you'll never see a narrow footpath. It's always a trail that is wide enough for a 4x4 SUV to drive on." But after this debate, Tapon decided "to add a helpful line to my #1 criticism. I added, 'It's almost never a narrow footpath where pilgrims are forced to walk in a single file.'"

Again, Tapon wrote, "About half the time you're on a paved road or on a dirt path right next to a paved road. Some of the paved roads have little traffic, but others are quite busy," again some readers took issue. In his correspondence to me, Tapon expanded on his original comment, "... when I write about traffic noise being 'within earshot,' [I don't mean] that there's constant noise in your ear. It just means that IF there is noise, you will hear it."

Of the Primitivo and Norte, we would estimate less than 20% is on dirt trail until you reach Galicia where it will be off pavement most of the time. When it is narrow, one-person wide track, it is often on soil that soon turns to muddy clay with standing water to pick your way through cautiously. That makes for slow-going hiking, but more memorable moments.

In our opinion and that of many others, the Primitivo and the Norte are considerably harder than the Francés. In fact, we consider them also more difficult than the Porto, Le Puy, Arles, and Vézelay routes.

Norte: The portion of the Norte that follows the coastline of the Bay of Biscay is a series of ascents and descents because of the rivers that drain to the northern coast. Therefore, you will find yourself dropping to gorgeous beaches and cities and climbing up into the hills. When the trail heads inland, at Ribadeo, the route goes into the mountains. The highest point of the route, which is after Miraz and unmarked, is 710 meters. The trail then gradually descends and levels out until it joins the Francés.

Primitivo: The Primitivo has many challenging days after it reaches San Juan de Villapañada and starts its ascent into the Cordillera Cantabria. It proceeds along an undulating route—down to farming communities, up to isolated villages or windmills in mountainous terrain. Those taking the Hospitales option after Borres will encounter a 990-meter total ascent on the twenty-seven kilometer stage. The descent 800-meter descent into Embalse de Salime is also impressive.

WHEREAS THE WAYMARKING of the well-traveled Camino Francés, from the Pyrenees to Santiago de Compostela is so good that it's almost impossible to get lost for any length of time (except in severe weather in the mountains), on both the Norte and the Primitivo the waymarks are more sporadically placed. Some sections are well-marked, others are not. There occasionally are road construction projects and related detours along the northern route that can add to the confusion. We noticed that sometimes the concrete Camino markers had been moved to show the way through temporary reroutes. Though these projects may be described in the guidebooks, since the sites of work change over time, you need to be sure that you have checked for up-to-date info.

Some pilgrims have commented about the difficulty of finding signs in Oviedo (along the Primitivo). We found brass scallop shells in the sidewalks indicating the way through the city; one just had be on the lookout for them.

Another difference between the Francés and the northern routes is that the Francés has very few alternative routes, but the Norte and Primitivo have several places where there both "official" routes and variants.

Traditionally in Galicia the scallop shells that are used to show the direction to Santiago have been placed differently than they have been in other regions. In Galicia, the rays point west, whereas in the other places, the rays point east. (Note that in some places in Galicia they are now being placed to match how they are elsewhere!) If in doubt, continue west.

Still, with all that, Ralph and I found ourselves off our route only a couple of times—once because we ignored our guidebook and followed the yellow arrows, and another time because we walked right past a proper sign.

There were also many times that we were helped by local people when we were standing by the road or trail looking puzzled, studying the online map, and hoping the way would be made clear. I have a great deal of gratitude for those people!

ALONG THE NORTHERN route, there are several places where you have to walk through fields, opening and closing gates as you go. Somehow we missed it, but it's rumored that one passes a weathered wooden sign that reads, *"Advertensia si a usted le parace que puede cruzar la finca en 8 minutos, my toro 'Bringo' lo hace in 4. Quico y a. lana . . . ."*

This translates to, "Warning: If it seems to you that you are able to cross the field in 8 minutes, my bull 'Bringo' can do it in 4. Keep to the path . . . . . . "

Passport, Credential, Compostela, and Certificate

Your travel passport: Most pilgrims are concerned about two passports—the one from their own country that lets them in and out of Spain and back home again, and the Pilgrim Passport, often called the *credential.* Before leaving home, make certain that your passport is valid for *at least* three months beyond your intended date of return—six months is better.

If visiting other countries, be certain that you check their entry requirements. The State Department says,

> Entry into any of the 26 European countries in the Schengen area for short-term tourism, a business trip,

or in transit to a non-Schengen destination, requires that your passport be valid for at least three months beyond your intended date of departure. If your passport does not meet the Schengen requirements, you may be refused boarding by the airline at your point of origin or while transferring planes. You could also be denied entry when you arrive in the Schengen area. For this reason, we recommend that your passport have at least six months' validity remaining whenever you travel abroad."

Being refused entrance by the airline, or being denied entrance to a country happens! A friend of mine, headed for Indonesia for two weeks, got some bad news when she arrived at the airport. Her passport's expiration day was only five months away; the airline would not let her travel. The US Passport service says, "This is not a new requirement, but it is only recently that the requirement has been more strictly enforced."

Interestingly, in my friend's case, neither the travel agent or the airlines that she worked with before the trip told her what would be needed. Be certain you know when your passport expires.

Another consideration, check to see if a round trip ticket is required. Spanish government regulations may require a return or on-going ticket or proof of funds. Sometimes airlines have this same requirement—so check.

American citizens can enter Spain or Andorra visa-free for periods of up to three months. Should an American citizen wish to remain longer than ninety days, then they will be required to obtain an extension of stay from Spanish immigration authorities. This extension, of no more than ninety days, must be requested at a police station at least three weeks before the initial entry period expires. It is only granted under exceptional circumstances. By law, foreigners who have overstayed their permitted time will not be allowed to leave without first obtaining an exit permit from the Directorate of Security of the State in Madrid or from the local police in another city. A fine, commensurate with the time overstayed, may be charged.

Should you be considering a stay longer than three months you should inquire with the Spanish embassy or consulate near your place of residence outside of Spain prior to entry. You may also write directly to the Spanish National Police at Calle Moratin, 43, 28014 Madrid; or check the Spanish Ministry of Interior's website. *madrid.usembassy.gov/citizen-services/information-for-travelers/traveling-to-spain.html*

If you are entering France prior to the Camino del Norte, you would need to abide by their regulations for passport validity and blank passport pages. The passport "must be valid for a minimum of six months at entry and valid for an additional three months beyond your planned date of departure from the Schengen area. Please note that 'emergency passports' issued by U.S. Embassies and Consulates overseas may not be accepted for entry into France."

'Blank Passport Pages' means that there must be one page blank to use for your entry stamp to that country. Check here for more info on passports and visas by various countries: *travel.state.gov/content/passports/en/country.html*

The Pilgrim Passport—the Credential (credencial). The Pilgrim Passport/Credential is a folding document that allows you to stay in pilgrim albergues (aka refugios) along the Camino routes. In it, pilgrims collect *sellos* (inked rubber stamps) each day from churches, municipal offices, museums, restaurants or other establishments they pass along the way. The credential, when properly filled out, allows you to obtain the Compostela from the pilgrim office when you arrive in Santiago.

You can get the credential before you leave home or once you set out on the Camino. If you live in the U.S., you may want to order a credential from the American Pilgrims on the Camino. From them, there is no charge, but donations are appreciated. Order online or by mail to: American Pilgrims on the Camino, 120 State Avenue NE # 303, Olympia WA 98501-1131, three months in advance of your trip, and allow a month for delivery. Other Camino associations can supply credentials. The APOC maintains this list: *americanpilgrims.org/internet-resources* You can also order from Ivar's Camino forum page:

tinyurl.com/IvarsPassport

Others prefer to obtain their passports from an albergue or pilgrim office in a larger city once they arrive in Spain. In general, you will only need to pay a couple of dollars (or euros). Those walking the Norte can obtain the credential at the pilgrim albergue in Irún. Those traveling the Primitivo can easily obtain a credential at the Cathedral in Oviedo, or in Lugo.

The Compostela—Most people who walk the Camino want to receive the Compostela, a certificate honoring their achievement, when they reach the Holy City of Santiago de Compostela.

When you reach the pilgrim office at Rúa Carretas, 33 in Santiago, you will present your Credential to a clerk with its record of your journey. If you have documented the required 100 km if on foot, or 200 if by bicycle or horseback, you will receive the Compostela. (There have been reports that you may also be asked to present your U.S. passport (or National ID), so bring it along.)

Those who start their walk at the 100 km point, in Galicia, are required to get two *sellos* (inked rubber stamps) entered into their credential) each day. If starting farther back, you will only need one sello per day until you reach the 100 km point, from there on, it is advisable to get the two stamps each day (reportedly this may or may not be enforced at the pilgrim office.)

You will be asked your motive for completing your pilgrimage. If you state it was for religious or spiritual reasons, you will be issued the Compostela. If for cultural or other reasons, you will receive an alternate certificate, the Certificate of Welcome, which is also written in Latin. There is also a certificate available for pilgrims completing the journey to Finisterre or Muxia.

The Compostela is not a new invention; it was introduced by the Catholic Church in the thirteenth century. Those who secured it then (as do many who secure it today) usually considered it more than a handsome souvenir written in Latin. It could used as proof that one had traveled to Santiago as a form of reference, or to show that one had paid their penance, or as a ticket to heaven. Some sources suggest that there was a good market for Compostelas during Middle Ages.

From time to time there is discussion of whether or not the

100/200 km requirement that currently exists should be changed to a greater number. Those who argue for it, believe that it would encourage pilgrims to start the Camino farther away from Santiago. This would stretch the number of people on the routes out more and lessen the impact on Galicia in particular. One proposal suggests that the minimum distance to obtain the Compostela be 300 km. If set into motion, this would mean that Norte pilgrims would start in Avilés and the Primitivo group would start in Oviedo.

The Certificate of Distance: In March 2014, another certificate was made available—the certificate of distance. It gives the starting point, the route, the distance walked/cycled, and the date of completion. This certificate is printed on parchment paper and ornamented with a Latin phrase from the Codex Calixtinus.

When you go to the Pilgrim Office in Santiago to request your Compostela, you can obtain the new certificate for three euros. This fee helps cover the costs of the reception service and the delivery of the Compostela, which are completely free. There are plans to make the certificate available online, but in the meantime, those who walked the Camino before that the certificate became available, can request the certificate of distance by emailing the Pilgrims Office in Santiago (be patient). *certificadodedistancia@catedralsesantiago.es*

ACCOMMODATIONS

Many pilgrims have reported that there are far fewer places for pilgrims to stay along the Norte and Primitivo than along the Francés. In particular, it's along the early stages of the Norte, in the Basque country, that it is most difficult to find albergues—especially those for pilgrims only. During the months that Spaniards take vacations, July and August, accommodations at the beaches and other places along the northern coast, will be more difficult to find. However, the number of accommodations continue to increase to meet the increased demand.

During our Norte and Primitivo journeys, we stayed in a variety of places—pilgrim albergues, pensions, and hotels large and small. Those desiring to always stay in pilgrim accommodations will have fewer options and more difficulty, but there are sources online that give contact information. Because we were able to be flexible (and pay the higher rates of private rooms when necessary) we never had problems finding a place to stay.

Generally, we found that advance reservations were optional along the Norte and Primitivo, but we usually made them for the day ahead especially when it would be a Friday and Saturday night. The downside of making reservations is, of course, losing flexibility and spontaneity because you have to get to, or stop at, the prearranged place.

Any reservations that you make should be kept if at all possible, or cancelled. Although increasingly reservations can be made online, Spain still has many places where a phone call is all that is required to have a host hold a room for you. Unlike the U.S. where a credit card is almost universally required when you call, here your word is often enough. If you don't show up, or don't notify management early enough, another pilgrim might be turned away for no reason. It addition, many of the places where one might stay are small—sometimes just a room or two. In such cases, the host will very likely have to purchase and prepare food for your meals ahead of time. If you don't show up, the host will lose money on the deal. It's important to play fair—both for the sake of other travelers and for our hosts.

Reservations can be reassuring if you find yourself walking during busy times of the year—vacation times, festivals, and holidays. Both pilgrims and other visitors tend to be on or near the trail towns and cities during the summer months; August is prime vacation time for Europeans. Some accommodations are only open seasonally, so if you are traveling during the winter months, you should check in advance. Hotels in major cities that you might visit, or fly into, such as Barcelona or Madrid, often fill up early—be sure to make reservations well in advance of need.

When the trails head inland and away from the coast there is greater likelihood of running into a "bed race," but not as frequently as occurs on the Camino Francés in all but the winter months.

The classification of lodgings. Wondering if it's hostal or hostel? There are both, plus a good many more kinds of accommodations and many of them are quite affordable on a hiker's budget. When you are traveling through the larger cities such a San Sebastián, or Oviedo, you will often find many options.

Another thing for couples to consider when choosing accommodations is whether the rate charged is by the room or per person—albergues usually charge per person, hotels usually charge for the room. Therefore, a couple might pay $25 each, totaling $50 in an albergue, or they might find a hotel room at the same price. If the place you stay serves meals, make certain you understand if the food is included with the room rate, or charged separately.

Another factor is the exchange rate, which can fluctuate. In some places you eat or stay, you will be asked if you prefer to have your bill charged in dollars or euros. If you have that choice, you should almost always pay in euros because the establishment will charge you a conversion fee for the service on top of the exchange rate cost.

On our 2015 pilgrimages, we spent from $40-$45 (donativo or albergue rate) to $125 (four-star hotel). For finding a place to stay, we used a number of sites or guides including *Booking.com*, *Gronze.com*, and *Wise Pilgrim apps* for the Norte and Primitivo. This simplified things although we found that their prices were sometimes higher than booking directly through the hotel. We also found that the less expensive albergues and hostels might not be included in online hotel listing sites.

As might be expected, prices are generally higher in larger cities and in resort towns along the Bay of Biscay. (And if you are staying in Madrid or Barcelona, either before or after the hiking portion of your trip, expect to pay even more.)

There are advantages and disadvantages to each level of accommodation. Those walking the entire Camino del Norte might be traveling four to six weeks or more and so they might look for more affordable accommodations than they might chose when on a one-week vacation elsewhere. Pilgrim albergues (hostels) rather than more expensive hostals and hotels save considerable expense on a lengthy walk.

However, dormitory-style/albergues rooms are usually more crowded, noisy, and less private than private rooms. On the other hand, there is often more of a sense of community or camaraderie in the hostels. Another factor is supply and demand—the Norte route has fewer places to stay than the Camino Francés, and even fewer are pilgrim-only.

There are not only noticeable differences between the following categories such as Basic and Extravagant, there are also often noticeable differences within each category. We have stayed in basic accommodations that were quite charming. That said, we have also stayed in ones with sheets that were too narrow for the bed, lights too dim to read by, and no heaters.

Basic accommodations include *habitaciones* (rooms) or *camas* (beds). These could be above a bar or room in a private home. In this category is also *pensión*, an official term with 1-2 stars given. Look for the "P" marking. Usually these are simple rooms, often well-worn, with perhaps bathroom down the hall. We have yet to stay in a *fonda* (F), but understand that they sometimes have a dining room onsite. The *casas de huéspedes* (CH) is a guest house, and that could mean anything from room in a private home to a separate facility. Though there are some *hostels* or *albergues juveniles* (youth hostels *albergues juveniles*) in Spain, there are few along the Camino routes. To use them, you'll also need a *hihostels.com* membership card, which you can usually buy at the hostels. Some will have dormitory rooms (either same sex or co-ed); some offer private rooms.

Basic accommodations for pilgrims also include *albergues.* These popular municipal or private facilities can range from private to dormitory-style rooms. The number of beds varies as does whether the sleeping rooms, showers, and bathrooms are single sex or co-ed. Sometimes you will find *monasteries* with pilgrim accommodations: These sometimes allow pilgrims to drop in and ask, but generally it is better to call or otherwise contact them ahead of time.

Included in the *Mid- and Higher levels* are *hostales* (Hs) and *hostal-residencias* (HsR Hostals). These are not the same as hostels. They are probably the most prevalent kind of accommodation along the Norte, and are what we most often chose. They're budget hotels, usually with private bathrooms, but sometimes offer less expensive rooms with shared bathrooms. The rooms generally are clean and comfortable, but not plush. Service is often very good and friendly.

Hotels (H), usually display a number of stars as determined by the government. They may or may not be a nicer than a hostal, but the price will usually be higher. Room-size, tub or shower, elevator (or not), and staffing help determine the number of stars, rather than how beautiful the room is. Like the AAA guidebooks and ratings in the U.S. the Spanish governments star-rating can indicate such things as whether or not there is staff on duty twenty-four hours a day, elevators, English-language TV channel, and fancier breakfast buffet. Reportedly, the Galician Council of Tourism has come up with a new system of rating hotels. The new ratings will be tourist hostel, of first or second category, instead of the current star rating of one, two and three stars.

In larger cities, you may find a room in chain hotels such as NH Hoteles, Accor, Sol Meliá. Prices are usually fairly reasonable. The décor of the chains' rooms tends to be contemporary and cookie-cutter style.

Because much of the Norte is along the Bay of Biscay with its dozens of beaches, there are also many resort areas. In many places you can find not only condos and apartments but also *Villas, Bed & Breakfasts,* and *Inns.* Some may include kitchens and sitting rooms. These could be listed on booking sides including *Airbnb.com.*

When the trail is more inland, rather than along the coast, one can occasionally find farm stays at an *Agriturismo.* This is not a dude ranch where visitors work as part of the deal; it means the owners still work the farm, but also may provide quite luxurious rooms for guests. Note: Regional terms for hotels, homes, farmhouses and so forth in the North include *pazos* (castles) in Galicia and other parts of Spain.

For the upscale stay in Galicia, you may find a new classification of hotels that can be applied to hotels, apartment hotels, spa hotels, and motels that have spas. The term *thalasso hotel* is applied to those hotels using natural sea water. In top of the line five-star hotels, you can expect to find such luxuries as spas, pools, and notable restaurants. These pricey *luxury hotels* can be listed as deluxe or *gran* classe (GL).

Finally, do not rule out the *paradores;* there are more than ninety in the country. Paradores/paradors are four to five-star hotels, which are usually in scenic locations and boast some history. You could stay in a *castillo* or *pazo* (castle); *alcazár* (a former fortress), palace, monastery, *casona* (mansion), or other historic building. These buildings have been remodeled enough to accommodate travelers and can be quite elegant, but they might not earn a five-star rating because they lack an elevator. The rates can be relatively reasonable—in the same range as other four- or five-star hotels and are in the $125-$150 range. Some of the paradores have discounted prices on food or lodging.

In Santiago de Compostela, you may be able to stay in the luxurious Hostal dos Reis Católicos on the Praza do Obradoiro. It is in what began as the pilgrims' Royal Hospital under the direction of King Fernando and Queen Isabel after they completed their own pilgrimage across Spain in the late 1400s. Originally, pilgrims who showed their Compostela could stay for up to three days. Nowadays, the hotel still provides free meals for three days to ten pilgrims holding Compostelas.

Finding places to camp is a bit more problematical. Along the initial stages of the Camino del Norte, you may find areas where camping is available for vacationers—perhaps even a tent, caravan (mobile home), or bungalow for rent. If these are in tourist areas, there may be a swimming pool, restaurants, and stores. However, these are usually not low-cost pilgrim accommodations; they more often are in pricey tourist areas. If you are interested, you can check out *vayacamping.net* for information.

"Free camping" is not legal in Spain (though some people have mentioned that during busy times on the Camino, authorities *may* be more lax). You can't just set up a tent in urban areas, military installations, or on the beach. While in national parks, you can camp in designated areas, but the northern trails don't take you through the parks.

Ivar's Camino forum has some Q & A about camping along the northern routes. Most postings are several years old, but probably little has changed. Kanga, one of the moderators, wrote that she did not find many places open when she and her companion were on the Norte in May and June of 2016 (though she thought there might be more open later in the season). "We also found it not so easy to camp in the grounds of albergues. Many do not have gardens and a couple with gardens were unwilling or not allowed to have campers. We would have paid the same as for a bed."

During our many weeks on the trails, we saw only one instance of people camping. If you want to give camping a try, the best bet is to ask at an albergue if you can set up near their building, ask the local *turismo*, or ask landowners for permission. We think that "stealth camping" would be difficult to pull off.

Packing lists and Hints:

Pack light: It's often recommended that you should carry no more than 10% of your body weight—a good rule of thumb, but not an absolute. People who are very fit might be able to carry more (but should they?), those with physical limitations such as back or knee problems, as well children or older hikers might be better off carrying less than the standard amount. Winter travelers will need more warm clothing; spring travelers will need more raingear; summer hikers will need more water. If you spend a few months training for your Camino—gradually increasing your distance walked, level of difficulty, and weight carried—you will have a very good idea of how much weight works for you.

Setting aside the weight of food and clothing for the moment, traditionally, the big three items a backpacker on a long-distance trail carries are the pack itself, a sleeping bag, and a tent. For Camino hikers, the big three might be the pack, bedding, and electronic gear. Camino travelers can find suitable packs weighing two pounds or less, few carry a tent, and their sleeping equipment can be a lightweight sleep sheet or a one-pound sleep quilt or bag.

Which kind of shoes to wear is controversial and everyone's

feet are different, but in our opinion, hiking boots are unnecessary on most Camino routes. I wore hiking boots on our first
Camino, and had nothing but problems with them. Subsequently
we changed to trail runners because they are lighter weight, more
comfortable, and adequately supportive.

There's a saying, that a pound on your feet is equal to five on
your back. Not sure how one proves this, but experience testifies
to its accuracy. Neither of us has exceptionally strong ankles, yet
have never twisted them. I'm of the opinion that the more support
your ankles get, the less strong and flexible they become—but
research is divided on the issue. We wear non-waterproof trail
runners; occasionally we wear waterproof socks if it looks like
we will encounter heavy rain.

Everyone has his or her "must have" items that make little
sense to others—a leather bound journal for some, laptops and
other electronic gear for others, a SLR camera for me. There's
no rule against carrying items that are wants rather than needs,
just make give safety priority over frivolous.

Susan's Packing List:

Keep in mind that Ralph and I usually start or end our Camino trips in a major city such as Madrid, Paris, or Barcelona. I
like to dress up a bit more in cities, do my laundry almost every
day, and prefer my change of clothes to be less utilitarian than
my hiking clothes, and pack accordingly.

Money Matters:

Currency, credit cards, and other important documents: We bring
with us sufficient euros to pay initial cab/shuttle/bus fare to a
hotel, etc. and also carry a minimal amount of U.S. currency for
homeward-bound travel. We carry both a credit and debit card
(which can double as a charge card). These are chip enabled. When
on the Camino, we have been able to find a town with an ATM
machine about every two or three days. In my around-the-waist
money belt (worn hidden under clothes). I also carry passport,
medical card, and airline info.

Basics:

Backpack: An Osprey Tempest 40, which weighs about two

pounds. Loaded, I was carrying about 12 pounds (including water) because I brought a single-lens reflex (SLR) and paperback books. Ralph currently carries a ZPacks Arc Blast 60L

Bedding: A ZPacks, down-filled, sleeping bag, which weighs about one pound. We know that many people on the Camino Francés don't bring sleeping bags, but we noticed that most people on the Primitivo did. Most albergues have blankets, so one might consider sleeping bags as optional. However, with increasing concerns about overcrowding in the albergues and about bedbugs, we prefer to bring this extra layer of insurance.

Hiking poles: We consider hiking poles essential. Others may consider them optional, but they are helpful on climbs, ease wear and tear on joints when going downhill, increase stability on uneven terrain (especially flooded trails). As a bonus, they give your upper body some workout, and keep your fingers from swelling. We are very pleased with our Black Diamond Carbon Z models because they fold, are very lightweight and strong. (We carry them in checked luggage in order to reduce problems at the airport. This is not a foolproof method (because luggage can get lost), but seems most likely for success.)

Umbrella: Though we have waterproof raingear, we find it's much more pleasant to walk in the rain if water is not pouring on our heads and down our faces. If it's only drizzling, we often find that using our umbrellas can alleviate the necessity of changing into raingear. Umbrellas also shield you from the sun and buffer the wind. To us, an umbrella is well worth the seven or eight ounces.

There are several models with our preferred silver-colored fabric: they often seem to be out of stock, but look for Gossamer Gear's Liteflex Hiking (Chrome) Umbrella, Campmor's euro-SCHIRM Swing Liteflex Trekking Umbrella, and the Chrome umbrella from My Trail CO. We recently found the Wing Trek Umbrellas' Liteflex Trekking Umbrella on Amazon and we liked the ribbed handle, which made holding onto it easier.

We attach the umbrella to our pack so our hands are free, using the technique suggested in ***sectionhiker.com/how-to-attach-trekking-umbrella-to-a-backpack***

Clothing:

I often make minor modifications to my list depending on the expected weather and my mood, but these are the basics. I chose one neutral color like navy blue, khaki, or tan and build around it. A neck scarves can add flair if desired. Clothes should perspiration away from your body so that you don't get chilled. Choose synthetic fibers or wool; avoid cotton because it's heavy and takes too long to dry.

Skirt: I usually carry a skirt of some kind--either a hiking one, or a lightweight one of knee-length or longer. I've noticed that women in rural areas tend to dress more conservatively than those in the large cities. To some, skirts fall in the optional category, but I've found having one is a welcome change when going to dinner in the evening, and during the day provide some degree of modesty when trying to pee behind the shrubbery. Some women carry a *pareo*, the Hawaii-style length of fabric that can be wrapped around the waist and used as a skirt, around the body as a sarong, or over the shoulders as a shawl.

Tee shirts and outer shirts: My favorite combination of tops for hiking is a long-sleeved shirt over a short-sleeved t-shirt.; I can easily take off the outer layer when it warms up. On cooler days, I wear a lightweight wool shirt because it doesn't stink like the synthetics, however, it does take longer to dry. Other people much prefer to wear a long-sleeved, synthetic hoodie, or similar, but I find this too hot.

Pants: Two pairs (of which one pair is optional), synthetic. Pair #1: Long with zip-off, or roll-up legs, Pair #2: Long, somewhat warmer, and more wind and water-resistant. (In the future, I may drop the second pair and keep with the hiking skirt option.)

Underwear: Panties (dark) three pair, Ex-officio. One pair to wear, one in the wash, one dry; bra; full-slip, black nylon. I sleep in this, and wear with my skirt.

Long underwear: Both top and bottoms. Black, Smartwool. The long-sleeved top can be an inner layer when it's cold, used as a lightweight sweater, or worn as a sleepshirt. Bottoms can also be used as an extra layer when hiking, or as sleepwear. Smartwool can be worn for days without washing and without getting stinky.

Rain gear: Jacket: Waterproof, breathable, with "pit" (underarm) zips. I'm back with a Goretex model and hoping it will remain waterproof over time. Rain pants: Waterproof. Full-length zippers are much easier to use because you can put the pants on and off without removing your shoes.

Cold-weather gear: Jacket: My 850-fill down model from L.L.Bean claims its "DownTek absorbs 33% less moisture and dries 66% faster than standard down." I haven't tested this, but I assume this means it is water-resistant, but not waterproof. Pants: fleece, black, nine-inch zipper at ankle for slipping on and off over shoes when necessary.

Hats: Two types: fleece and fabric. The fleece cap has a flap that can be pulled down to cover the neck and nose. My Sunday Afternoons hat has a large brim to offer protection from the sun.

Footwear: Trail runners: Both Ralph and I have now moved to Altra Lone Peak shoes. These are "zero drop" running shoes—meaning the heel is level with the front. Even better is that the toe-box has room for your toes to spread out naturally. Everyone's feet are different and what works for one person may or may not work for another. Whatever shoes you get, be sure you get them big enough. Feet generally swell on long-distance hikes and it is not unusual to have them get a half-size or more larger. I wear men's shoes because they have more room in the toe-box.

Second pair of shoes or sandals: Many people like to bring a pair of flip flops or similar for use in the shower room. I substitute a second pair of shoes that I can use for walking around town to find food and see the sights after the day's hike. My black, suede Mephisto sandals or my Noat flats work well (but they are comparatively heavy.

Socks: I think I have tried about every combination known to man or woman. Socks should be quick-drying synthetics or wool (no cotton). Three pairs usually means one pair on your feet, one clean pair, and one drying on a short line on your pack.

Currently both Ralph and I wear very light-weight socks or only sock liners. If it's cold, I switch to Injinji toe-socks and put the sock liners over them. The Injinjis keep the toes separated; the liner sock provides a second layer to prevent the abrasion that creates blisters.

Sundries:

Eyeglasses: Sunglasses and regular prescription glasses

Soap: Campsuds™ is a biodegradable, concentrated clothes washing liquid for those times when we run out of tiny containers of shampoo, conditioner, soap, and lotion from hostals where we have stayed. We wash some clothes every night.

Towel: A Packtowel™, but don't skimp too much on the size because it's not pleasant to get chilled in unheated shower rooms.

Bandanna: The one item that can be cotton! This essential item can be used for many purposes beyond covering your head or tying around your neck. Alternately it can be a washcloth, a hankie, a picnic placemat, pee-rag, and a bandage. It can also be used to hold a splint in place or to wrap a sprained ankle. For *pee stops*, women can carry a ziplock bag for their used t.p., wear a mini-pad to absorb drips, or use a pee-rag (hang it on the back of your pack to dry; wash it frequently). Another option is a urination device, which allows one to stand while peeing as does a skirt or specially-designed pants that have a zipper in the seam of the crotch.

Toiletries: Toothbrush, toothpaste (we found three of the .75 oz. tubes was a perfect amount for the two of us), floss, comb, prescriptions drugs, OTC meds such as Tums, Motrin, and Pep-to-Bismol. Sunscreen, anit-fungal cream, and lip-gloss. Optional: lipstick, cosmetics, lotions, and disposable razor. Toilet paper.

Melatonin can be helpful for jet lag. If traveling two or more hours, suggest 3-mg around the bedtime of your new destination. (So if you are traveling from California to Spain and want to go to bed at 11 p.m. take it at 11 p.m. their time.)

Bandages and tapes: Omnifix and Medipore. Blisters used to be a problem for me on the Caminos. It may have been the boots I wore, the trail surfaces, the heat, the many hours day after day. Whatever the cause, I was not alone. People were glad to share their remedies. From a French woman, we learned of a flexible tape that I began to use extensively years ago. I now often wrap Omnifix around the ball of my feet and Medipore (or similar) around some toes before problems arise. I highly recommend reading John Vonhof's *Fixing your Feet* to learn how to ward off foot problems. We also carry a few standard bandages.

Water containers: We generally use water hydration bladders and reuse a soda container for extra water. There is no need to add dozens of empty plastic bottles to the trash stream while walking across the country—bring a container or at least reuse your plastic bottles over and over.

We saw few fountains with potable water on the northern routes, but there was always plenty of water available at the places where we stopped for lunch or stayed overnight. We carry a few purification tablets with our emergency supplies.

Swiss Army knife: Ralph carries one with a couple of blades, a corkscrew, nail file, toothpick, tweezers, and several other tiny tools. I carry a smaller version. At this time, such items should be carried in *checked* luggage or purchased in Spain.

Flashlight: We use headlamps. When in albergues, it's important to restrict your lamp's light to your immediate area. Your fellow bunkmates might object to your lighting up the whole room while you read your dime-store novel. A mini LED light is light and can be clipped to your pack.

Electronics: An area continuing to evolve—and by some considered optional. For me, it has been a help to have the electronic gear. I carry an android smart phone for sending most emails, but more often use Ralph's iPad mini because it makes keeping my journal easier.

Maps and guidebooks: Ralph carries paper maps and guidebooks, as electronics can fail, but finds both the iPad mini and android smart phone useful. Keeping your phone/device in airplane mode greatly extends battery life. We used the *Northern Caminos* guidebook, the Wise Pilgrim apps for Norte and Primitivo, *maps.me* app and *gronze.com* website. The Wise apps and Gronze both have route elevation profiles.

Maps.me is a very useful app. With that app, you preload the maps for any area when you have Wi-Fi, and then you can use them in airplane mode. You can load kmz/kml routes as bookmarks and they appear as overlays on the maps you've loaded. To download the routes you want see *santiago.nl/smartphone-on-the-camino.*

(more info under *Guidebook and other resources* (pg 289)
More Optional, but nice:

Books: Leisure reading. Make them expendable so you can tear off pages as you go or leave them behind at some albergue for another traveler to enjoy.

Notebook paper and pen: for journal writing.

Camera: I currently use a SLR Canon with zoom lens and we both carry smartphones.

SELDOM DO WE lack anything we need and by washing clothes each night, we are fairly presentable. If for some reason clothing doesn't dry by morning, we always have a back-up. When I get tired of wearing the same clothes day after day, I look for a new neckscarf or shirt.

BEFORE YOU LEAVE home:

Though at first glance, this section—with its comprehensive lists of how to get ready, and how to get your home ready for an extended trip—may seem overwhelming, in actuality you probably do most of these things intuitively. However, we have found that no matter how many times we have traveled, without a checklist it's quite easy to overlook some small matter that would've been much more easily handled at an earlier stage. Breaking the list into tasks requiring smaller chunks of time will make it much easier to fit your preparations into your normal routine in the few weeks preceding your trip.

Obviously, everyone taking a Camino trip will need not to consider all items. For example, if you have a house-sitter, you will not need to set the timers and alarms nor move the indoor plants to one location. Do the chores a bit at a time, and let your trip be one with smooth sailing.

As SOON AS you decide on your itinerary:

Purchase airline, ship, or other transportation tickets (inquire if you will be able to get at least a partial refund if the tickets go on sale after they are initially ordered). Note that, unfortunately, airline fares for stays of thirty days and longer usually cost more than shorter visits and that sale prices seldom apply.

Arrange travel and medical insurance, if needed. Your first step in considering travel or medical insurance will be determining how much risk you will be facing financially and physically on your trip. Consider these scenarios: Money lost if your entry hotel or other place of lodging goes out of business. Cost and inconvenience if your backpack is lost, damaged, or stolen. Cost of transportation to medical facilities and subsequent hospital care. Monetary penalties for postponing or canceling your transportation costs to and from your destination, and costs incurred if your airline flight is delayed or you miss a connecting flight. Extra food and lodging if travel is delayed.

Even though in past years I have traveled blissfully unaware of the risks I was taking by not having insurance, I'm somewhat older and wiser now. I've found that for some trips, travel or medical insurance may be worthwhile. Airlines and other service providers are less likely to refund your money than they once were.

But, before you rush out to buy a new policy, check what coverage you already have. For example, your homeowners' insurance policy may cover your clothing and luggage, though probably not your smartphone, camera or money. Check what coverage your VISA/MasterCard/American Express offers. Some cards offer long-term coverage on past purchases. Supplement your existing coverage with trip cancellation insurance (TCI) unless you determine you want to self-insure.

Determine what medical coverage you already have while traveling. Carry your health plan card; some plans require notification before you depart. Even if your policy is in effect outside your coverage area or outside of the country, you may be required to pay medical costs when service is provided and submit a claim to your carrier for your reimbursement later on.

If you do decide to order trip cancellation insurance, order your insurance promptly after ordering your plane tickets. Many plans will not cover pre-existing medical conditions after your initial enrollment. Some popular websites offering comparisons of TCI include: *squaremouth.com, travelinsure.com, and insure-mytrip.com*

Start a training program if you haven't already got one in place.

UP TO THREE months in advance

Book accommodations for lodging. We like to know where we will stay the first night and the last night; others may want more extensive arrangements. Request confirmation numbers, or at least note with whom and when, you made reservations. Note that on the Camino itself, you are not allowed to make reservations in pilgrim albergues—it's first come, first served (though there is discussion that this may change).

Sign up for a conversational Spanish class, or study on your own with books, CDs, tapes, apps such as Duolingo, or TV programs. Spanish-language *telenovelas* ((soap operas) use fairly predictable dialog.

Order or download guidebooks.

Order or renew passport if required (valid for six months minimum).

Check with your health-care provider regarding updating immunizations. Since you will be hiking through farming areas on the Camino, check that your tetanus vaccination was within the last ten years. Those over 50 years of age are the group *least* likely to have up-to-date tetanus immunizations, putting themselves at unnecessary risk.

Make necessary doctor and dental appointments.

Plan house-sitting or pet care if needed.

Video house contents for insurance purposes and store elsewhere (i.e. in the cloud)

Consider yard maintenance. In our case, we elected to install a drip-irrigation system to simplify watering.

If you are planning to buy a new camera, begin your research.

Revisit your insurance requirements; update your will.

Stay organized: create a file folder and keep all correspondence and trip notes in one place (including this checklist).

Decide on backpack.

Purchase footwear. Whether you are taking trail runners (our preference) or boots, try them on with the type of socks that you will wear on your trip. Your feet will swell, so buy shoes at least a half-size larger than your usual. Allow time to break in boots.

Convert credit and debit cards to chip enabled, if appropriate.

Join Ivar's Camino forum to get familiar with many aspects of the trip and get advice. Join American Pilgrims on the Camino. Sometimes you can read messages from people who are on the trip and learn about current weather conditions, refugio conditions, etc.

One month in advance

Inventory your clothing list and make necessary purchases.

Locate money belt.

Enlist trusted neighbor or house-sitting service to keep an eye on your place—to pick up the mail, to call the newspaper if they forget to stop the paper, to put the trash barrels back in place as needed, etc.

Determine watering system for *indoor* plants. Put them together in a protected spot outdoors? Buy self-watering containers? Give them away? Ask a friend or neighbor to care for them at their place, or yours? Have a house sitter take care of them?)

Pack your backpack and weigh it. With a quart of water, it shouldn't exceed fifteen pounds. If you are doing training hikes (recommended!), make some of those hikes with your pack.

Two weeks in advance

Arrange pet care, whether dog-walking services, pet boarding, or a visiting pet-sitter.

Prepay utility and other regular bills (double up) that are not on-line payments.

Leave a couple of pre-signed checks with a *trusted* person to send off to pay any bills that you may have overlooked.

Set up newspaper vacation hold/stop. If you request, some newspapers will deliver to public schools during your absence.

Contact post office to have them hold mail, or arrange for a trusted person to pick-up it up.

Obtain euros sufficient to pay for taxis and a middle of the night arrival. As with many foreign countries, Spain offers limited access to banks on weekends, but ATM machines are widely available. Most ATM machines accept a *maximum* of four characters, and the keys only have numbers. If you normally remember your PIN number by letters, be sure you learn the corresponding numbers on the keys.

Update family's /friends' email and phone numbers.

Make two copies of your passport, itinerary (hotel numbers), traveler's checks, credit cards (front and back so you'll have a contact number if needed). Leave one copy at home with a trusted person and carry one copy separate from your money and cards for your protection in case of loss or theft.

Put jewelry and valuables you are leaving behind in a bank safety-deposit box.

Refill needed prescriptions (best to carry in original, labeled containers).

List medical information—doctor's and dentist's phone numbers, prescriptions of drugs and eyeglasses, lists of allergies or medical conditions.

One week in advance

Purchase memory cards.

Inventory and fill any needed over-the-counter (OTC) medications—Lomotil, ibuprofen, and so forth.

Purchase sunscreen, toiletries, cosmetics, etc.

Consider sleep mask and neck pillow for airline travel

Obtain earplugs for use in crowded refugios.

Get needed supply of pet food if pets will be staying home (or leave money for your pet sitter).

Update your security system. Give a trusted neighbor a copy of your itinerary and contact numbers. If you have a security service, be sure they have up-to-date emergency numbers. Tell them your departure and return dates if warranted. Some communities suggest notifying the local police of your absence.

Arrange transportation to airport or other departure point.

Within last week

Confirm flights.

Gather documents of travel: passport (and a copy carried in a separate place—could be your travel partner); record of immunizations as required, travel tickets, hotel confirmations.

Check yard and indoor watering systems.

Check your refrigerator. Use or dump food that will be too old by the time you return. Fill liter soda bottles with water and place in freezer to keep food frozen in case of a short-term brownout.

Clean perishables (onions, potatoes, fruit) out of the pantry.

Disconnect TV and VCR and other appliances that consume electricity in the "ready-on" mode.

Set indoor and outdoor lights for self-timing.

Wash clothes.

Remove any wet laundry from the washer or hamper.

Lock windows and doors and shut skylights.

Set radio, or similar, to play at determined times.

Set alarms.

Take a photo of luggage contents for insurance purposes. We always *carry-on* our fully-packed backpacks, but we *check* a lightweight duffel bag that contains our hiking poles, umbrellas, and Swiss Army knives. In general this has worked well, *but* we learned a lesson when our duffel bag was lost on our flight to Bilbao—take a photo of the contents of your luggage before packing. When we filed our claim, we forgot to list some items and had to file a revised claim. We were reimbursed for all losses, but the process would have been smoother if we'd had a photo to jog our memories.

Pack!

Transporting Baggage and People

There are several options for those who arrive in Spain with extra luggage. Sometimes you may want to bring things with you to Europe that won't be needed on the Camino. Let's say you want to travel to Paris to see the museums or you want to end your time in Madrid dancing in the discotheques—how do you pack those extra clothing items?

Sending extra items home before or after your walk is a very expensive option. The least expensive way to send items back to the U.S., or anywhere outside of Europe, is by surface mail rather than air mail, but the packages will be transported by ship and take one to three months to reach the destination.

Stay in the same hotel coming and going to Europe. Often hotels will store your extra piece of luggage until your return, and at no charge (but check beforehand).

Mail things ahead. If while walking the Camino de Santiago you find you have packed some items that you aren't using, the *Correos* (Spanish postal system) offers a handy and relatively inexpensive solution. *"Lista de Correos."* At the Correos, ask for the *paquete peregrino* (pilgrim package) to get the discounted rate. Packaging is also available for reasonable prices there.

For example, this is how you should address your package if the destination was Santiago de Compostela:

(Your name)
Lista de Correos
15780 Santiago de Compostela   (postal code, then city)
A Coruña   (province}

When you arrive at the destination, you would go to the post office, with your passport, to pick up the package. The length of time that it would be held was given as fifteen calendar days in December 2016, but this can change from time to time. After the hold period ends, the post office sends the parcel back to the office of origin, so make sure you get to your destination in time.

In December 2016, Correos announced many new services to Camino pilgrims—including package service, backpack transport, and issuing the pilgrim passport.

Alternately, you can use the service of Ivar Rekve (Camino forum) to ship items to Santiago. This is how to address your package to Ivar.

Ivar Rekve
For: Your last name, first name (this is you)
Travesía da Universidade, 1 (street name, house number)
15704, Santiago de Compostela (postal code, then city)
A Coruña (province)

Ivar allows you to store your things for up to sixty days and at a very reasonable fee. *caminodesantiago.me/ luggage-storage-in-santiago-de-compostela*

Carry the extra stuff, but carry it in a lightweight duffel bag, rather than a suitcase. If you need an inexpensive bag in Europe, you can probably find one at a Chinese/Chino store.

Hire a service to transport your backpack from place to place. Increasingly on the Camino Francés, people are sending their gear ahead. It is not as widespread a practice on the Northern routes, but it's an option.

Typically these services cost about around seven or eight euros to pick up a pack at one place and deliver it to the next. If you have additional packs, you may be able to get a reduced rate on them. There are usually distance limits: twenty-five kilometers or less is typical.

Generally you will make these arrangements with private albergues or hotels, because you cannot reserve beds in pilgrim albergues and because they usually don't open until mid-afternoon your luggage would not be secured. If you do decide to use a luggage transfer service, you can ask the receptionist at the hotel where you have been staying to contact the service you want to use (or they suggest). You will fill out a form and leave the fee for the service to pick up and deliver your luggage.

Keep in mind that besides the restrictions of weight, distance, and which lodgings you can use, there are other considerations—namely that you have to walk or otherwise get yourself to the place where your baggage has been sent.

These services have been used by thousands of people and there seldom are problems, but even so there are some things you need to keep with you. Write down the name of the service and your destination, and keep important documents (such as passports, cash, and airline tickets) with you. You should also keep some snacks, water, maybe sunscreen, and any additional clothing that you might need during the day (such as raingear).

Not all of these services operate year round. They generally offer transport to pilgrims from Easter until late October. This period may be extended in special cases and as the number of pilgrims increases, services will expand.

To send luggage ahead a short distance where none of the services operate or when none are available when you need them, you can probably find a cab that will transport luggage and/or you. Ask at your hostel, a tourist office, the local bar, or restaurant for recommendations.

Companies that transport backpacks or other luggage along the Norte:

Hike-Tech can arrange your bag transfers for part of, or all of, your stages all along the route. They book the independent contractors for you for a fee. *hike-tech.com*

Le Petit Bag has a compilation of drivers (with different email addresses and phone numbers) who transport baggage from stage to stage along the north coast. *greencartrans.webcindario.com/* or email: *g.car.trans@gmail.com.*

The Peregrine Express transports luggage along specific sections of the Norte—primarily Irún to Santander, but for a larger group, Irún to Oviedo. *caminodesantiago.me/community/threads/ the-peregrine-express-luggage-transfer-Irún-to-santander.10057/*

Jacotrans on the Norte has a service called *Sherpaontheway. com* to take your bags from Ribadeo to Santiago de Compostela.

Companies that transport backpacks or other luggage along the Primitivo:

Jacotrans on the Primitivo uses *Sherpaontheway* to transport luggage along the stages between Oviedo and Santiago.

Taxicamino.com offers service from the Asturias airport and also transports luggage and backpacks.

Companies that transport people along the Camino del Norte or the Primitivo:

When you look into personal transportation, a few names will most commonly pop up: *Lurraldebus.eus/eu*; *ALSA.com* (bus company); and *RENFE.com* and *Euskotren* train (Cercanías is the commuter train) (*euskotren.eus*).

Castilian maintains an excellent site that gives public transit (other than taxis) info in greater detail. *caminodesantiago.me/ community/resources/camino-del-norte-public-transportation.516/*

Rome2Rio.com is a great help in finding your options.

Transport of luggage or people on the Camino Francés:
Once you join the Camino Francés at Arzúa, you can utilize these additional services:

Jacotrans covers the entire Camino Francés (except late fall-spring). Luggage and passenger transport, bike rentals, mailing assistance, equipment rentals, and more. *jacotrans.com*

Express Bouricott has a menu of services from transporting passengers to transferring luggage. Based in France, they will take luggage over the Pyrenees from St. Jean-Pied-de-Port, France to Roncesvalles, Spain. They also carry passengers from Biarritz Airport, Biarritz train station, and Bayonne train station. They attempt to arrange carpools for their clients to reduce costs. *expressbourricot.com*

TaxiBelorado.com will transport individuals, groups and/or luggage between all towns on the Camino Francés starting at Roncesvalles and ending at Santiago de Compostela.

Associated with Taxi Belorado is *Caminofácil.net*—luggage and backpack transport only.

BICYCLES ON THE Northern Routes

There are definitely bicycles on the Northern Caminos, though not as many percentage-wise as on the Camino Francés. If you consider that in 2016, only 8.6% of those who applied for their Compostela in Santiago stated that they had completed their pilgrimage on bicycle—and that most of those were on the Francés—it is clear that the percentage on the northern routes is quite small.

However, there are some excellent websites for bicyclists and a supportive community of riders. The company, Camino de Santiago en bicicleta, *bicigrino.com/en* has a great deal of useful information about the routes, packing, accommodations receptive to bicyclists, and more.

Other information is available on Facebook with the group Cycling - American Pilgrims on the Camino and on Ivar's Camino forum. Other rental companies include: *cycling-rentals.com* and *BikeIberia.com*. These not only have bikes to rent, but also will deliver them and pick them up at different locations.

Bringing your own bicycle for the Camino is possible, but according to most reports, an expensive and challenging proposition.

A new service, called *Paq Bicicleta,* is a way to transport your bike with the *Correos* (post office). This service is from 42,37 € (VAT, packaging and insurance of 300 € included). Correos takes your bike to the point where you start the Camino de Santiago and sends it back from Santiago, Fisterra/Finisterre or any other point where you end it. Delivery time: from 48 to 72 hours.

The Norte route is doable. Those who want to make the miles stick to paved highways, but it is also possible to take the same pathways as the walkers (but not infrequently returning to paved highway). Either way, it pays to be an experienced bicyclist.

Kiwi Suz reported on Ivar's Camino forum when she and her companion returned from their bike trip from Santander to Santiago in August 2016. *caminodesantiago.me/community/threads/del-norte-in-high-season-2016-we-biked.44078/* They took nineteen days and averaged thirty km. a day, mainly on the Camino hiking trails. She commented that those who were doing fifty km. a day stuck to the roadways. Staying on the Camino requires frequent getting off the bike and walking, but it also allows you to take in your surroundings and talk to other pilgrims.

The Primitivo is much more challenging. It can be done, but it's extremely difficult as one of the Bicigrono's owners, Tomas Sanchez says, "When I did it in 2010, I could see firsthand its stunning beauty, but also its extreme hardness." His advice should not be taken lightly. The rocky and muddy trails in the mountains on a bicycle, especially with saddlebags, make for a grueling expedition.

It's All about the Food; Tipping

"Blessings on him who invented…food that satisfies hunger, the drink that slakes thirst…" Cervantes in *Don Quixote*

The food in the Basque regions of the Norte (and Primitivo if you start in Irún) is exceptionally good. This is the land of pintxos and tapas. The restaurant Mugaritz, in Errenteria (near San Sebastián), ranked #7 on the 2016 World's 50 Best Restaurants list, and the Asador Etxebarri, in Axpe, Spain (halfway between San Sebastián and Bilbao) ranked #10. The two might not fit a pilgrim's budget at €185 (USD: $240) and €135 (USD $175) respectively, but it gives an indication of the world-class cuisine that can be found in the region. There are four additional Spanish restaurants in the top fifty.

Along the Norte's coastline there are many fishing villages and cities where seafood and fresh fish will be found on the menus. On the Primitivo, because it travels inland and through a lot of farmland, you will more often find meat and potatoes (the ever-present fritos/French fries) similar to what you find on the Camino Francés. As might be expected, the larger cities have more extensive menus.

Servings often are huge. If you find that you are getting far more food than you want, you can ask to share it with a companion—but do not take it for granted that your request will be accepted. Some people do not realize that you can usually order two starters (appetizers) instead of the usual order of one starter and one entrée on the Pilgrim Menu or the Menu of the Day. Again, ask if you are not certain.

Many places, especially in big cities, serve bread without your asking for it and then charge for it. If it makes a difference to you, ask if it is *gratis* or not. (In Spanish, *gratis* means free of charge; *libre* means available.)

Some definitions

General:

Ayuntamiento = Town hall. Sometimes there is no Turismo for information and the town hall can provide information on where to stay or where to find a computer to use.

Barrio = neighborhood/parish

Tienda = shop or small market/grocery

Food related

Tapa = small plate. Tapas are small amounts of food. They can be anything from a bit of cheese to a layered stack of foods such as chopped hard-boiled egg, shrimp, and olives. In places such as Madrid or Granada, tapas may be complimentary with a glass of wine. In other cities, there may be a charge, but generally the quality and innovation are superior.

Pintxo (peen-cho) = Pintxo is the Basque word for tapa. In general, pintxos in Basque country are more elaborate than tapas. Think of a snack of goat cheese and caramelized onions on a round of crusty rustic bread with a skewer through the entire thing and you have the picture.

Racion = shared plate. Raciónes are simply larger amounts of tapas served on a plate. Dishes are often served family style and raciónes, are often shared. As in the U.S. when ordering Chinese and other Asian plates to share, the general practice in Spain is to order one plate of raciónes per person.

Menu del dia = The daily lunch, the Menu of the day, is often a delight and usually a bargain. You will find several choices for your first plate, second plate, and dessert. All this is usually accompanied by a bottle or carafe of wine or water and bread. Typical cost is typically ten to twelve euros.

Cana = a serving of draft beer, usually about 200 ml (almost seven ounces).

Cuenta (pronounced "kwen-tuh") = "La cuenta, por favor." "The check, please." You have to ask for it!

Postre = Dessert may be a piece of fruit, a dish of flan, a slice of chocolate cake, or a pre-packaged ice cream treat of some sort. Order *Casero* (homemade) when possible.

En su punto, poco hecho, muy hecho = Rare, med-rare, or well-done steak

Vaso de agua de grifo = glass of tap water. If you simply ask for *agua*, you will almost always get bottled water. If ordering or buying bottled water, you can get it either *con gas* (carbonated) or *sin gas* (still water). Tap water is perfectly fine to drink. We didn't try any public fountains on these routes because we always had plenty of water from where we had stayed, but I would not have worried about using them (unless, of course, they were posted as non-potable).

Cortado = A cortado coffee is a shot of espresso "cut" with a splash of steamed milk and topped with a spoonful of milk foam.

Tipping in Spain is not as widespread, or at as high a percentage, as it is in the U.S., but it seems to be catching on. Many are of the opinion that Americans are spoiling things by leaving 20% and higher tips. Looking through comments by travel agents, writers and others online, I found a wide variety of opinions on whether to tip or not. If you are comfortable doing so, ask or watch what other patrons do and follow the local customs. On, you might find the following suggestions helpful:

In bars and similar places: Leave the small change that you get from your bill (or round up the amount charged.) For example, if your bill comes to 4.75 euros, leave 5. In fine restaurants tip around 10 percent. Note: It is preferable to tip in euros, and in cash rather than on your credit card because otherwise the server may not get it. If service was unsatisfactory, it is not expected to tip.

In hotels the amount of a tip may vary. Suggested is 1-5 euros per day for the cleaning staff. If you will be in a place for more than one day, it is wise to tip well and at the start. For taxi drivers, round up the fare.

Tipping in France:

At restaurants: Oftentimes a tip has already been included in your bill at a restaurant. The words *service compris* mean the tip is already included, but you can add up to 10% for special service. In bars, tipping is not expected. At hotels, tip one to two euros per night for housekeeping. For taxi drivers, tip 10–15%

Guidebooks and other Sources of Info:

Apps (download from your device's App store):
Bookings.com Used extensively for reservations
Maps.me Used extensively for route finding
WisePilgrim Norte
Wise Pilgrim Primitivo
Books:
The Confraternity of Saint James has guidebooks to many Camino routes including the Norte and Primitivo. Also some free PDF updates. The Confraternity is a UK-based charity that promotes the pilgrimage to Santiago de Compostela. *csj.org.uk/*

Perassoli, Laura and Whitson, Dave. *The Northern Caminos: The Norte, Primitivo, and Ingles routes.* Cicerone, 2015. Our main guide book. *cicerone.co.uk* Whitson frequently posts updates to the route and the accommodations (see below under Internet)

Picaud, Aymeric. *Codex Calixtinus*. A translation of the document to English is available here: *Sites.google.com/site/caminodesantiagoproject/home*

Wise Pilgrim, *Camine Del Norte* Used the app frequently, book was published after our hikes. Primitivo book is due out in 2018. *www.wisepilgrim.com/*

Internet:

Americanpilgrims.org American Pilgrims on the Camino (APOC). Support and information for those interested in the Camino. You can order a Pilgrim Passport, free of charge, but donations are always appreciated.

Asturnatura.com has photos and brief descriptions of sites of historic, archaeological, scientific, or cultural interest primarily in Asturias but also other places on the Iberian peninsula.

Backpack45.com/norte-primitivo.html Our website has a wealth of current information on the Norte and Primitivo.

Santiago-compostela.net Site owned by Alex Simon.

Gronze.com has information on many Camino routes including stages, distances, route elevation profiles, and accommodations on the North Way and the Primitive Way. We used this frequently.

Mundicamino.com A valuable site for finding accommodations on the Camino routes. They also have information on luggage transfer and much more.

Northerncaminos.com/updates.html Homepage of Cicerone's The Northern Caminos guidebook, by Dave Whitson and Laura Perazzoli. (See previous listing under Books.) Updates to the book, changes to the Northern routes, and lists of accommodations.

Tourism.euskadi.net/x65-19143/en/ Northern Routes to Santiago. Free online and downloadable guides in English to the Northern Routes including Caminos Norte and Primitivo and more. Published by the governments of Basque Country, Cantabria, Asturias, Galicia, Navarre, and La Rioja. Descriptions of the routes, section maps, distances between towns, elevation profiles, but not accommodations.

Pilgrim Routes to Santiago de Compostela in Northern Spain. Homepage of Eric Walker, Confraternity member and six-time

Santiago pilgrim. Author of several guide books available through the Confraternity of Saint James. Walker's website includes some basic information about the pilgrimage, practical advice for those contemplating walking the coastal route, and detailed descriptions of all branches of these less frequented routes to Santiago. *camino-norte.co.uk/pages/pilgrimwalks.htm*

Santiago.nl/smartphone-on-the-camino This site is an excellent source for the kml/gpx routes that you need for maps.me and similar apps.

Turismo.gal/ The Xunta de Galicia's site has articles about the history, albergues, and other services of the Caminos. Some are limited to info about the Galician portion of the trail, but not all. Sometimes the translations to English are a bit perplexing, "The last stages of this road ran for more giggly lands for Baamonde and Guitiriz."

Norte only:

Northerncaminos.com/accommodations.html Whitson, Dave. Guidebook author Dave Whitson provides links to accommodations on the Norte.

Turismo.euskadi.eus/es/rutas/el-camino-de-santiago-por-la-costa/aa30-12379/es/ Euskadi: Basque Country. Also check out *turismo.euskadi.eus/es/* for a wealth of information on the Basque country including extensive information on the Camino del Norte in their region.

Primitivo only:

Northerncaminos.com/2/category/camino%20primitivo/1.html Guidebook author Dave Whitson provides up-to-date links to accommodations along the Primitivo

Lizb82657.wordpress.com/2015/08/02/my-updated-guide-to-the-camino-primitivo-and-the-camino-muxiafisterra-august-1-2015/ Camino Primitivo to Santiago and then to Muxia & Finisterre Guide. Liz Brandt. Start with the link and then download the PDF. Thorough guide lists albergues and other accommodations including phone numbers. Site shows places of interest, maps, distances, and profiles. Liz and her husband Tom walked the Primitivo in 2015.

Sanfroilan.info/ Fiestas de San Froilán de Lugo. The biggest

festival in Lugo is held early every October. Festa de Interese
Turistico Galego. Municipal de Turisimo on Praza do Campo,
11 Tel. 982 251 658

*pilgrimagetraveler.com/camino-primitivo.html Pilgrimage
Traveler.* Elle Bieling's blog includes topics such as a pilgrim's
purpose and spiritual journey. Practical information about the
Camino Primitivo, Ingles, and Finisterre.

The Camino forums:

*Facebook.com/groups/AmericanPilgrims/ American Pilgrims on
the Camino* on Facebook, as are various local chapters, including
ours, Peregrinos - Northern California. *facebook.com/groups/
Peregrinos.Northern.California/*

Caminodesantiago.me/community Camino de Santiago forum
Ivar owns the most widely used forum site, where you can get
opinions on anything from blister care to where to find the best
flights.

*Norte route forum: caminodesantiago.me/community/forums/
el-camino-del-norte.21/*

*Primitivo route forum: caminodesantiago.me/community/
forums/the-camino-primitivo.34/*

Video links:

Our roads to Santiago A Camino video series by the Spanish
television channel TVE. North Road, part 1: *rtve.es/alacarta/vid-
eos/nuestros-caminos-a-santiago/nuestros-caminos-santiago-cami-
no-del-norte-1/681576/.* North Road, part 2: *rtve.es/alacarta/videos/
nuestros-caminos-a-santiago/nuestros-caminos-santiago/687263/*

Where Is Asturias? vimeo.com/whereisasturias (Spanish speak-
ing) has almost 100 vimeos on the region focusing on history.
Two of particular interest: The Coastal Route in Asturias and
Asturias: The Original Way of Saint James, El Camino Primitivo
vimeo.com/53604076 and Asturias: The Way of Santiago on the
North, The Way of the Coast. *vimeo.com/88175826*

EMERGENCY NUMBERS

112 - Emergency number in Europe. They will answer very
quickly even if there is no credit on your phone. Explain slowly
and clearly that you need to speak to an operator in English if

that is the case. Emergencies: *Socorro* (help) or *accidente* (accident).

061 (or 112) – Health Emergencies. *Urgencias*. Or visit the emergency department of any hospital. On the phone, you would say, *"Necesito una ambulancia."*

062 – The Guardia Civil. A military force that operates mostly in rural areas and is responsible for dealing with drug offenses, fatal car accidents, robberies and murders.

091 – National Police

092 – Local Police

080 – (or 112) – Fire Department

010 – Local information

+34 902 102 112 – Servicio de Atención al Turista Extranjero (SATE) handles security of foreigners. Tourist helpline and emergency number (in English, French, German and Italian). For victims of crimes who wish to make a police report, but don't speak Spanish. Operates from 8 a.m. to 12 a.m. daily. Report crimes, lost property/documents, damage, assault, robbery, break-in or an accident to a tourist police. After calling, you will typically have 48 hours to visit your local police station to ratify your complaint.

+34 915 872 200 (or online: *madrid.usembassy.gov/*– Advice and assistance from your Embassy

900 580 888 – Support for women: 24-hour helpline. Domestic violence and abuse (Mujeres Maltratadas) **900 100 009**

Acknowledgments

Thanks to friends and family: Helena Bernardo, Andrea Boyd and Terry Street, Melanie Clark, Barbara Close, Diana and Scott Cole, Lynn and Tom Cole, Tom Coroneos, Tracy Dordell, Lorinda Ferland, Annie Gardiner, Karen Herzog, Bill and Louise Lidicker, Amy Racina, Rui Ribeiro, Suzie Rodriguez, Nancy Rutledge, Amanda Schaffer, Patricia Schaffarczyk, Justine and Michael Still, Deborah and Dennis Sullivan, Joanne Vincent, and Clem and John Underhill. As much as we enjoy traveling, we even more enjoy coming back to be with you.

Thanks also for professional care and guidance from: Lydia Bird, Manuscript Consultant; Fran Alcorn and Scott Williams, copy-editing; my medical team at Kaiser; Richard Teel at Nine Corners, Novato, CA; Joseph Cristofalo, MA, Oakland, CA.

The following people have granted permission to use some of their work and have added knowledge and insight to this book:
Anemone del Camino, *caminodesantiago.me/community/threads/are-there-are-any-parts-of-the-norte-stages-that-people-consider-dangerous.37745/*
Pete Berg *bootstrappin.com*
Elle Bieling *pilgrimagetraveler.com/camino-primitivo.html*
Kanga *caminodesantiago.me/community/threads/camping-along-the-camino-del-norte.18835/*
William Z. Lidicker *ib.berkeley.edu/people/directory/detail/125*
Peter Robins, *peterrobins.co.uk/*
Randall St.Germain   *caminomyway.com/camino-del-norte-spain-Irún-albergue-guadalupe*

Rebekah Scott of Peaceable Kingdom *moratinoslife.blog-spot.com/*

Francis Tapon *FrancisTapon.com and francistapon.com/ Travels/Spain-Trails/10-Reasons-Why-El-Camino-Santiago-Sucks*

Index

A

Abadín 151–154
Alfonso II, King of Asturias 8, 170, 172, 176
Alfonso XIII, King of Asturias 63
Alto de la Cruz 118
American Pilgrims on the Camino (APOC) 12, 249, 261, 279, 285, 290, 292
A Roxica 235- 241
Arzua 213-215, 223, 241-242
As Seixas 210- 211
Asturias 8, 68, 105 -146, 165-, 198, 227, 248-254, 284, 292
Avilés 120-126
Aymeric Picaud, FR scholar 8

B

Baamonde 77, 144, 227-229, 231, 291
Balenciaga, Cristobal 31
    Cristobal Balenciaga Museum 31
Barcelona 15-18, 24, 93, 200, 253-254, 264-265, 270, 273
Barredo, Cerezo (artist) 95
Basque Country 14-55, 79, 80, 100, 248, 249-252, 256, 263, 286, 288, 290, 291

Bean, Vivien W. (Mom) 4-5, 23, 24, 27, 38-39, 41-42, 45-46, 49, 50-52, 55-56, 59-61, 65-75, 162, 244
Berducedo 187-189
Biarritz, FR 253
bicycles 11-12, 152, 262, 285-286
Bilbao 44, 47-60, 77-80, 134-135, 141, 248, 253-256, 281, 287
    Basilica de Begona 50
    Basque Museum of Bilbao 79
    Guggenheim Museum 44, 53, 54
        Gehry, Frank 50
        Maman (Bourgeois, Louise) 54
        Puppy (Koons, Jeff) 53- 54
Black Madonna
    Monserrat 15
bridges
    Ponte de Gallegos, Oviedo 176
    Ponte de Saa nr. San Xoán de Albaz 229
    Puente de los Santos, Ribadeo 146
    Puente Medieval de Recuna, El Berrón 169
    Puente de Pentaflora, nr. Venta del Escamplero 177
    Rio Labrada nr. Baamonde 229
    Vizcaya Transporter nr Portugalete 80
Bufones de Arenillas (blowholes) 108
bus lines
    ALSA 166, 254, 284

C

Cabueñes 118
Cadavedo 131, 133, 135
Camino forum (Ivars's)132, 261,
    269, 279, 282, 285-286
Campiello 183-184, 186
Cantabrian 63, 103, 106, 132, 167,
    249-250
Casquita 118, 165
Castro 193-195
Castro-Urdiales 84-86
    Saltacaballo, fatality 85
Castroverde 200, 202, 313
Cathedral de Santiago 7, 9, 220
    botafumeiro 12
    Plaza de las Platerias 218
    Plaza del Obradoiro 217, 225,
        242-243
    Portico de la Gloria 12
    Tree of Jesse 12
Cávado Baleira 196, 198, 200
Celts 7, 204
    Celtic 62-63, 145, 160, 206,
        209, 231, 248, 252
Codex Calixtinus 8, 9, 263, 290
Colombres 105, 313
    Casa Indianas 105
    Indianos 105, 106
    Museo de la Emigracíon 105
Colunga 114-115
Comillas 102-104
Compostela 12, 135, 216-218, 220,
    254-255, 261- 263, 285, Certifi-
    cate of Completion 220, 263
Confraternity of Saint James
    232, 249, 289, 291
Cosa, Juan de la
    Christopher Columbus 89
Crusades 8-9

Cruz de Ferro 118

D

Deba 33
    Church of Santa María 33-34
dolmen 37, 121, 197, 313

E

El Berrón 169-171
Elcano, Juan Sebastián-explorer
    31
El Pito 129
    Quinta de Selgas 129
Embalse de Salime 189-193, 258,
    314
Ermita de la Atalaya, Luarca 139
ETA (Euskadi Ta Askatasuna)
    53
Ethnographic Museum of Gran-
    das de Salime 193
Euskara, Basque language 248

F

Ferdinand (King of Spain) 10, 59
fiestas and celebrations
    Arde Lucus, Lugo 206
    Dia Infantil de Cantavaria,
        Santander 61-62
    Feast of Transhumance 252-
        253
    Fiera of the Butelo of the
        Fonsagrada 196
    Fiestas de San Froilán, Lugo
        160, 291
    Saint James Day 251
Fonsagrada
    A Fonsagrada 195, 196
Franco, Francisco
    Franco 17, 42-43

G

Galician 106, 139, 176, 186, 196-223, 236, 249, 252, 267, 291
games played 34, 48, 51, 62, 104, 160, 248
gardens
    Quita de Selgas 41, 42, 47, 53, 119, 129, 232, 249, 269
Gaudi 15, 103, 104
    El Capricho 103
Getaria 31, 32
    Balenciaga, Cristobal 31
Gijón 118-119, 256
Goya, Francisco 59, 129
Grandas de Salime 193
    Ethnographic Museum Grandas de Salime 193
Güemes 91-97
    Ernesto (Father Ernesto Bustio Crespo) 91-97, 103
    La Cabaña del Abuelo Peuto
Guernica (Gernika) 42, 43, 44, 46, 47, 64, 314
    Father Tree 43

H

Hendaye, FR 17, 20, 253
Herod the Great
    Herod Agrippa, grandson 7
hórreos (corn cribs) 149, 210
Hospitales Route 186, 188, 249, 258
hospitals 10, 186, 196
    Fanfaron 186
    Paradiella 186
    Valparaiso 186
Hotel Palacio de Magdalena 127

I

Iberian ham 203
indulgence 9, 11

Irún 8, 16-19, 79, 233, 249, 253-254, 262, 284, 286
Isabella (Queen of Spain) 10
Itziar 31, 33
Izarbide 33-34, 36

J

Jerusalem 7, 9, 10, 172

L

Lavacolla 216-217, 254
La Vega de Sariego 167-169
Le Puy, FR 2, 9, 234, 257
Lezama 46-49
Liendo 86-88
Llanes 107-109, 132
Lourenza 148-149
Luarca 132-141, 314
Lugo 154-161, 171, 198, 202-, 207, 248, 256, 262, 291
    Fiestas de San Froilán 160
    Saint Mary's Cathedral 159

M

Madrid 52, 54, 55, 63-65, 144, 156, 159, 161-162, 166, 248, 253- 254, 264, 270, 287
    Prado Museum 63
Magellan, Fernando 31
    Elcano, Juan Sebastián 31
Markina-Xemein 36-39
    Miguel de Arrechinaga 37, 39
Meakaur Turnoff 47
Melide 5, 211-213
Menu of the Day, Pilgrim Menu 287
Miraz 231-235, 258
Mondoñedo 149-151
    Slaughter of the Holy Innocents 150

Monte de Gozo 217
Monte Urgull 25
Montserrat 15
Moors
   Muslim 8-9, 101, 142, 150,
      165, 177
Munitibar 39, 42
Murray-Wakelin, Janette 234
museums
   Basque Museum, Bilbao 79
   Ethnographic Museum
      Grandas de Salime 193
   Guggenheim, Bilbao 44, 53-54
   San Telmo Museum, San
      Sebastian 25-26
   Museo de Calamar Gigante/
      Giant Squid Museum,
      Luarca 140
   Museo de la Emigracíon,
      Colombres 105
   Prado, Madrid 63

N

Navia 141-145
Neolithic era 20, 197, 204
Noja
   El Brusco 76, 88, 90, 91
Nueva 51, 109, 110

O

Ortuella explosion 81
Oviedo 5, 117-118, 165, 170-179,
   248, 250, 254, 256, 258, 262-265,
   284
   Cathedral of San Salvador 172
   Sudarium (Shroud) 172

P

Pacific Crest Trail 1, 47, 75, 99,
   104, 134, 304

Padrón 7- 8, 140, 220
pain 24
Pasajes de San Juan 22
   Pasai, Pasaia 19-20, 22
Peñaflor 177
   Battle at Peñaflor Bridge 177
   The Battle of Lutos 177
Pendueles 105-107
Peninsular War 25
Picasso, Pablo 43, 64, 315
Picos de Europa 8, 71, 93, 108,
   250
Pilgrim Office (Oficina de Pere-
   grinos) 11-12, 254-255, 263
Pilgrim Passport 12, 130, 259
Pobeña 80, 84
Pola de Allande 186-188, 191
Puerto de Palo 188

R

Reconquista (Reconquest) 9
Rekve, Ivar
   Ivar's Camino forum 132, 261,
      269, 279, 282, 285-286
Ribadeo 144-148, 227, 258, 284
   Puente de los Santos 146
Ribadesella 68, 110-114
   Cueva (Cave) de Tito Bustil-
      lo 113
   frescoes(los hermanos, Uría
      Aza) 111
   Santa Maria Magdalena 111
rivers
   River Miño 203
   Río Navia 191
Roman 9-10, 17, 97, 127, 154, 168,
   197, 199, 203-204, 206

S

Saint James 7-8, 12, 142, 202, 231,

243, 249, 251, 292
Salas 178-180
Salinas 126
    Philippe Cousteau Anchor
        Museum 126
San Juan de Villapañada 177, 258
San Román da Retorta 207- 208,
    210
San Sebastián 16-17, 21-29, 34,
    44, 134, 141, 253, 256, 265, 286-
    287, 315
    Basilica Santa Maria 24
    San Telmo Museum 25-26
Santa Irene 215-216
Santander 16, 52-62, 66, 95-98,
    208, 256, 284, 286
    Dia Infantil de Cantavaria
        61-62
    Peninsula of Magdalena 61
Santiago de Compostela 5, 7-12,
    135, 217, 219-223, 225, 242-245,
    252, 254, 262-263, 268, 282,
    284-285, 289-290
Santiago Matamoros (St. James
    the Moor-Slayer) 142, 200
Santillana del Mar 97-100
    Altamira Cave 100
    Claustro Romanico de La
        Colegiata 102
Santoña 88-90
    Juan de la Cosa 89
    Columbus, Christopher 89
Santuario (Sanctuary) de Guada-
    lupe 20
San Vicente de la Barquera 104
    S. Maria de Los Angeles 104
Sebrayo 115, 254
sellos 12, 25, 261-262
September 11, 2001 (9/11) 83
Serdio 104-105

sidra 114-116, 171-175, 222, 316
Sobrado dos Monxes 239-241
Somo, ferry 96
Soto del Barco 126-129, 316
Soto de Luiña 129, 131
Spanish Civil War 17, 43, 64
Stations of the Cross 111

T

Tineo 180, 183
trains
    Cercanías 284
    Euskotren 284
    FEVE 97, 254
    RENFE 63, 284

U

Uberuaga Etxebarria, Jose Angel
    Ube 41
UNESCO World Heritage sites
    100, 113, 154, 175, 204

V

Valdediós 167-168
    Holy Savior of Valdediós 168
Venta del Escamplero 176, 177
Vilalba 144, 154, 156-157, 159, 223,
    225-229
Villapañada 177-178
Villaviciosa 5, 115-118, 165-167,
    249, 254

W

wildlife 132
    Anguis fragilis (lizard) 193
    snake, asp 132, 133, 193
    storks 229

Z

Zarautz 28, 29, 31

About the author

A FAMILY TRADITION of journalism got Susan Alcorn into writing at an early age. It was a family joke that—because both her father and paternal grandparents were in the newspaper business—she was born with printer's ink in her veins.

Susan Alcorn lives in the San Francisco Bay Area with her husband, Ralph, where she can pursue her hiking year-round while continuing to write and maintain close connections with friends and family. She retired from teaching in 2001 to devote more time to travel and her publishing business, but still shares her interests in language arts, travel, and the outdoors as a volunteer in a third-grade classroom.

She's an accomplished, professional photographer and seldom leaves behind her digital SLR camera when traveling—the exception to her usual "packing light" practice.

Long distance hiking has become a passion for her, and in mid-2017 she passed the six-thousand-mile mark. The longer trips included the Pacific Crest Trail, the Camino de Santiago and many other pilgrimage routes in Europe, as well as Torres del Paine in Chile and Mt. Kilimanjaro in Tanzania.

She has given more than a hundred talks and digital presentations about long-distance hiking and the Camino de Santiago at bookstores, REI sporting-goods stores, Sierra Club dinners, libraries, travel group programs, and more.

Susan Alcorn's recent books include—
We're in the Mountains Not Over the Hill: Tales and Tips from Seasoned Women Backpackers

Camino Chronicle: Walking to Santiago
Patagonia Chronicle: On Foot in Torres del Paine
Available from your local or online bookstore.

The Alcorns have given back to the hiking community by sharing their knowledge on ***backpack45.com***. You can sign up for Susan's free monthly newsletter on hiking and backpacking "tales and tips" at backpack45@yahoo.com

CPSIA information can be obtained
at www.ICGtesting.com
Printed in the USA
BVHW030815310119
539136BV00001B/5/P